CW00794715

BUILDING
THE
REVOLUTION

BUILDING THE REVOLUTION

SOVIET ART AND ARCHITECTURE 1915–1935

ROYAL ACADEMY OF ARTS

First published on the occasion of the exhibition *Building the Revolution: Soviet Art and Architecture 1915–1935*, organised by the Royal Academy of Arts in collaboration with the SMCA – Costakis Collection, Thessaloniki. Based on an exhibition at the SMCA, Thessaloniki, curated by Maria Tsantsanoglou, David Sarkisyan and Hercules Papaioannou, with the collaboration of Richard Pare.

CaixaForum Barcelona, 3 February – 17 April 2011
CaixaForum Madrid, 26 May – 18 September 2011
Royal Academy of Arts, London, 29 October 2011 – 22 January 2012

2009–2013 Season supported by

The Royal Academy of Arts is grateful to Her Majesty's Government for agreeing to indemnify this exhibition under the National Heritage Act 1980, and to Resource, the Council for Museums, Archives and Libraries, for its help in arranging the indemnity.

EXHIBITION CURATORS
MaryAnne Stevens
Maria Tsantsanoglou
with the collaboration of Richard Pare

CURATORIAL ASSISTANT
Sarah Lea

EXHIBITION MANAGEMENT
Sunnifa Hope

PHOTOGRAPHIC AND COPYRIGHT CO-ORDINATION
Trine Lyngby Hougaard

CATALOGUE
Royal Academy Publications:
David Breuer
Beatrice Gullström
Carola Krueger
Sophie Oliver
Peter Sawbridge
Nick Tite

Project Editors:
Tom Neville, Vicky Wilson
Design: Unlimited
Colour Origination: DawkinsColour
Printed by Graphicom

British Library Cataloguing-in-Publication Data
A catalogue record of this book is available from the British Library

ISBN 978-1-905711-92-5 (paperback)
ISBN 978-1-905711-91-8 (hardback)

Distributed outside the United States and Canada by Thames & Hudson Ltd, London

Distributed in the United States and Canada by Harry N. Abrams, Inc., New York

Illustrations (details): page 2: Cat. 73.1; page 6: Cat. 77.3; page 9: Cat. 71.2; pages 10–11: Cat. 75.7; pages 92–93: Cat. 62.2; page 100: Cat. 66.5.

Works reproduced on pages 30–91 courtesy the SMCA – Costakis Collection, Thessaloniki.

Richard Pare's photographs courtesy the artist and Kicken Berlin.

Archival photographs on pages 112–243 courtesy the Department of Photographs, Shchusev State Museum of Architecture, Moscow.

Works shown only at CaixaForum Barcelona and Madrid: Cats 9, 11, 21, 38, 40.1, 40.2, 58–60, 62.5, 64.4, 65.2, 66.1, 71.2, 75.7, 75.8, 77.3, 78.5, 79.7, 80.1–80.4, 81.6, 92.10

Videos of buildings by Richard Pare copyright © Richard Pare

Tatlin's Tower – Monument to the Third International (3 min 11 sec)
© 1999 Takehiko Nagakura
Producer/Director: Takehiko Nagakura; Computer Graphics: Andrzej Zarzycki, Takehiko Nagakura, Dan Brick, Mark Sich

Tatlin's Tower (3 min 28 sec)
© Lutz Becker
Reconstruction 1971 by Christopher Cross, Jeremy Dixon, Peter Watson and Christopher Woodward

CONTENTS

IN MEMORY OF DAVID SARKISYAN
1947–2010

EDITORS' NOTE

Architects' biographies:
The indispensable source of information on avant-garde Soviet architects is S.O. Khan-Magomedov, *Pioniere der sowjetischen Architektur*, Dresden, 1983; English translation by A. Lieven, *Pioneers of Soviet Architecture: The Search for New Solutions in the 1920s and 1930s*, ed. C. Cooke, London and New York, 1987.

Dimensions: Richard Pare's photographs are given in centimetres, height before width. For all other works, dimensions are given in millimetres, height before width. The majority of photographs lent by the Department of Photographs, Shchusev State Museum of Architecture, Moscow, are mounted on index cards measuring 197 x 288 mm.

Place names: In Russia these are liable to change, in some cases several times (for instance, St Petersburg – often just called Petersburg – was renamed Petrograd in 1914 and Leningrad in 1924, reverting to St Petersburg in 1991). We have used current place names throughout (thus St Petersburg, and Ekaterinburg, which was known as Sverdlovsk between 1917 and 1991) though we have retained Russian forms (thus Kharkov, not Ukrainian Kharkiv).

Transliteration: There are a number of ways to transliterate Cyrillic; we have followed the simplified Library of Congress system, which dispenses with diacriticals and provides a fairly straightforward letter-for-letter procedure. However, we have kept the familiar forms of the names of artists and others who lived and worked in the West: Wassily Kandinsky, not Vassilii Kandinskii, Leon Trotsky but Noi Trotskii.

Authors of catalogue entries, biographies and glossary:
AC Angelica Charistou
MC Marie Collier
NDBdeM Nicholas Bueno de Mezquita
RP Richard Pare
All artists' biographies by Angelica Charistou
Glossary by Nicholas Bueno de Mezquita except where otherwise indicated.

Richard Pare's colour photographs were made between 1993 and 2010 using negative film in three formats: 35 mm, 6 x 6 cm, and 20 x 25 cm. The negatives were scanned and the digital files output on a laser printer at Color Space Imaging, New York, under the supervision of the photographer.

ACKNOWLEDGMENTS

The curators would like to thank the following for their assistance in the making of this exhibition and its catalogue:

Neale Albert
Maria Ametova
Eugene Asse
Kiril Asse
Yuri Avvakumov
Lutz Becker
Barry Bergdoll
Neil Bingham
Betty Blair
Alexander Brodsky
Maria Brodsky
Clementine Cecil
Centre Canadien d'Architecture/ Canadian Centre for Architecture, Montréal
Irina Chepkunov
Susan Compton
Ben Diep/Colour Space Imaging
Jeremy Dixon
Kate Goodwin
The Graham Foundation for Advanced Studies in the Fine Arts
John and Eileen Harris
Pavel Khoroshilov
Rudolf and Annette Kicken
Irina Korobina
Pavel Kusnetsov
Phyllis Lambert
Antonia Mamina
John Milner
Yuri Mostovoy
Vacheslav Nechaev
Sergei Nikitin
Ekaterina Pachina
Hercules Papaioannou
Lev Rassadnikov
Maria Rogozina
the late David Sarkisyan
Howard Schickler
Irina Sedova
Vitaly Stadnikov
Olga Sviblova
Exeniager Vytulera
William Webster
Irina Zaraisky

PRESIDENT'S FOREWORD

Russia in the 1920s witnessed a period of intense innovation and creativity in the fields of art and architecture. Influenced by the deliberate rejection of figurative art in the years immediately preceding the October Revolution of 1917, artists and architects sought to forge a new visual language that would proclaim the political ideals of the new Socialist era. Architects responded to the bold abstractions of pure, geometric form being pursued by artists – who also made excursions into sculpture, constructions and architectonic structures. From 1922 until Stalin's imposition of a heavy-handed Neoclassicism in the early 1930s, they produced radical and highly innovative designs for buildings created to fulfil new functions of the state, new Socialist canons for living, work and recreation, and new economic and industrial programmes.

Building the Revolution: Soviet Art and Architecture 1915–1935 brings together three elements that demonstrate the close interrelationship between art and architecture, and its exceptional manifestation in built form during this period. It presents a conversation between important works of art from the Costakis Collection, Thessaloniki, vintage photographs from the Shchusev State Museum of Architecture, Moscow, which clearly articulate the novelty of the new architecture as it sat within older urban textures, and a major selection of photographs made by Richard Pare of the buildings as they are today.

The exhibition has its origins in two earlier shows which focused solely on Richard Pare's photographs, at the Shchusev State Museum of Architecture, Moscow, and the Museum of Modern Art, New York, and a third, more recent exhibition curated by Maria Tsantsanoglou, Director of the State Museum of Contemporary Art, Thessaloniki, the late David Sarkisyan, then Director of the Shchusev State Museum of Architecture, and Hercules Papaioannou, Curator of the Thessaloniki Museum of Photography. In that last exhibition, Richard Pare's photographs were juxtaposed with work from the Costakis Collection and modern prints of photographs made more or less contemporaneously with the buildings themselves. For this exhibition, we have been exceptionally fortunate in being able to borrow the original vintage photographs from Moscow, which convey the atmosphere of those extraordinary pioneering years.

We are most grateful to our colleagues at the State Museum of Contemporary Art, Thessaloniki, and the Shchusev State Museum of Architecture, Moscow. In particular to their respective directors Dr Maria Tsantsanoglou and Dr Irina Korobina. The generosity of both institutions in lending major works from their holdings is sincerely acknowledged. We also wish to record our collegial partnership with the Fundació LaCaixa, Spain – initially established in association with the exhibition *Andrea Palladio* (2009–10) – which has made possible the presentation of the exhibition in Barcelona and Madrid prior to its showing at the Royal Academy.

This exhibition could not have been completed without the energy and commitment of Richard Pare to the cause of recording these innovative structures and his talent in creating a portfolio of exceptional photographs which show them decayed yet still capable of evoking their earlier roles as manifestations of the new political and social order. The exhibition has been curated by Dr Tsantsanoglou and MaryAnne Stevens, with the collaboration of Richard Pare. For its presentation in London, the Royal Academy is most grateful to JTI, our Season Supporter of exhibitions in the Sackler Wing of Galleries.

The initial discussions about the configuration of this exhibition and its preparation for presentation in Spain and London were undertaken in close collaboration with the late David Sarkisyan. A gifted and committed visionary, he contributed in no small measure to the making of an exhibition which we feel certain will reveal new understanding about the art and architecture of the heroic early years of post-Revolutionary Russia. We hope it will alert our public to the current condition of the buildings that were intended to proclaim their vision and achievement. The exhibition catalogue is dedicated to David Sarkisyan's memory.

Sir Nicholas Grimshaw CBE PRA
President, Royal Academy of Arts

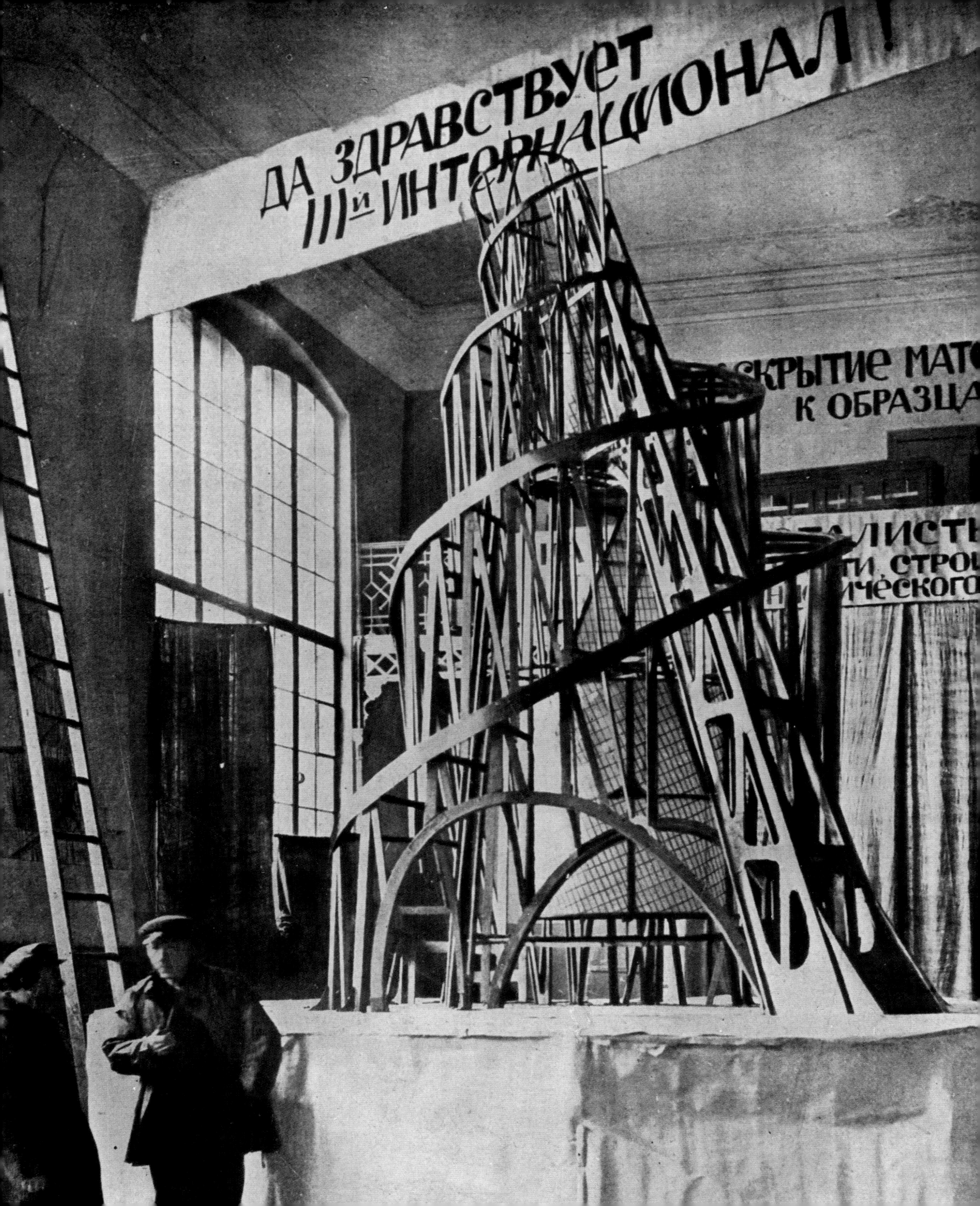
ДА ЗДРАВСТВУЕТ
III-й ИНТЕРНАЦИОНАЛ!

UNEASY CROSSINGS
THE ARCHITECTURE OF THE RUSSIAN
AVANT-GARDE BETWEEN EAST AND WEST

Jean-Louis Cohen

From the time of the seminal show *Art in Revolution: Soviet Art and Design since 1917*, held in 1971 at the Hayward Gallery in London – where several rooms had to be closed, censored by the Soviet Ministry of Culture, which still saw the topic as subversive – most exhibitions on the architecture of the post-Revolutionary Russian avant-garde have documented it as if it were a quasi-autonomous phenomenon. According to most interpretations, designs and buildings had apparently evolved in parallel to the chronicle of Western architecture, but with minimal interaction between the two, both in the early years of post-Revolutionary culture and in the later years when Socialist Realism blossomed. There have, however, been some exceptions to this interpretative trend, both in the form of books, such as the study led by Manfredo Tafuri of the contribution of European architects in the 1920s and 1930s, and of such exhibitions as the memorable *Paris–Moscou* held at the Centre Pompidou in Paris in 1979.[1]

Buildings from the first fifteen years of Soviet Russia's history have now been documented in their present – and often appalling – condition thanks to Richard Pare's exceptional photographic campaigns, the results of which were first exhibited in 2007 in New York and the following year in Thessaloniki. The spectrum of buildings shot by Pare goes beyond the canon of radicalism defined by the structures most closely identified with the explicitly Constructivist group OSA, since his campaign has included buildings for which eclectic or opportunistic architects of some talent borrowed from the radical groups. In terms of documentation, a new phase can also be perceived in the widespread recognition of the innovative architecture imagined and sometimes implemented between the October Revolution of 1917 and the consolidation of Stalin's absolute power over culture and society at large around 1932. There is now also

much better access to the archives that were often off limits for Western scholars before Mikhail Gorbachev's *Perestroika* twenty years ago.

TURBULENT DECADES

Earlier interpretations of a unique cycle of transformation in politics, culture and architecture have not been significantly altered by this new context, and need to be briefly mentioned. As Bolshevik power emerged, latent patterns of modernisation in pre-1914 Russian culture were activated through the response to new forms of patronage, and found their architectural expression in a particularly intense and pluralist Modernist culture. In the two decades between World War I and World War II, transformations in the discourse, in the institutional role of architecture and in built production happened rapidly, engaging three generations of professionals. Major figures of the pre-Revolutionary establishment, such as Igor Fomin, Aleksei Shchusev or Ivan Zholtovskii, modernised their language. Young professionals, such as Moisei Ginzburg, Ilia Golosov, Konstantin Melnikov or the Vesnin brothers, built careers by responding to the new regime's programmes. Alumni of reformed educational institutions such as VKhUTEMAS, created in 1920 in Moscow, included visionary radicals such as Ivan Leonidov as well as cynical eclectics such as Karo Alabian.

Theoretical investigation and building work kept changing in these intense years, during which the design professions metamorphosed from private practice to state organisations, changes that can be briefly summarised as follows. During the Civil War, from 1918 to 1920, architects joined forces with painters and sculptors to create utopian factions such as ZhivSkulptArkh (painting-sculpture-architecture), aspiring to create global works of art that translated into built form the dynamics of the

1 A.A. Rosa, M. Tafuri *et al*, *Socialismo, città, architettura URSS 1917–1937, il contributo degli architetti europei*, Rome, 1971; *Paris–Moscou*, K.G. Pontus Hultén (ed.), exh. cat., Centre Georges Pompidou, Paris, 1979.

Figure 1 Vladimir Tatlin, *Model for a Monument to the Third International*, 1920. Documentary photograph. Moderna Museet, Stockholm

Figure 2 El Lissitzky, first page of *Izvestia ASNOVA*, 1926

Revolution. Most participating architects, such as Vladimir Krinskii and Nikolai Ladovskii, became influential educators at VKhUTEMAS. In parallel, within INKhUK the nucleus of what would soon be called Constructivism was shaped, revealing its radical proposals in 1921 in exhibitions such as *5x5=25* or at the third OBMOKhU show.

With the resumption of actual construction in the early 1920s, thanks to building programmes implemented by local Soviets or by the commercial firms flourishing under the New Economic Policy, pre-Revolutionary groupings such as MAO in Moscow or its counterpart in St Petersburg attempted to take control of professional life but were prevented from doing so by more radical organisations. The first was ASNOVA, created in 1923 by Ladovskii and Krinskii with a distant contribution from El Lissitzky, a former junior colleague of Kazimir Malevich in Vitebsk. Its members favoured the expressive interpretation of the new programmes and were not particularly focused on addressing the potential of new technologies. In contrast, OSA[2] addressed developments in building technology and expectations of the rapid 'reconstruction' of daily life. Led by Aleksandr Vesnin and Moisei Ginzburg, OSA's Constructivist architects researched building types meant to accelerate the emergence of a collective lifestyle: in the residential sphere, communal houses, with remote echoes of Charles Fourier's *phalansteries*; in the sphere of social interaction, workers' clubs, which continued the tradition of People's Houses initiated by the Social Democrats in the late nineteenth century. A loner such as Konstantin Melnikov, who never joined any organisation, was nonetheless responsible for designing five of these clubs in Moscow, all based on provocative structural and spatial concepts.

With the launch of the First Five Year Plan (1928–33) promising accelerated industrialisation, factory architecture became the focus of much attention both in the schools and in the profession. Plans for hundreds of urban extensions and new towns were drafted and the limits of the discourse of collectivisation in the domestic sphere were measured, even if shared domestic quarters would remain dominant for decades. In contrast to their previous enthusiastic endorsement of communal life, OSA's leaders shaped the alternative vision of a 'disurbanised' territory, in which loose villages of single-family houses would replace existing cities. This position contributed to OSA's marginalisation, just when the young members of VOPRA, founded in 1929, were fighting for control of the architectural profession.

These internecine battles gave the leadership of the Communist party a wide window of opportunity to 'reorganise' architecture as well as art and literature, and in 1932 it put an end to pluralism, merging all the associations into a party-controlled union. Despite this firm push from above, recent research shows that the Stalinist grip over the profession would not be totally achieved prior to the Congress of Soviet Architects staged in Moscow in 1937, three years after the Writers' Congress, while ideas and themes developed by the avant-garde still sometimes found their way into buildings constructed immediately before World War II.[3] However, it would take fifteen more years before there was an attempt to bring the energy of early radical projects back into public discussion, when Nikita Khrushchev used his 1954 'Discourse to the Builders' to engage in de-Stalinisation.[4] Architecture had been the last profession to be converted to Socialist Realism, and it was the first to be freed of its doctrine.

2 OSA was the Union of Contemporary – or Modern – Architects. The term 'modern' could not be used by Russia's radical architects of the 1920s as it was too closely related to Art Nouveau. Hence 'contemporary' became the main epithet used to denote the new trends.

3 The best analysis of the 'normalisation' of architectural life is R. Anderson, *Toward a Socialist Architecture: Politics, History, and Theory in the Soviet Union, 1928–41*, PhD dissertation, Columbia University, 2010.

4 C. Cooke, 'Modernity and Realism, Architectural Relations in the Cold War', in S.E. Reid (ed.), *Russian Art and the West: A Century of Dialogue in Painting, Architecture and the Decorative Arts*, DeKalb, Ill., 2007, pp. 172–94.

POROUS CULTURES

Chronicling the response of the architectural community to the pressures of an intense, sometimes tragic, political life is one of the avenues scholars have taken in writing a history of Soviet architecture.[5] Rather than monitoring the complex interaction between architects and their Bolshevik rulers, the actual patrons of architecture in the municipalities, ministries and in the economy, here I propose to look at the no less complex fabric of relationships established with the West between the 1917 Revolution and Hitler's 1941 invasion of Russia. Despite the widespread perception of the USSR as a 'closed' empire, the architecture produced between the October Revolution and the advent of Socialist Realism in the 1930s never dissociated itself from Western models and parallels, nor did it fully escape the attention of the rest of the world. Emerging from vibrant polemics at home, the innovative structures of the period were rooted in precedents built in capitalist Europe and North America, and remained present in the background of Western debates, though with some understandable eclipses and limits. If the body of work erected was by no means negligible quantitatively, as Richard Pare's photographs and recent Russian publications confirm, its echoes in the scholarly world, in criticism and in public opinion abroad, were diverse – though often focused on a rather narrow corpus.

Over a relatively short period a sequence of cycles can be identified in which the discourses developed in the USSR and those constructed abroad do not necessarily coincide in time, and even less in their perspective. The novelty of Russian schemes was recognised at the time and still discussed decades later abroad, whereas Western theories and buildings, given an immediate reception in the early USSR, would later be somewhat repressed.

Defining the meaning of the useful notion of 'reception' in the field of architecture can be problematic. However, I would suggest a broad encompassing understanding of the processes through which Soviet designs and projects were received by professionals, critics and historians, through direct experience as well as through publications and other media such as film.[6] Inversely, the Soviet reception of Western architectural culture was a no less labyrinthine process in which slogans, ideas and spatial constructs were imported in parallel with the purchase or imitation of building methods and patents. Much more than a case of 'influence', this process can best be understood as a case of intertextuality,[7] of themes and forms circulating across the then permeable border between the Soviet Union and the rest of the world.

LOOKING WESTWARD

The first historical cycle, extending conventionally from the Revolution to the 1932 'reorganisation' of architectural associations, which coincided with the judging of the Palace of Soviets competition, saw a wide and unashamed assimilation of Western culture by Russian architects, the swan song of which corresponds with the publication in 1932 of David Arkin's book *Arkhitektura sovremennogo Zapada* (*Contemporary Western Architecture*). In the fifteen years after the Revolution, buildings erected by commercial organisations, ministries, municipalities and cooperatives represented the hopes for a new life promised by the New Economic Policy. These facilities were widely published in the Russian popular press and in new magazines such as *Stroitelnaia promyshlennost* (*Construction Industry*) and *Stroitelstvo Moskvy* (*Construction of Moscow*), created in 1924 and relatively generally disseminated.[8] In comparison, OSA's remarkable magazine *SA* (*Contemporary Architecture*) would

5 H.D. Hudson, Jr, *Blueprints and Blood: The Stalinization of Soviet Architecture, 1917–1937*, Princeton, 1994.

6 On the notion of reception and modern architecture, see *Image, usage, héritage: la réception de l'architecture du mouvement moderne, Actes de la VIIe Conférence internationale de Docomomo*, St-Etienne, 2005.

7 On the notion of intertextuality, see G. Genette, *Palimpsests*, trans. by C. Newman and C. Doubinsky, Lincoln, NB, 1997.

8 J.-L. Cohen, 'Avant-garde et revues d'architecture en Russie, 1917–1941', in *Revue de l'art*, No. 89, 1990, pp. 29–38.

have only a very limited print run between 1926 and 1930.[9] Few of these magazines were read in the West except in Czechoslovakia, where the left-wing critic Karel Teige published many reports on Soviet experiments.[10]

The Soviet press was not only a vehicle for the dissemination of Russian projects, but also made it possible to discover works produced abroad. German experiments, from those developed at the Weimar and Dessau Bauhaus to the urban expansion programmes of cities such as Frankfurt, as well as buildings designed in France by Auguste Perret, André Lurçat or Le Corbusier, were regularly documented. Also, despite the lack of diplomatic relations with the United States, American projects and technical inventions mobilised attention. Highlights of the 1920s for the Russian context were the 1922 competition for the *Chicago Tribune* headquarters, which inspired many projects in the USSR, and images of the New World published in 1926 by Erich Mendelsohn in *Amerika: Bilderbuch eines Architekten* and by Richard Neutra in *Wie baut Amerika?* in the following year.[11] Architectural associations were keen to legitimise their theories and designs by referring to Western precedents and parallels. The clearest case is the exhibition of contemporary architecture organised in 1927 by OSA at VKhUTEMAS, in which radical works by Ginzburg, Leonidov and their colleagues were juxtaposed with German, Dutch, Belgian and French projects.[12]

Along with the circulation of forms, sometimes stigmatised by the conservatives as an indulgence in 'Korbusianizm' or 'Amerikanizm', building technology imported from Germany provided the basis for most innovative structures erected in the Soviet Union.[13] Occasionally foreign designers were invited to build complex ensembles, as in St Petersburg, where Erich Mendelsohn designed a significant part of the Red Banner Textile Factory (Cat. 71).

THE SOVIET EXPERIMENT OBSERVED

The Western reception of Soviet architecture went well beyond professional circles and was shaped not only by the direct experience of many foreign visitors – activists, politicians, engineers, writers and architects – whose impressions were recorded in essays and innumerable books, but also by Soviet exhibitions mounted abroad and films that had wide foreign distribution. The early projects were known quite quickly in the West, thanks to the efforts of Ilya Ehrenburg, a writer then operating in Berlin, who published the short-lived magazine *Veshch/ Gegenstand/Objet* with El Lissitzky. Vladimir Tatlin's Tower was reproduced almost immediately by Bruno Taut in *Frühlicht* and by Le Corbusier in *L'Esprit nouveau*.[14] El Lissitzky wrote an essay on 'Architecture in the USSR' for *L'Esprit nouveau*, which featured a vigorous attack on the structures of the 1923 Moscow All-Union Agricultural Exhibition, a subtle critique of Russia's 'mecanomania', and was eventually published in German by the Berlin *Kunstblatt* in 1925 after being rejected by the French magazine.[15]

Also in 1925, the existence of a new Russian architecture was unveiled to a large audience by Soviet participation in the *Exposition Internationale des Arts Décoratifs et Industriels Modernes* in Paris. The star of the show was Konstantin Melnikov's Soviet Pavilion, hailed as a glass house by the left and perceived as a stylised guillotine by conservatives. The workers' club built by Aleksandr Rodchenko also created a sensation, but the presentation of more than a hundred architectural drawings hung around a model of Tatlin's Tower in the galleries of the Grand Palais was no less influential. Here, for the first time, projects for the

9   See the collection of the journal's major essays edited by Guido Canella and Maurizio Meriggi: *SA Sovremennaja Arkhitektura 1926–1930*, Milan, 2007.

10 K. Teige, *Sovětská kultura*, Prague, 1927; R. Švacha, 'Sovětsky konstruktivismus a česká architektura' ('Soviet Constructivism and Czech architecture'), in *Umění*, No. 36, 1988, pp. 54–70; O. Mácel, 'Paradise Lost: Teige and Soviet Russia', in *Karel Teige, Architecture and Poetry, Rassegna*, No. 53, March 1993, pp. 70–77.

11 E. Mendelsohn, *Amerika: Bilderbuch eines Architekten*, Berlin, 1926; Richard Neutra, *Wie baut Amerika?*, Stuttgart, 1927. A Russian translation of the latter was published in 1929.

12 K.P. Zygas, 'OSA's 1927 Exhibition of Contemporary Architecture: Russia and the West Meet in Moscow', in G.H. Roman, V.H. Marquardt (eds), *Avant-Garde Frontier: Russia Meets the West, 1910–1930*, Gainesville, Fl., 1992, pp. 102–21.

13 A. Zalivako, 'Soviet Avant-Garde – Origin of New Materials and Construction Methods or Extension of Europe's Modern Movement? A Critique', in *Proceedings of the Third International Congress on Construction History*, Cottbus, 2009, pp. 1533–37.

14 Ilya Ehrenburg, 'Ein Entwurf Tatlins', in *Frühlicht*, Vol. 1, No. 3, 1921–22, pp. 92–3; 'La Tour de Tatline', in *L'Esprit nouveau*, Vol. 3, No. 14, January 1922, p. 1680.

15 El Lissitzky, 'SSSRs Architektur', in *Das Kunstblatt*, Vol. 9, No. 2, February 1925, pp. 49–53.

Figure 3 A building site, as reproduced in
E. Mendelsohn, *Russland–Europa–Amerika:
ein architektonischer Querschnitt*, Berlin,
1929

competitions held in Moscow since 1923 and works from VKhUTEMAS studios were exhibited abroad.[16]

These materials were later used in Jean Badovici's magazine *L'Architecture vivante*, which devoted many plates to Soviet projects and buildings between 1926 and 1932.[17] In Germany, Russian work was discussed in *Wasmuths Monatshefte*, published by the conservative critic Werner Hegemann, who was himself more interested in the Neo-Classical work of Alexander Klein than in the radical projects of the avant-garde. Hegemann also suggested a provocative parallel between German pre-1914 memorials and Aleksei Shchusev's wooden Lenin Mausoleum (Cat. 92.5). Recently completed buildings such as David Kogan's Mosselprom commercial building in Moscow were discussed by St Petersburg architect Aleksandr Dmitriev.[18]

In the second half of the 1920s major Western architects discovered Russian cities. Travelling regularly to St Petersburg to monitor his factory site, Mendelsohn published his album *Russland– Europa–Amerika* in 1929, making no mystery of his astonishment at the primitive condition of building in the USSR.[19] After his first trip to the USSR in 1928, Le Corbusier wrote several articles for French and Swiss newspapers, all rather enthusiastic about the emergence of a new urban society and supportive of his Constructivist 'soulmates', whose work he had previously scorned.[20] But the most important book was unquestionably El Lissitzky's *Russland: die Rekonstruktion der Architektur in der Sowjetunion*, published in Vienna in 1930, which remained for several decades the main source of Western architectural interpretation and had a new lease of life with its 1965 reprint and a subsequent English edition.[21] Interestingly, no comparable book giving a global and strikingly illustrated view of developments since 1920 would ever be published in Moscow.

In the November 1931 issue of the recently founded magazine *L'Architecture d'aujourd'hui* Aleksandr Pasternak discussed 'the problems of building Socialist cities in the USSR'. The article was illustrated with images of Aleksandr Fufaev's Dukstroi apartment building in Moscow and several Constructivist schemes. In the same periodical Mikhail Ilyin wrote about 'The Architecture of the Workers' Club', devoting space to Melnikov's buildings and Leonidov's projects.[22] The Russian avant-garde also had a significant impact in Japan where, for instance, Aleksei Gan's *Konstruktivizm* (1922) and Moisei Ginzburg's *Stil i epokha* (*Style and Epoch*, 1924) were translated as early as the 1920s.

Numerous writers discovered the cities of Russia, Ukraine or the Caucasus. To mention only the French, Georges Duhamel perceived that 'Constructivism, a rigorous art, is without hypocrisy',[23] while Marc Chadourne saw in Melnikov's Rusakov Workers' Club (Cat. 85) 'a baroque studio-set for German cinema'.[24] In 1930 Henri Barbusse wrote notes on the Kharkov Gosprom Building, DneproGES and the new Baku (Cats 63, 68, 66, 86). He described the 'Cyclopean skeleton' of the 'monstrous house' of the Gosprom Building and the limits encountered by the photographer standing in front of it: 'with its foreshortenings, its sharpened perspectives, and its flattening and distortion of curves, [it] does no justice to this achievement of artistic realism. You can only photograph the building effectively in sections.'[25] Alfred H. Barr was one of the few American art historians to spend time in Moscow. During his trip of 1927–28 he visited the writer Sergei Tretiakov in Ginzburg's Gosstrakh apartment building and was merciless in his criticism, even though he considered it 'one of the four "modern" buildings in Moscow – an apartment house built in the Corbusier–Gropius style. But only the superficials are modern, for the plumbing,

16 S.F. Starr, *Le pavillon de Mel'nikov, Paris, 1925*, Paris, 1981.
17 J. Badovici (ed.), *L'Architecture vivante en URSS*, Paris, 1930.
18 A. Dmitriev, 'Zeitgenössische Bestrebungen in der russischen Baukunst', in *Wasmuths Monatshefte*, Vol. 7, No. 8, August 1926, pp. 331–36.
19 E. Mendelsohn, *Russland–Europa– Amerika: ein architektonischer Querschnitt*, Berlin, 1929.
20 See J.-L. Cohen, *Le Corbusier and the Mystique of the USSR: Theories and Projects for Moscow, 1928–1936*, Princeton, 1992.
21 El Lissitzky, *Russland: die Rekonstruktion der Architektur in der Sowjetunion*, Vienna, 1930. Translated as *Russia: An Architecture for World Revolution*, Cambridge, Mass., 1970.
22 A. Pasternak, 'Les problèmes de l'édification des villes socialistes en URSS', in *L'Architecture d'aujourd'hui*, Vol. 2, No. 8, November 1931, pp. 4–16; M. Ilyine, 'L'architecture du club ouvrier en URSS', *ibid.*, pp. 17–19.
23 G. Duhamel, *Voyage de Moscou*, Paris, 1927, pp. 170–71.
24 M. Chadourne, *L'URSS sans passion*, Paris, 1932, pp. 53–54.
25 H. Barbusse, *One Looks at Russia*, London, 1931, p. 54; originally *Russie*, Paris, 1930.

Figure 4 Moisei Ginzburg, Ignatii Milinis, Narkomfin Communal House, Moscow, as reproduced in *L'Architecture d'aujourd'hui*, November 1931

Figure 5 S. Kravets, M. Felger and S. Serafimov, the Gosprom Building in Kharkov, on the cover of J. Badovici (ed.), *L'Architecture russe en URSS*, Paris, 1930 (a portfolio of plates previously published in *L'Architecture vivante*)

18

heating, etc. are technically very crude and cheap, a comedy of the strong modern inclination without any technical tradition to satisfy it.'[26]

During this early period cinema was one of the most powerful media through which the new architecture was diffused. It appeared in the montage films of Dziga Vertov and played a significant role in Sergei Eisenstein's *Old and New*, or *The General Line*, released in 1928. The hero is the peasant Marfa Lapkina, who dreams of an ideal modern farm designed for the set by OSA architect Andrei Burov and subsequently often published in the West as if it were a real building. But in order to get permission to obtain a tractor for the collective farm Marfa goes to the city to overcome the resistance of the bureaucracy, seated in the fortress-like Gosprom Building in Kharkov, filmed like an American skyscraper.

FOREIGN SPECIALISTS AT WORK

Importing technology was no longer sufficient; foreign designers were invited to compete in several competitions. In 1928, thanks to the unanimous support of his local admirers, Le Corbusier won the commission to build Tsentrosoyuz, the headquarters of the cooperative movement (Cat. 65). This, his largest structure of the interwar period, would not be completed until 1936. The failure to implement the sophisticated air-conditioning and heating system he had envisaged was a sign of the backwardness of Russian building technology, while the challenge of accommodating hundreds of clerks led him to design novel circulation systems using ramps throughout the scheme. The Berlin architect Bruno Taut and former Bauhaus director Hannes Meyer, both present in Moscow in the early 1930s and whose political sympathies for the regime were openly declared, made fun of Le Corbusier's lack

of realism when confronted with the dire state of local building sites.[27]

Meyer had arrived in the Soviet Union with a 'brigade' of young architects and worked primarily on the planning of new towns in the east of the country. He designed the plan of Birobidzhan, the capital of the Jewish territory created near the Pacific. Simultaneously, the most successful of the planners hired by the Soviet organisations was Ernst May, former head of Frankfurt am Main's city planning and housing administration, who arrived in Moscow in 1930 with an even more numerous 'brigade'. Enthusiastic about the campaign launched under the aegis of the Five Year Plan to build hundreds of new towns, May took part in numerous competitions, for instance in Magnitogorsk, the new metallurgical centre created east of the Urals, and his planning work gave a decisive impetus to the formulation of design standards that would remain in place for several decades. He also brought to the Russian sites the experience of heavy prefabrication developed in Frankfurt's *Siedlungen*.[28]

But the most prolific of all the Western *spetsy* (specialists) engaged in the Five Year Plan's expansive programme was the Detroit firm of Albert Kahn Associates, widely known in Russia through its buildings for General Motors and Ford. Other American firms, such as the Austin Company, were also active, but the output of Kahn's office was staggering: in a few years it was responsible for nearly 600 plants across the country. The most important was a tractor factory in Cheliabinsk, which Andrei Burov helped to design.[29] During World War II this American-looking facility switched to the production of military equipment and became the nucleus of a gigantic arsenal nicknamed 'Tankograd'. Significantly, the very centre of

26 A.H. Barr, Jr, 'Russian Diary 1927–28', republished in *October*, Vol. 3, No. 7, 1978, p. 13.

27 'Hannes Meyer über Sowjetrußland', in *Die Baugilde*, No. 30, 1931, p. 1602; H. Meyer, 'Bauen, Bauarbeiter und Techniker in der Sowjetunion', in *Das neue Russland*, Nos 8–9, 1931, p. 49.

28 M. de Michelis and E. Pasini, *La città sovietica*, Venice, 1976.

29 A. Kopp, 'Foreign architects in the Soviet Union during the first two five-year plans', in W.C. Brumfield (ed.), *Reshaping Russian Architecture: Western Technology, Utopian Dreams*, Cambridge and New York, 1990, pp. 176–214.

Figure 6 Cover of P.M. Bardi, *Un fascista al paese dei Soviet*, Rome, 1933

Soviet power for decades was a product of the work of US designers and technology.

AVANT-GARDE DÉNOUEMENT

The year 1932 was in many ways a watershed in Soviet architecture. The polemics between rival groups aspiring to monopolise the ruling party's support provided a good excuse to replace the pluralist milieu with a pyramidal and monolithic union. However, the critics lined up against Constructivism by the party's leadership and OSA's opponents in the profession did not secure the marginalisation of its leaders, who continued to control some architectural output. Ilia Golosov, Nikolai Kolli – Le Corbusier's Moscow partner – and Konstantin Melnikov were still among the heads of the new design studios established in 1934 by the Moscow municipality, and the debates with Lazar Kaganovich, the party leader in charge of architecture, continued to be vibrant and confrontational.[30]

Yet the tide had turned with two significant events in which foreign architects were engaged. The first was the competition held in 1931–32 for the Palace of Soviets, which was intended to become the forum of a Socialist Moscow. Invited Western architects, such as Walter Gropius, Erich Mendelsohn, Auguste Perret or Le Corbusier, were sidelined and severely attacked in the press, and a winning trio of Boris Iofan, Ivan Zholtovskii and the unknown American Hector Hamilton was announced. In the end Iofan, an architect trained in Rome, where he had initially practised, would get the job. Simultaneously, projects for replanning Moscow submitted by Hannes Meyer, Ernst May and other Western urbanists were turned down in favour of a scheme by Vladimir Semionov, a planner who had acquired significant experience of the British Garden City movement in London before 1914.[31]

Large Modernist projects continued to be built throughout the decade, such as the Vesnins' Palace of Culture for Moscow's Proletarskii district. Yet extremely aggressive attacks targeted 'Korbusianizm' and 'Leonidovizm', the latter term derived from the name of Constructivism's *enfant terrible*, and in the mid-1930s the 'infamous heritage' of Ernst May came under fire.[32] To avoid being sidelined, Vesnin, Ginzburg and Kolli had to criticise the 'abuses' of Constructivism at the 1937 Congress. During this period, the press campaigned against an architecture of 'boxes', pleading for a return to architecture understood as an art. Paradoxically, the Western reception of the Soviet avant-garde was beginning to take on a broader dimension as the path to regression was being traced in the USSR. Until 1936 the large-format illustrated magazine *USSR in Construction*, edited by journalist Mikhail Koltsov, regularly published images of factories, housing and public buildings. Laid out by avant-garde artists such as Aleksandr Rodchenko, El Lissitzky or Solomon Telingater, it was broadly circulated in its German, English and French editions, and displayed the buildings in use within their urban context.[33]

Western magazines started to feature more extensive records of Soviet architecture. In 1932 *L'Architecture d'aujourd'hui* published an account of a study trip to the USSR by some thirty professionals. The civil engineer Jean-Jacques Coulon wrote on building technology, Georges-Henri Pingusson on the spirit of the huge construction sites, and the planner Donat-Alfred Agache on the new towns.[34] Two books resulted from the journey: Marius Boyer's *Au pays des tovaritchi*, published in Casablanca, and Pietro Maria Bardi's *Un fascista al paese dei soviet*, published in Rome.[35] In London, *The Architectural Review* discussed the 'Russian Scene' in May 1932, documenting the competition for the Palace of Soviets. Robert Byron suggested provocative

30 Otdel Proektirovania Mossoveta, *Raboty arkhitekturnykh masterskikh (Portfolio of Architectural Workshops)*, Moscow, 1935.

31 H. Bodenschatz, C. Post (eds), *Städtebau im Schatten Stalins: die internationale Suche nach der sozialistischen Stadt in der Sowjetunion 1929–1935*, Berlin, 2003.

32 A. Mordvinov, 'Leonidovshchina i ego vred' ('Leonidovizm and its damage'), in *Isskustvo v massy (Arts of the Masses)*, No. 12, 1930, pp. 12–15; V. Lavrov, V. Popov, 'Protiv nekriticheskogo otnoshenia k eksperimentam zapadnykh arkhitektorov' ('Against uncritical relationships with the experiments of Western architects'), in *Stroitelstvo Moskvy (Construction Moscow)*, No. 9, September 1930, pp. 8–12; A. Mostakov, 'Bezobraznoe nasledstvo arkhitektora Ernsta Maia' ('The infamous heritage of Ernst May'), in *Arkhitektura SSSR*, Vol. 4, No. 9, September 1937, pp. 60–63.

33 E. Wolf, '*SSSR na stroike:* From Constructivist Visions to Construction Sites', in *USSR in Construction: An Illustrated Exhibition Magazine*, Sundsvall, 2006, n.p.

34 J.-J. Coulon, 'Les problèmes techniques en Russie soviétique' and G.-H. Pingusson, 'Un formidable champ d'expériences', in *L'Architecture d'aujourd'hui*, Vol. 3, No. 8, November 1932, pp. 66 and 77–78.

35 M. Boyer, *Au pays des tovaritchi*, Casablanca, 1932 and P.M. Bardi, *Un fascista al paese dei Soviet*, Rome, 1933.

Figure 7 L. Rempel, *Arkhitektura poslevoennoi Italii*, Moscow, 1935

comparisons of 'dwellings and porches through four centuries', featuring the Melnikov House (Cat. 83) and Mikhail Barshch and Mikhail Siniavskii's Planetarium entrance (derived from Le Corbusier's first Tsentrosoyuz design). Berthold Lubetkin questioned 'Architectural Thought Since the Revolution', reproducing, among other buildings, the Narkomfin Communal House and the Kharkov Gosprom Building (Cat. 75, 63). He analysed 'The Recent Developments of Town Planning in [the] USSR', focusing on DneproGES and the nearby city of Zaporozhye, including a caricature from *Krokodil* mocking the way residents customised new repetitive buildings by adding individual features.[36]

Contemporaneously, however, Soviet hostility led CIAM (Congrès internationaux d'architecture moderne) to cancel its intended fourth congress in Moscow in 1932; it would take place the following year in Athens. Sigfried Giedion, CIAM's general secretary, did not help by reacting to the new course set by the Palace of Soviets competition with a critical photomontage, which was sent to Stalin. In this uncertain phase it is remarkable that Melnikov was invited to show his work in the foreign section of the 1933 Milan Triennale. Another Soviet figure met a warm response in the West: Nikolai Miliutin's book *Sotsgorod*, propagating the concept of the linear industrial city featuring parallel ribbons of industrial facilities, housing and parks, was partially translated into German and fully published in a Czech version in Prague.[37]

SOCIALIST REALISM AND WESTERN INPUTS

In the mid-1930s, while the German specialists invited in 1930 left Russia in their hundreds, new guests from the West legitimised the turn towards Socialist Realism's historicist doctrine. Le Corbusier's arch-rival André Lurçat worked in Moscow from 1934 to 1937 and theorised about the 'absence of maturity' in building technology in order to justify the new course. Leftist French writers Paul Nizan and Jean-Richard Bloch argued respectively against the 'skeletal' character of Constructivist buildings and in favour of the 'right of the people to columns'.[38] However, designs and buildings from abroad continued to be discussed in various ways. The journal *Arkhitektura za rubezhom* (*Architecture Abroad*), published from 1934 to 1936 with Hannes Meyer on its editorial board, disseminated images of European and North American work, with particular emphasis on schemes such as the Rockefeller Center in New York. Germany almost vanished from the Soviet worldview, but Fascist Italy attracted attention and led to the publication in 1935 of Lazar Rempel's *Arkhitektura poslevoennoi Italii* (*Postwar Italian Architecture*), a book so embarrassingly positive that it led to its author's deportation. Among the heroes newly celebrated in Moscow were the French architects Auguste Perret, Michel Roux-Spitz and Marcel Lods, the first two because of their search for a modernised Classicism, and the last because of his experiments in prefabricated housing. While predominantly centred on the Renaissance, the historical investigations undertaken under the aegis of the Academy of Architecture, created to foster research, did not ignore modern Western work when it could be used to justify the marginalisation of the avant-garde. It is symptomatic that the only translation of Sigfried Giedion's 1928 book *Bauen in Frankreich*, which related the work of Le Corbusier to nineteenth-century iron buildings, was published in Moscow in 1937.[39]

In the second half of the 1930s Constructivism continued to cast a shadow over built work that could be defined as an early expression of Post-Modernism – that is, an architecture trying to distance itself from the 'excesses' of the previous period by 'critically' assimilating the legacy of

36 R. Byron, 'The Foundations'; 'The Competition for the Palace of the Soviets, Moscow'; B. Lubetkin, 'The Builders'; 'The Planning of Towns', in *The Architectural Review*, Vol. 71, May 1932, pp. 196–208.

37 J.-L. Cohen, 'Le commissaire prend le crayon', foreword to N. Milioutine, *Sotsgorod, le problème de la construction des villes socialistes*, Paris, 2002, pp. 5–39.

38 P. Nizan, 'Problema monumentalnosti, proekt André Lurçat' ('The problem of monumentalism, design by André Lurcat'), in *Literaturnaia Gazeta*, 28 December 1934, p. 3; J.-R. Bloch, 'Discours aux écrivains soviétiques', in *Moscou–Paris*, Paris, 1947, p. 120.

39 S. Giedion, *Arkhitektura zheleza i zhelezobetona vo Frantsii* (*Iron and Concrete Architecture in France*), Moscow, 1937.

history. The freedom of vast compositions such as the Ordzhonikidze Sanatorium built by Ginzburg in 1934–37 in Kislovodsk, a spa resort in the Northern Caucasus (Cat. 91), owed much more to the investigations of OSA than to the Classical schemes then *de rigueur* in the USSR.[40]

The project that best epitomised the new course towards Socialist Realism, with its emphasis on monumentality and the recycling of linguistic fragments collected in historical structures, was Iofan's final design for the Palace of Soviets, which generated vibrant opposition in the West. The French novelist André Gide was unsparing in his criticism of the appalling situation of the Russian people in his 1936 bestseller *Retour de l'URSS*, and its 1937 postscript *Retouches à mon retour de l'URSS*, writing that 'the Russian worker will know why he starves in front of this 415-metre-high monument crowned by a statue of Lenin in stainless steel, one single finger of which will be ten metres long.'[41] A guest of honour at the 1937 Congress, Frank Lloyd Wright, whose architectural and planning work was widely known in the Soviet Union thanks to writings by Ginzburg and Iofan, also scorned his young colleague's Palace of Soviets but had not a single word for the repressed avant-garde.

The first Western narratives historicising Modern architecture were generally ignorant of Soviet production. If Henry-Russell Hitchcock reproduced Burov's set for *Old and New* in his 1929 *Modern Architecture: Romanticism and Reintegration*, Nikolaus Pevsner did not include any Russian building in his *Pioneers of the Modern Movement* of 1936, which celebrated the figure of Walter Gropius. Giedion's influential *Space, Time and Architecture: The Growth of a New Tradition* of 1941 stopped at Germany's eastern border, and only in 1950 would Bruno Zevi mention some Russian works in his *Storia dell'architettura moderna*, essentially in order to

construct a parallel with the architecture of Nazi Germany. Symmetrically, Russian publications started to erase the traces of the architecture imagined or built between 1917 and 1932, or trashed it completely. In his 1952 book on the 'realist foundations' of Soviet architecture Mikhail Tsapenko barely tolerated the Gosprom Building in Kharkov, and the Sokol garden-settlement in Moscow (completed in 1930) was the only acceptable example. The house Melnikov had built for himself (Cat. 83) and his own and Leonidov's entries in the Commissariat for Heavy Industry competition of 1934 were pictured only to be condemned.[42] Barely two years later Khrushchev started the campaign that led in 1955 to the final demise of Socialist Realism in architecture.

Almost all the buildings through which architects had tried to embody their own and their patrons' 'revolutionary dreams', to use Richard Stites' expression,[43] are still standing, albeit in the miserable condition documented by Richard Pare.[44] But the dense network of interaction between East and West that gave birth and meaning to many of them has been too long forgotten: during the Cold War period, admitting a previous association with the USSR was difficult in the West and many architects repressed their Russian experience, while on the other side of the Iron Curtain contact with the West could take you to the Gulag. Fortunately, recent research has brought back into the frame materials that vouch for a different picture: that of a specific architecture, shaped as much by the response to political power as by constant interaction with the main poles of Modernist innovation worldwide.

40 D. Udovicki, 'Between Modernism and Socialist Realism: Soviet Architectural Culture Under Stalin's "Revolution from Above": 1928–1938', in *Journal of the Society of Architectural Historians*, Vol. 68, No. 4, December 2009, pp. 467–95.
41 A. Gide, *Retouches à mon retour de l'URSS*, Paris, 1937, p. 157.
42 M. Tsapenko, *O realisticheskikh osnovakh sovetskoi arkhitektury (On the Realist Foundations of Soviet Architecture)*, Moscow, 1952.
43 R. Stites, *Revolutionary Dreams: Utopian Vision and Experimental Life in the Russian Revolution*, Oxford and New York, 1989.
44 A vibrant movement for the preservation of avant-garde architecture has developed in Moscow, most notably thanks to MAPS (Moscow Architecture Preservation Society), founded in 2004. Among its publications are: Aleksandr Kudriavstev, Natalia Dushkina (eds), *20th Century Preservation of Cultural Heritage*, Moscow, 2006; Edmund Harris (ed.), *Moscow Heritage at Crisis Point*, Moscow, 2007 (updated, expanded edition 2009).

THE SYNTHESIS OF ART AND ARCHITECTURE IN THE RUSSIAN AVANT-GARDE
THE COSTAKIS COLLECTION TESTIMONY

Maria Tsantsanoglou

In 1913 the Futurist poet Aleksei Kruchenykh wrote: 'I call a lily e-u-y, and thus restore its original innocence,' going on to conclude that 'the new verbal form creates a new content'.[1] In the short period between 1912 and 1921 the artists of the Russian avant-garde would make abstract form the key element to be explored in a work of art, defining the main components of the visual arts as line, volume, light, colour and texture.[2] This fascination with abstract form led to a logical synthesis of painting and sculpture with architecture. In 1919 IZO, the Visual Arts Section of the Commissariat for Education, set up the ZhivSkulptArkh collective, the name created from the initials of the Russian words for painting, sculpture and architecture. Its purpose was the definition of a new language for architecture that would incorporate the new experimentation in painting and sculpture. The focus on abstract form created a new style of painting free from naturalistic description and a new sculpture that replaced the statue with the construction; these definitions generated concepts that would, in turn, be applied to a new architecture.

Flying Sculptures and *Flying Cities*, *Axonometric Painting* and *Painterly Architectonics*, *Planetary Objects* and *Dynamic Cities*, *Tectonics* and *Spatial Force Constructions*: these are just some of the titles of works of art that refer directly to architectural terms. When abstract form becomes the primary concern of the artist, then it is abstract form that redefines, and often creates, content. In painting, the background functions as a void, governed by laws of tension, gravity and rhythm. Likewise, in sculpture the organisation of space and use of pure materials generated new methods of construction and modes of perception; a new approach to the relationship between the viewer and the three-dimensional work could be brokered.

The artists of the Russian avant-garde were determined to redefine the concept of space. Seven years before the 1921 OBMOKhU exhibition in Moscow at which Constructivism triumphed, Vladimir Tatlin had declared his position in respect to traditional sculpture, creating three-dimensional non-objective works which he described as 'counter reliefs' (Cats 2, 3). At *The Last Exhibition of Futurist Painting: 0.10*, held in St Petersburg in 1915, where Kazimir Malevich presented his manifestation of Suprematism, *Black Square*, Tatlin showed a series of flat and corner wall constructions based on the relationship between form and materials. These represented one of the first attempts to create a three-dimensional work that sought to differentiate itself from the traditional concept of a sculpture – hence the artist's determination to find an alternative name for his work. As the Modern Movement has evolved, Tatlin's 'counter reliefs' have led to 'constructions', and 'constructions' to 'installations'.

From 1917 Tatlin turned to architectural design, culminating in 1919 with the plans for the *Monument to the Third International*, a glass and steel building intended to house the operations of the Comintern on three levels, each with a different geometric form revolving at a different speed. Although the building was never realised, it was celebrated for its radicalism by writers such as Nikolai Punin, who declared that 'the basic idea for this monument evolved from the organic synthesis of the principles governing architecture, sculpture and painting, thus providing a new pattern of monumental construction that combined the purely creative form with the functional.'[3]

At *The Last Exhibition of Futurist Painting: 0.10*, Ivan Kliun presented a series of works he called *Flying Sculptures*. These may have been the earliest 'mobiles' in the history of modern art. Unfortunately,

1 A. Kruchenykh, *Deklaratsiya slova kak takovogo* (*The Declaration of the Word as Such*), published as a leaflet, Moscow, 1913.
2 Much was written by artists and theorists of the avant-garde in the debate on form and content. For example: W. Kandinsky, 'Soderzhanie i Forma' ('Content and Form'), first published in the catalogue of the Second Artistic Salon organised by Vladimir Izdebskii in Odessa, 1910; D. Burliuk, 'Faktura' ('Texture'), in the anthology/manifesto *Poshchechina obshchestennomu vkusu* (*A Slap in the Face of Public Taste*), Moscow, 1912; V. Markov, *Faktura* (*Texture*), St Petersburg, 1914; W. Kandinsky, 'O linii' ('About Line'), in *Iskusstvo* (*Art*), Moscow, 1919; A. Rodchenko, 'Liniia' ('The Line'), first published in S.O. Khan-Magomedov, *INKhUK i Ranii Konstruktivism* (*INKhUK and Early Constructivism*), Moscow, 1994.
3 N. Punin, *Pamiatnik Tretevo Internatsionala* (*Monument to the Third International*), published as a leaflet, St Petersburg, 1921.

none of the works has survived nor is there any photographic record. Thus Kliun's careful drawings in the Costakis Collection (Cats 4.1–4.7) are crucial to the study of experimentation with form, materials and design during the early years of the Russian avant-garde. Dating from 1914–15, the *Flying Sculptures* are constructions free of any attempt at figurative representation; they seek to foster a new perception of space, as defined by objects suspended in space, like the planets of the solar system.

Flying cities, the cities of the future, fascinated both artists and architects: in 1928, for example, the architect Georgii Krutikov designed just such a flying city of the future. A subject of particular interest to the European architectural avant-garde, it was also frequently found in the designs of the Italian Futurist architect Antonio Sant'Elia, the utopian architect Wenzel Hablik and others. The idea of space flight attracted artists, engineers, philosophers and physicists, inviting them to engage in extensive experimentation and speculation; although this may have seemed utopian at the time, it was eventually to become a reality.[4]

From 1919 to 1921 Gustav Klutsis was working on the idea of the painted representation of a planet moving through space where the rules of gravity are observed, while at the same time the various planes intersecting the sphere seek to convey messages about the possibilities of technological advances. The painting is called *Dynamic City* (Cat. 12) and is of particular interest because of the way materials – oil mixed with concrete, sand and tar on wood – are used to transform texture. Klutsis also presented the painting under the titles *Plan for the City of the Future* and *Dynamic City of the Future*, and described his artistic method as 'axonometric painting'. Similarly, Mikhail Plaksin created his own *Planetary World* and El Lissitzky the *Proun* series.

El Lissitzky, painter, photographer, book designer and architect, was one of Malevich's closest collaborators at UNOVIS in Vitebsk. During the period 1919–21 he produced a series of paintings depicting floating spheres: the spectator is invited to make the spheres revolve in his or her mind's eye, creating an illusion of spinning, of turning around some hypothetical centre of gravity (Cats 14, 15). These paintings and drawings, which El Lissitzky described as 'the transitional stage from painting to architecture', present utopian constructions that seem to hover above a substratum we are invited to see as the universe. He named the series *Proun*, an acronym derived from *Proekt utverzhdeniia novogo* (Project for the affirmation of the new). 'When we turn the canvas, we have the sensation of entering the space and ourselves becoming part of the construction,' the artist explained in a lecture in 1924. The same rationale was followed in the design for the *Monument to Rosa Luxemburg* (Cat. 13), probably done for a competition announced by the Commissariat for Education in 1919. The *Proun* works study the relationship between form and material, colour and material, material and construction.[5] These concerns, as well as the formalist, revolving conception of the series, later influenced El Lissitzky in his architectural work, such as the *Wolkenbügel* project, a series of horizontal skyscrapers in Moscow (1925), or the plans for an international aviation fair in Paris (1932).

It should be noted that both Klutsis' *Dynamic City* and El Lissitzky's *Proun* series were informed by Suprematist theories. Later, as a teacher at VKhUTEMAS, Klutsis became a militant champion of Constructivism, declaring that Suprematism had given all it had to offer.[6] El Lissitzky, on the other hand, who taught interior design at the VKhUTEMAS-VKhUTEIN workshops from 1925 to 1930, combined his experience of the application

4 See J. Bowlt, N. Misler, M. Tsantsanoglou, 'Engines of the Russian Cosmos', in *The Cosmos of the Russian Avant-Garde: Art and Space Exploration, 1900–1930*, exh. cat., Fundación Marcelino Botín, Santander, 2010, pp. 321–30.
5 On the connection of art and architecture in El Lissitzky's *Proun* project, see V. Rakitin, 'El Lissitzky 1890–1941', in O.A. Shvidkovsky (ed.), *Building in the USSR 1917–1932*, New York, 1971, pp. 35–41.
6 See G. Klutsis, S. Senkin, 'Masterskaia Revoliutsii' ('The Workshop of the Revolution'), in *LEF*, No. 1 (4), 1924, pp. 155–59.

of Suprematism to graphic design and architecture with the new, Constructivist vision of Klutsis.

When Malevich first presented his 'suprematism of painting' in 1915, extolling, among others, Olga Rozanova for her 'fittingly Suprematist' sculptures, he essentially denied the artists who followed him any legitimate possibility of engaging in figurative representation, even in the form of Cubofuturism. Suprematist sculpture replaced Cubist sculpture and quickly became associated with architecture.

Between 1919 and 1927 Malevich ceased to paint, declaring that he had taken painting to its limits and no longer had faith in its representational value. To explain this shift, it is necessary to explore in some detail the ideas that informed his decision. During the first phase of Suprematist painting (1915–18) he had created flat, two-dimensional artworks, in which he ignored the third dimension altogether while engaging in philosophical and aesthetic exploration of a fourth dimension. In the mind of the artistic community, this fourth dimension was a parameter in a non-Euclidean geometry, the exploration of which offered wide scope for experimentation and enquiry, appealing to both philosophers (Petr Uspenskii) and artists (Kazimir Malevich, Mikhail Matiushin).

From 1919 onwards Malevich began to refer in his writings to the new architecture, mainly in relation to proposals for celebratory decorations for the town of Vitebsk. From 1921 to 1927 he created works which carried Suprematist theory into the third dimension. In this period he constructed white architectural models of fantastic buildings, evoking cities of the future, which he named *Architectons*, titled using the letters of the Greek alphabet (Cat. 21). The *Architectons* were created in tandem with the *Planit* series, which was also three-dimensional. The former are studies in volume and form, while

the latter also takes into account the practical needs of human habitation. From 1921 Malevich wished to show that Suprematism had a practical application in order to rebut growing criticism from the Constructivists, who asserted that the programme delivered art that was merely metaphysical and decorative. *Suprematist Skyscraper*, a photomontage created by Malevich in 1925, represents an attempt to demonstrate the practical role of Suprematism in the design of structures for a new way of life.

Malevich's *Architecton* works seem to come from the world of science fiction. Their influence on modern architecture has been demonstrated and studied,[7] but their application to the design of utilitarian objects should also be noted, for it began in the 1920s. A characteristic example is the Suprematist inkwell in the form of an *Architecton* (Cat. 22) designed by Malevich's student, Nikolai Suetin.

The *Architectons* inspired many artists in Malevich's circle to move from painting to architecture. The application of Suprematism to the urban environment had already been made, under the guidance of Malevich, by the students at UNOVIS in Vitebsk. From late 1919 to 1921 they had undertaken to decorate the city for the celebrations of the anniversary of the October Revolution. The ground plans they drew for buildings were combined with proposals for Suprematist decoration, and painted buildings and train carriages (Cat. 17).

In 1919 Malevich sent his associate, the artist Ivan Kudriashev, to Orenburg to set up a branch of UNOVIS and to teach the philosophy and methodology of Suprematism. The Costakis Collection contains a letter from Malevich to Kudriashev referring to the latter's work in Orenburg, where the artist was invited to design

7   See, for example, C. Lodder, 'Living in Space: Kazimir Malevich's Suprematist Architecture and the Philosophy of Nikolai Fedorov', in C. Douglas, C. Lodder (eds), *Rethinking Malevich*, London, 2007, pp. 172–202.

the interior of the First Soviet Theatre. Kudriashev's three drawings (Cats 18–20)[8] are studies for the design for the stage and were presented at the First State Fair in Orenburg in 1920. 'Painting,' Kudriashev wrote when the plans were made public, 'in the form defined by this work of mine, ceases to be an abstract, formalist, chromatic construction, and becomes the realistic expression of the contemporary perception of space, the material reality. This is the essential new element which is now represented by the painting of space.'[9]

There is no better evidence of the organic relationship between painting and architecture than the work Liubov Popova made between 1916 and 1921, and particularly the *Painterly Architectonics* and *Spatial Force Constructions* series (Cats 5–8, 10). Influenced by Malevich's dynamic Suprematism, she created relief paintings in which forms combine to suggest structurally unified components, with emphasis on the diagonal motion that directs the structure upwards, reinforcing the dynamism of the composition as a whole. The study and interpretation of space are the main preoccupations of these works, which annihilate the boundaries between painting and architecture. They place the former at the service of the construction, and subject the latter to a logic of synthesis.

The concept behind Popova's *Architectonics* transcends the strict limits of architecture and is related to the dynamic combination of geometrical forms, volumes and materials. Popova's paintings offered architects original propositions about painterly geometry. Her interest in architectural forms was undoubtedly stimulated by her friend and colleague, the architect Aleksandr Vesnin; they had collaborated, for example, in 1921 on designs for a mass festival to be held in Moscow to honour the Third Congress of the Comintern.[10]

This exploration and study of the relationship between composition and construction was articulated in an open discussion between artists and architects held from January to April 1921 at INKhUK in Moscow. INKhUK was founded in 1920, the same year as VKhUTEMAS, and operated for almost four years. Its first director, Wassily Kandinsky, encouraged dialogue and synthesis between the arts, going so far as to claim that before long there would be created 'an edifice which is the result of thinking in all kinds of art, adapted for all kinds of art, those that exist already and those that we still only dream of.' Kandinsky named this ideal edifice the 'Great Utopia'.[11]

In 1923 most members of INKhUK's architectural department came together to found ASNOVA. Although INKhUK was the breeding ground for the elaboration of Constructivist theory and practice, during its short life it promoted a robustly Rationalist approach. This was expounded primarily by Nikolai Ladovskii, who challenged the aesthetic principles of Constructivism, as advocated chiefly by Aleksandr Vesnin. Without altogether dismissing the relevance of the new developments in painting and sculpture, the Rationalist architects claimed that Constructivist architecture remained very closely related to visual Constructivism and was therefore limited to the expressive rendering of form without recognising the critical importance of such architectural issues as space, materials and function. It should be noted that Constructivism was still a very new movement, having first emerged from the VKhUTEMAS and INKhUK workshops, specifically from the First Working Group of Constructivists (Aleksei Gan, Aleksandr Rodchenko, Varvara Stepanova, the Stenberg brothers, Konstantin Medunetskii and Karel Ioganson), which had participated in OBMOKhU's exhibition in May 1921.[12] Constructivism, the last major movement of the Russian avant-garde, was also a politicised

8 A fourth drawing in the same series, originally in the Costakis Collection, now belongs to the State Tretyakov Gallery in Moscow.
9 See V. Kostin, *OST: Obshchestvo Stankovistov* (*OST: The Society of Easel Painters*), St Petersburg, 1976, p. 25.
10 See C. Lodder, above, p. 98.
11 W. Kandinsky, 'Velikaia Utopiia' ('The Great Utopia'), an article in *Khudozhestvennaia Zhizn* (*Artistic Life*; a magazine published by IZO (the Visual Arts Section of the Commissariat for Education), No. 3, Moscow, 1920.
12 This was followed in January 1922 by an exhibition under the title *Constructivists* by the Stenberg brothers and Konstantin Medunetskii, held at the Poetov café in Moscow, and by Aleksei Gan's book/manifesto, *Konstruktivizm*, Tver, 1922.

movement. Utterly loyal to Marxism, it championed materialism over idealism, and the union of art and life – art should meet social needs, should be functional and should express Bolshevik ideology, in which art has its role in the foundation of a new Communist society.

The original group of Constructivists was made up mainly of visual artists who had renounced pure painting in favour of art as a utilitarian product. A group of equally innovative architects, headed by Ladovskii, raised questions of Rationalist and Formalist architectural practice, asserting that Constructivism was of use only in design, not in pure architecture. When those who worked only as architects, however, such as the Vesnin brothers, Konstantin Melnikov, Mikhail Barshch and others, adopted the Constructivist approach, it soon became apparent that Constructivism could transcend the limits of representation and be given practical application.

Launched between January and April 1921, a series of discussions took place at INKhUK on the analysis and definition of the concepts of 'composition' and 'construction'. The portfolio of drawings that resulted from these discussions was preserved by George Costakis (Cats 24–36). The artists and architects taking part in the dialogue had a variety of approaches: some perceived construction as the process of technical and mechanical drawing and composition as drawing for sculpture (aesthetic), while others regarded construction as the organisational framework of structures in space and composition as the combination of planes. Ladovskii was the only practitioner whose drawings represent both aspects within the same architectural design, proposing a duality of construction and 'synthesis'. He claimed that construction combines the development of material elements with a specific plan, and hence produces a synthesis of construction and composition; for Ladovskii, the proof of a successful construction lay in the absence of unnecessary materials and features, while for synthesis he was committed to coordination and hierarchy.[13] Konstantin Medunetskii created a flat (two-dimensional) representation of the form of an object, reminiscent of the musical lyre, as an example of synthesis; this becomes three-dimensional, with precise measurements, in the case of the construction. Boris Korolev used representation in the case of synthesis and was non-objective (abstract) in that of construction; his proposal concerns a study for a public sculpture derived from the Cubist statue of Mikhail Bakunin that he had created in 1918.[14]

Having now broken the relationship with their traditional tools – oil paint and canvas – artists turned to the study of science, mechanics, physics and geometry in order to offer, through their work, ideas and practical solutions that might be viable in the fields of design, graphics and, finally, architecture. In doing so, they sought to revolutionise art by placing it at the service of mass production. This was the ideology underlying the work of, for example, Gustav Klutsis, who designed and built impressive constructions – of which only photographs have survived.

After graduating from VKhUTEMAS, in 1921–24 Klutsis became an active member of INKhUK. He advocated the rejection of pure painting and sought to expand the range of possibilities open to artists through deep knowledge and application of the rules of architecture and engineering. From 1924 to 1930 he taught graphic design and architecture at VKhUTEMAS. He replaced the term 'axonometric painting', which he had used in 1920 to describe his artistic works, with 'construction' in 1922 (Cats 54–57). In the same year, as a member of INKhUK's Production Art group, he designed

13 See S.O. Khan-Magomedov, *Nikolai Ladovskii*, Moscow, 2007, pp. 31–32.
14 This was one of the first propaganda statues created in the experimental aesthetic erected in Moscow, but it was too extreme for its time; it provoked a fierce public reaction and did not remain on display for long.

a series of propaganda kiosks (Cats 48–53). Two were constructed for the Fourth Congress of the Comintern in November 1922 and the kiosks subsequently enjoyed great popularity when their plans were published in books and magazines and models were shown at exhibitions.

In 1921 the art critic and fervent advocate of Production Art, Nikolai Tarabukin, declared: 'The Pegasus of the Ancients is dead. His place has been taken by the Ford automobile. The style of our times is not created by the Rembrandts, but by the engineers. The men who build the ocean liners, the airplanes, the express trains are not yet aware that they are the creators of the new aesthetic.'[15] The cause of 'art in production' was also championed by Communist theorists such as Osip Brik and Boris Arvatov. Many artists of the avant-garde turned their creative energies to this mission, looking for work in book design, fabrics and furniture as well as in advertising, propaganda and theatre design. They even attempted architecture, as is demonstrated in a very rare original model by the artist and architect Aleksei Babichev which is preserved in the Costakis Collection (Cat. 47); it was made in 1924 and entered for a competition for the design of an arch intended for the open space in front of the Bolshoi Theatre in Moscow. The arch was to be made of metal and glass with a monument dedicated to the Communist activist Iakov Sverdlov at its centre. Similarly, in 1917 Aleksandr Rodchenko had begun to take an interest in the projection of flat surfaces in space and to design folding constructions that would help in the formulation of new functional furniture; he subsequently applied himself to graphic and porcelain design, theatre and cinema interiors, and architecture. His design for a 'construction', dated 1921 is his contribution to the debate on synthesis and construction at INKhUK and is related to a study for the design of a table lamp.

A discussion of the relationship between visual arts and architecture in the 1920s must include consideration of the theory of tectonics, a theory based on three principles: the application, the organisation and the manipulation of industrial materials. The painting *The Connection of Painting to Architecture* (Cat. 23) by Solomon Nikritin dates from the period when Nikritin had started using the term 'tectonic' in order to transcend the narrow concept of architectural design and to declare his commitment to a typological organisation of materials. In this he was alluding to the theory of 'tectology', derived from the management theories of the American engineer Frederick Winslow Taylor and propounded by the Russian politician, philosopher and writer Aleksandr Bogdanov. Like Russian artists and architects of his time, Bogdanov moved like a prophet between science and fantasy: he is regarded as the precursor of cybernetics, the designer of the state programme for proletariat education (*Proletkult*) and one of the most important writers of science fiction of the 1920s. All three of his preoccupations would inevitably lead, one way or another, to the conception and construction of the City of the Future.

15 N. Tarabukin, *Ot molberta k mashine* (*From the Easel to the Machine*), Moscow, 1921.

ART

ARCHITECTURE

ВИДЪ ИЗЪ МОЕГО ОКНА НА ДОМА....

ИЗЪ Кварширы Мытнинская наб.

1906

Cat. 1
Liubov Popova
View from My Window onto Houses, 1906
Pencil on paper, 157 x 740 mm

This drawing depicts the view of houses
seen from the window of the 16-year-old
Popova's home. The representation of
the buildings seen 'from the apartment
on Mitninskaia ulitsa, beside the river'
in Moscow indicates the young artist's
impressions of the urban landscape of the
Russian capital. Popova and her family
had moved to Moscow from Yalta that year.

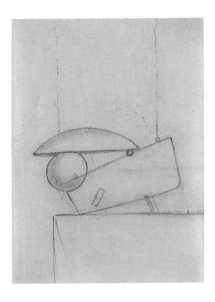

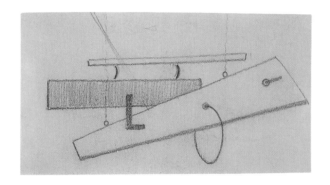

32

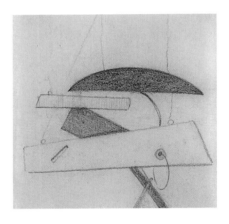

Cat. 4.1 top left
Ivan Kliun
Study for 'Three-Dimensional Construction',
c. 1915
Pencil on paper, 104 x 73 mm

Cat. 4.2 bottom left
Ivan Kliun
Study for 'Three-Dimensional Construction',
c. 1915
Pencil on paper, 76 x 76 mm

Cat. 4.3 top right
Ivan Kliun
Study for 'Three-Dimensional Construction',
c. 1915
Pencil on paper, 64 x 109 mm

Cat. 4.4 bottom right
Ivan Kliun
Study for 'Three-Dimensional Construction',
c. 1915
Pencil on paper, 100 x 94 mm

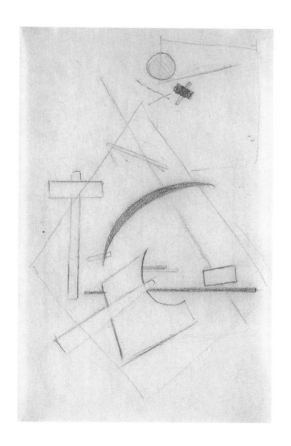

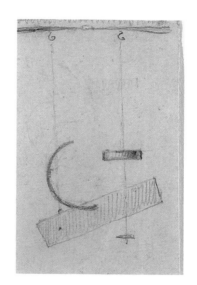

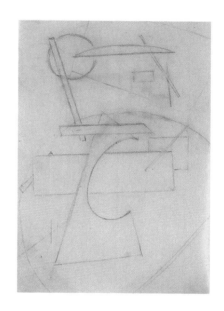

Cat. 4.5 left
Ivan Kliun
Study for 'Three-Dimensional Construction',
c. 1915
Pencil on paper, 153 x 94 mm

Cat. 4.6 centre
Ivan Kliun
Untitled, *c.* 1915
Pencil on paper, 100 x 67 mm

Cat. 4.7 right
Ivan Kliun
Untitled, *c.* 1915
Pencil on paper, 86 x 63 mm

Cat. 5
Liubov Popova
Painterly Architectonics, 1915–16
Oil on canvas, 435 x 439 mm

Cat. 6
Liubov Popova
Painterly Architectonics, 1918–19
Oil on canvas, 708 x 581 mm

Cat. 7
Liubov Popova
Painterly Architectonics, 1918–19
Oil on canvas, 731 x 481 mm

Cat. 8
Liubov Popova
Spatial Force Construction, 1921
Oil and marble dust on plywood,
710 x 639 mm

Cat. 9 opposite
Aleksandr Rodchenko
Linearism, 1920
Oil on canvas, 1029 x 696 mm

Cat. 10
Liubov Popova
Spatial Force Construction, 1920–21
Oil and marble dust on plywood,
1123 x 1125 mm

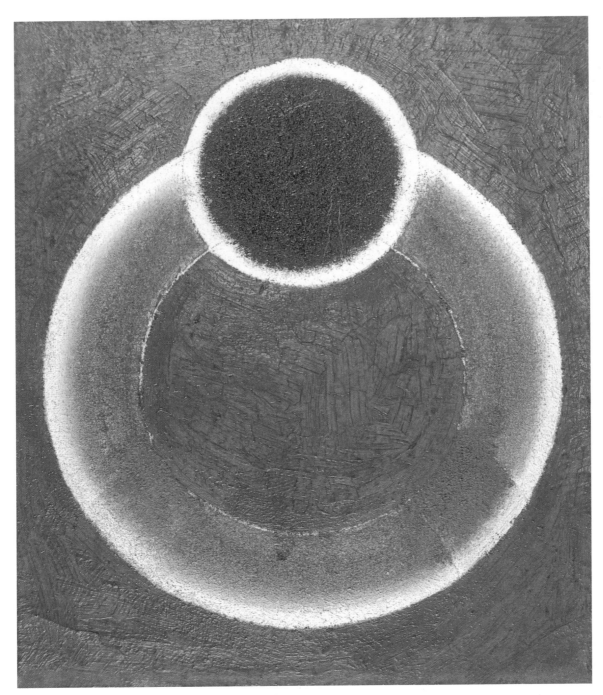

Cat. 11
Aleksandr Rodchenko
Untitled (Two Rings), 1918
Oil on canvas, 254 x 213 mm

Cat. 12
Gustav Klutsis
Dynamic City, 1919–21
Oil with sand and concrete on wood,
870 x 645 mm

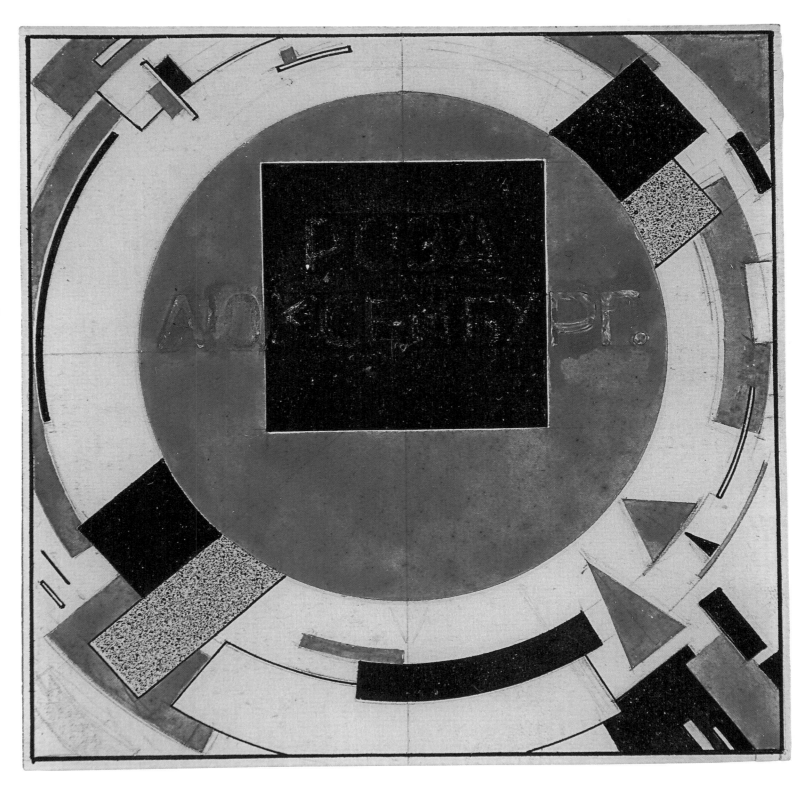

Cat. 13
El Lissitzky
Monument to Rosa Luxemburg, 1919–21
Pencil, ink and gouache on paper,
97 x 97 mm

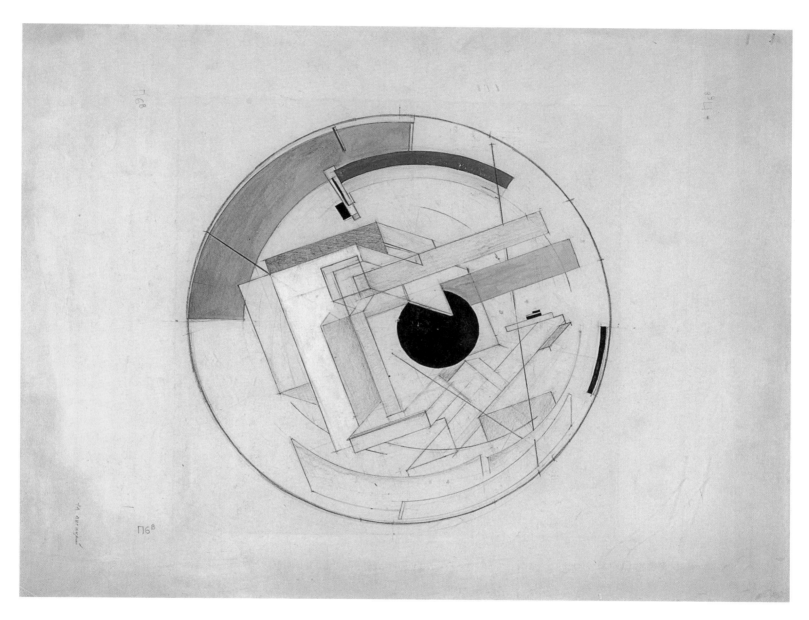

Cat. 14
El Lissitzky
Sketch for Proun 6B, 1919–21
Pencil and gouache on paper,
346 x 447 mm

Cat. 15
El Lissitzky
Sketch for Proun 10⁰, 1921
Pencil and gouache on paper,
279 x 231 mm

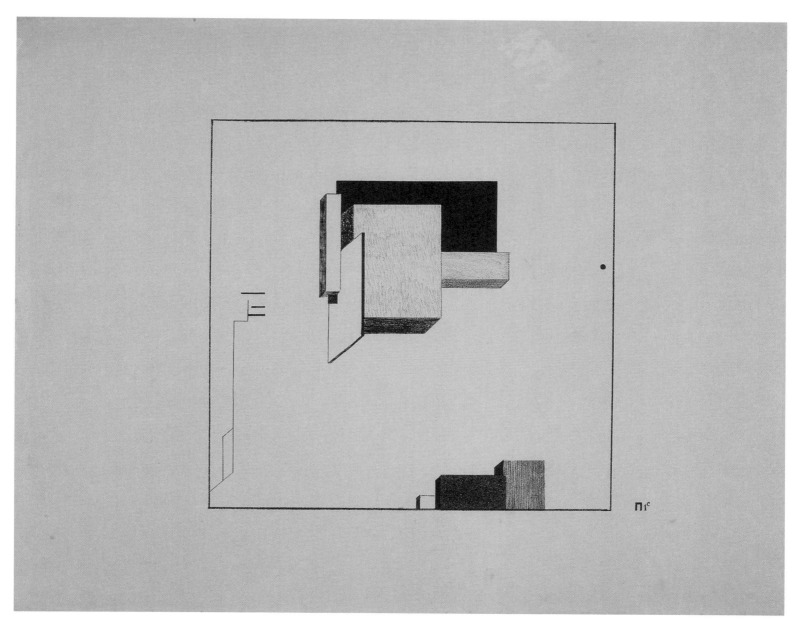

Cat. 16
El Lissitzky
Untitled, 1919
Lithograph on paper, 360 x 454 mm

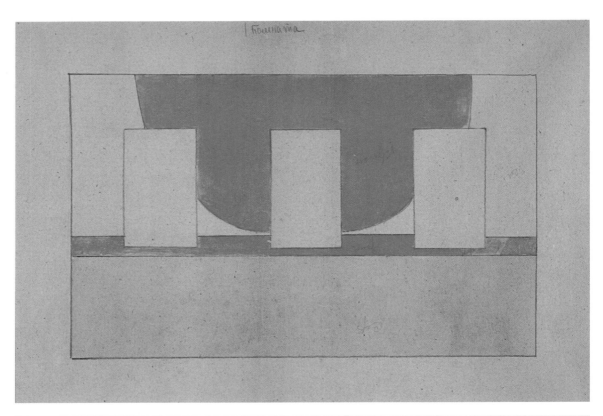

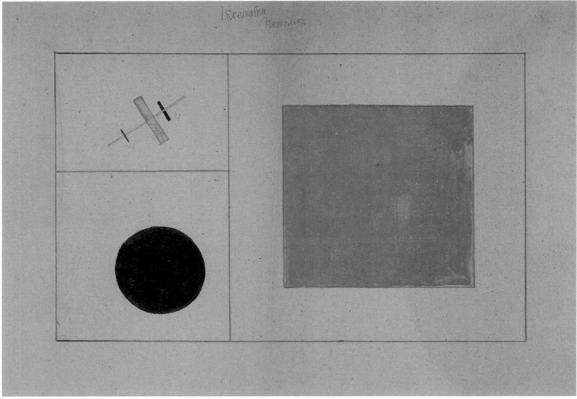

Cat. 17.1 top
Anon. (UNOVIS students, Vitebsk)
Untitled, c. 1919
Pencil and gouache on paper,
374 x 577 mm

Cat. 17.2 bottom
Anon. (UNOVIS students, Vitebsk)
Untitled, c. 1919
Pencil and watercolour on paper,
377 x 578 mm

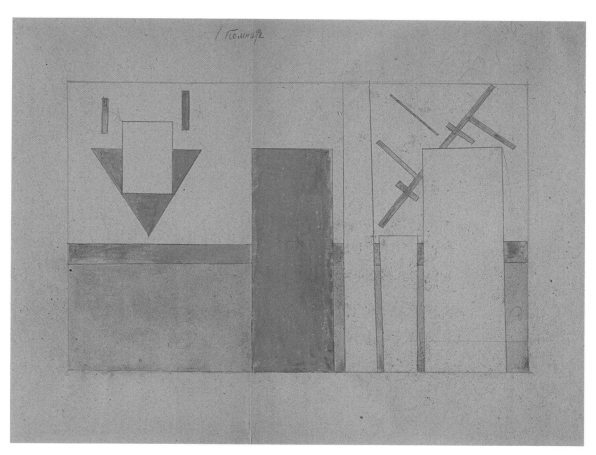

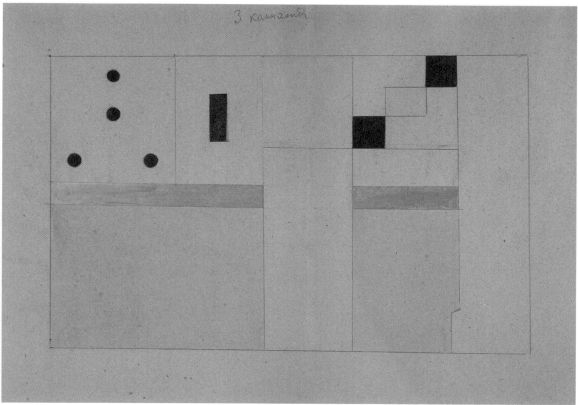

Cat. 17.3 top
Anon. (UNOVIS students, Vitebsk)
Untitled, *c*. 1919
Pencil and watercolour on paper,
379 x 576 mm

Cat. 17.4 bottom
Anon. (UNOVIS students, Vitebsk)
Untitled, *c*. 1919
Pencil and gouache on paper,
378 x 536 mm

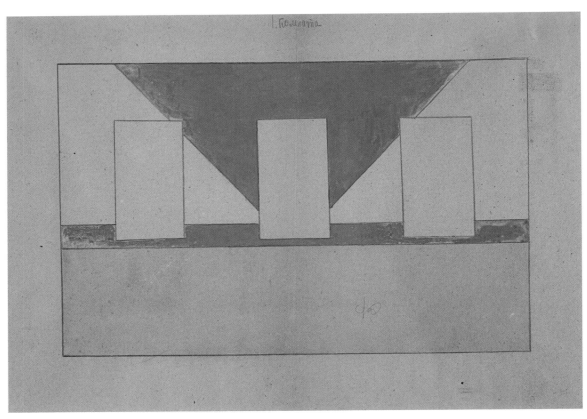

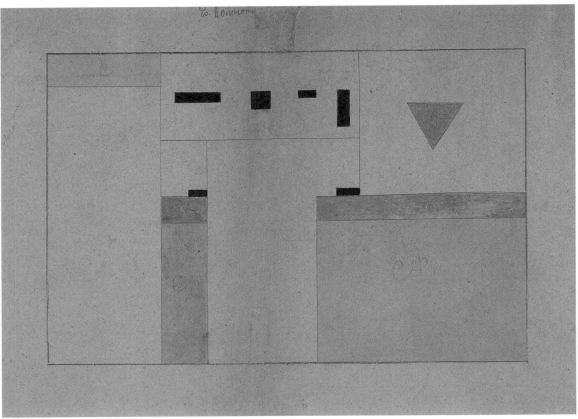

48

Cat. 17.5 top
Anon. (UNOVIS students, Vitebsk)
Untitled, *c.* 1919
Pencil and watercolour on paper,
375 x 576 mm

Cat. 17.6 bottom
Anon. (UNOVIS students, Vitebsk)
Untitled, *c.* 1919
Pencil and gouache on paper,
379 x 536 mm

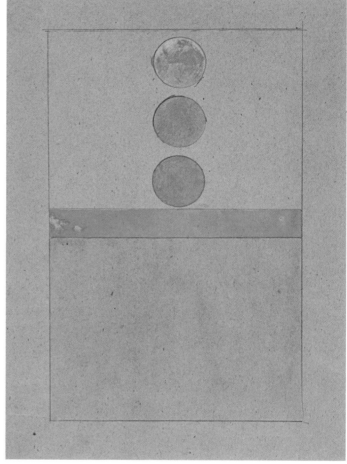

Cat. 17.7
Anon. (UNOVIS students, Vitebsk)
Untitled, c. 1919
Pencil and gouache on paper,
378 x 289 mm

Cat. 17.8
Anon. (UNOVIS students, Vitebsk)
Untitled, c. 1919
Pencil and gouache on paper,
375 x 287 mm

Cat. 18
Ivan Kudriashev
Drawing for the decoration of the
First Soviet Theatre in Orenburg (II), 1920
Pencil, ink and watercolour on paper,
133 x 390 mm

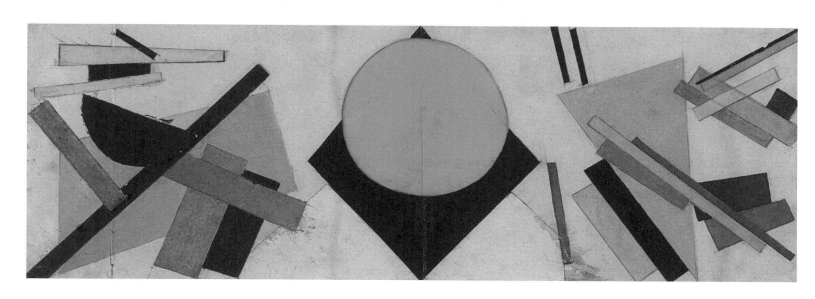

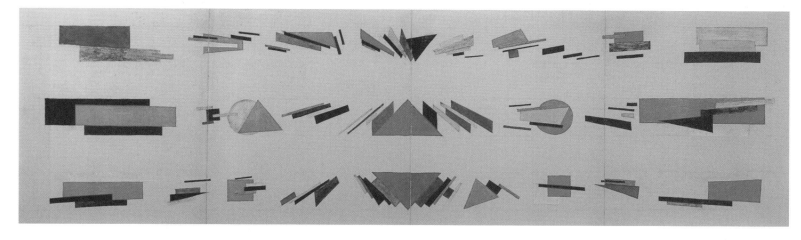

Cat. 19 top
Ivan Kudriashev
*Drawing for the decoration of the First Soviet
Theatre in Orenburg (I)*, 1920
Pencil, ink and watercolour on paper,
212 x 534 mm

Cat. 20 bottom
Ivan Kudriashev
*Drawing for the decoration of the First Soviet
Theatre in Orenburg*, 1920
Pencil, ink and watercolour on paper,
212 x 534 mm

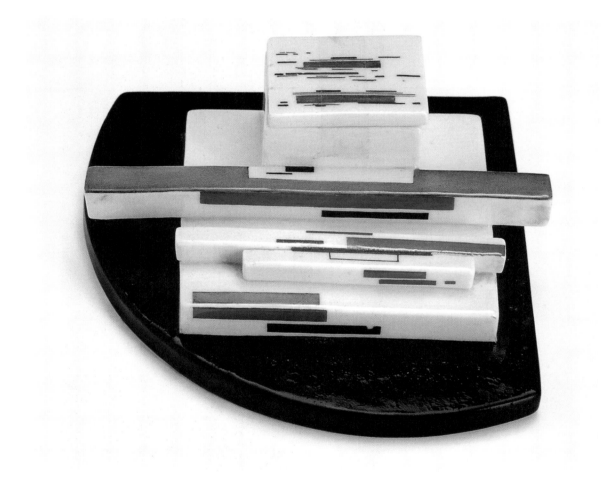

Cat. 21 opposite
Anon.
Photograph of Kazimir Malevich's
Architecton Zeta, 1926

Cat. 22
Nikolai Suetin (1897–1954)
Inkwell, mid-1920s
Porcelain, base 145 x 145 mm

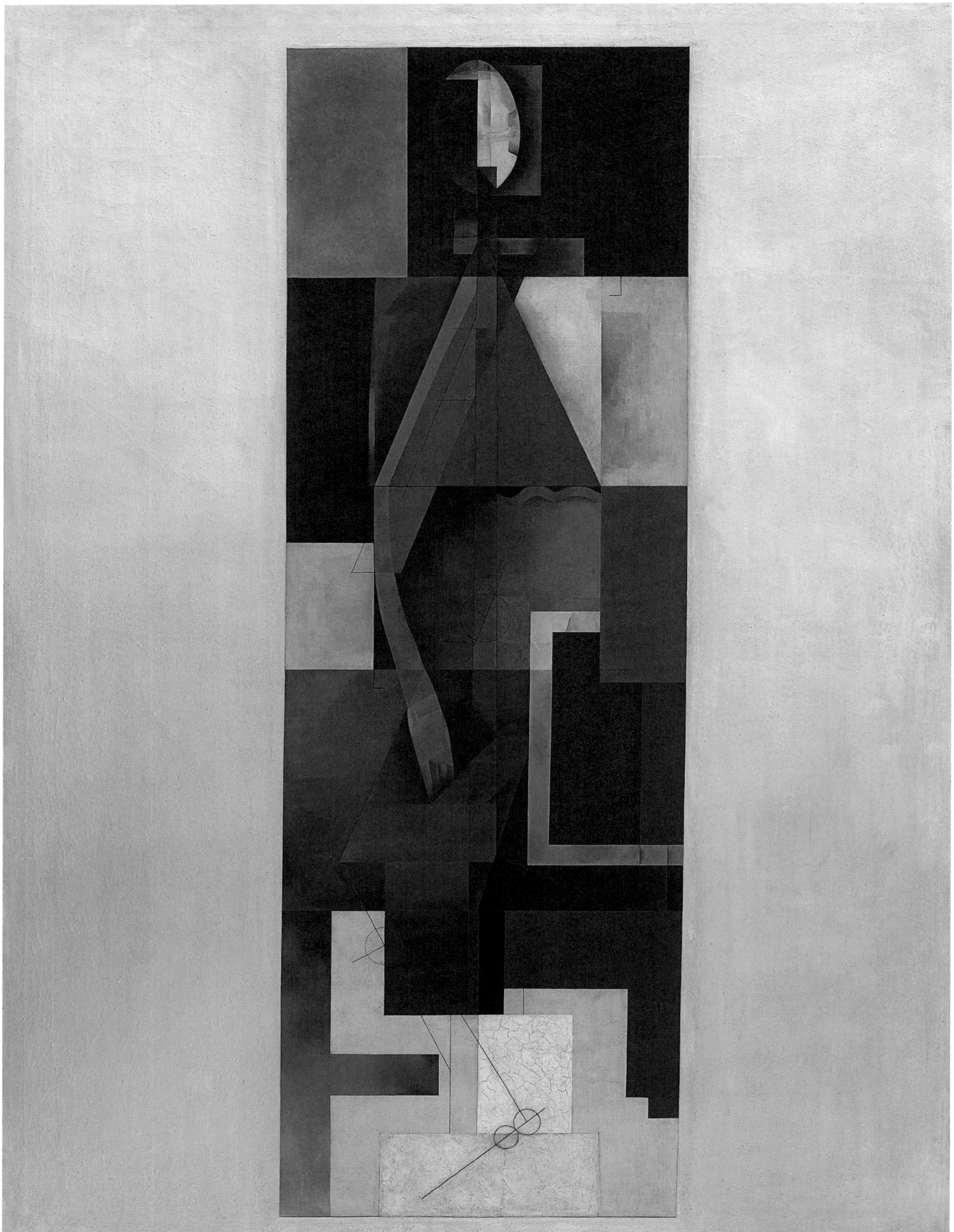

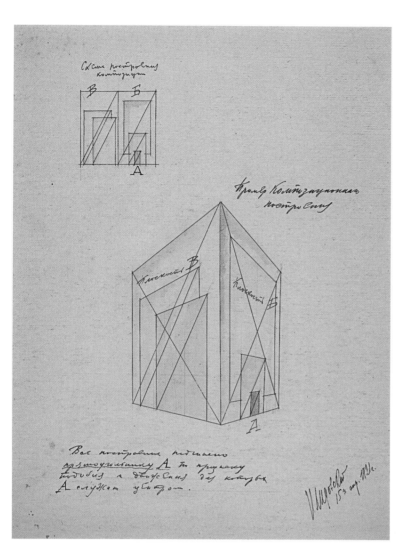

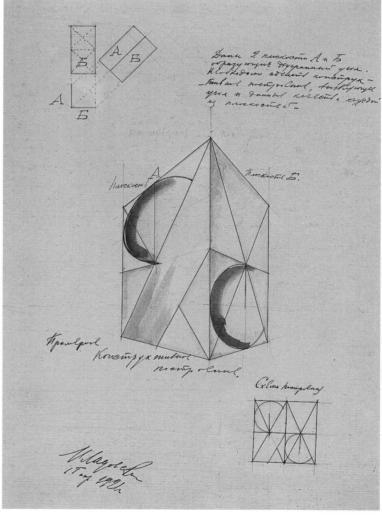

Cat. 24.1 above left
Nikolai Ladovskii
Model of a Constructive Structure, n.d.
Pencil, ink and wash on cardboard,
380 x 273 mm

Cat. 23 opposite
Solomon Nikritin
The Connection of Painting to Architecture,
1919–21
Oil on canvas, 1751 x 1311 mm

Cat. 24.2 above right
Nikolai Ladovskii
Example of a Composed Structure, n.d.
Pencil, ink and wash on cardboard,
380 x 275 mm

Cat. 25
Boris Korolev
Composition, 1921
Pencil and gouache on paper,
161 x 106 mm

Cat. 26
Boris Korolev
Construction, 1921
Pencil on paper, 354 x 259 mm

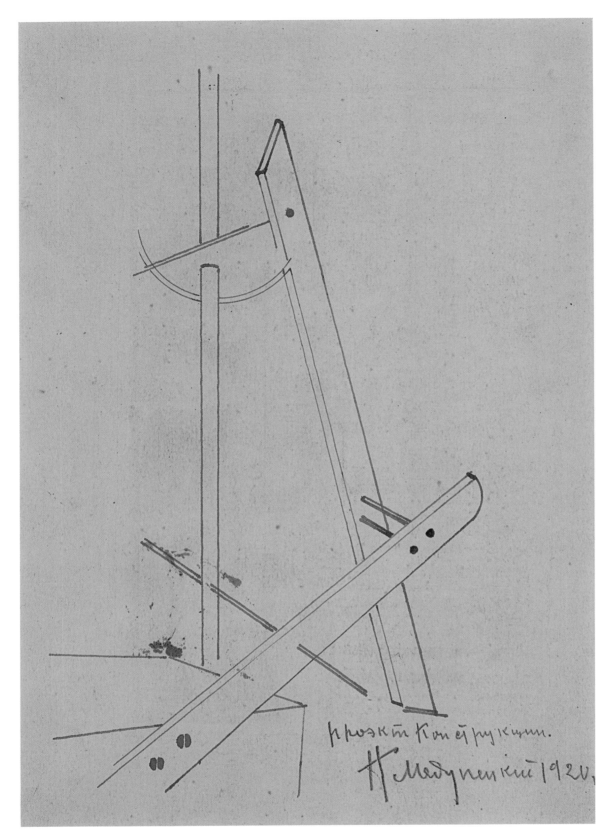

Cat. 27
Konstantin Medunetskii
Construction, 1920
Brown ink on paper, 270 x 191 mm

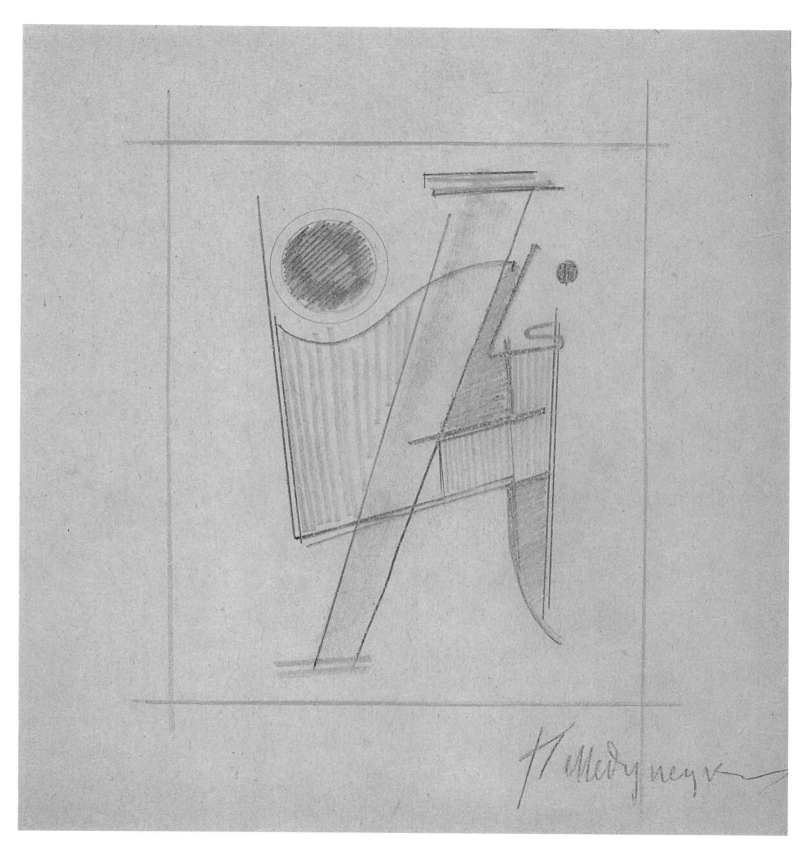

Cat. 28
Konstantin Medunetskii
Composition, 1920
Pencil and orange crayon on paper,
268 x 238 mm

Cat. 29
Aleksei Babichev
Construction, 1921
Pencil, ink and gouache on paper,
521 x 282 mm

Cat. 30
Aleksei Babichev
Construction, 1921
Pencil on paper, 495 x 345 mm

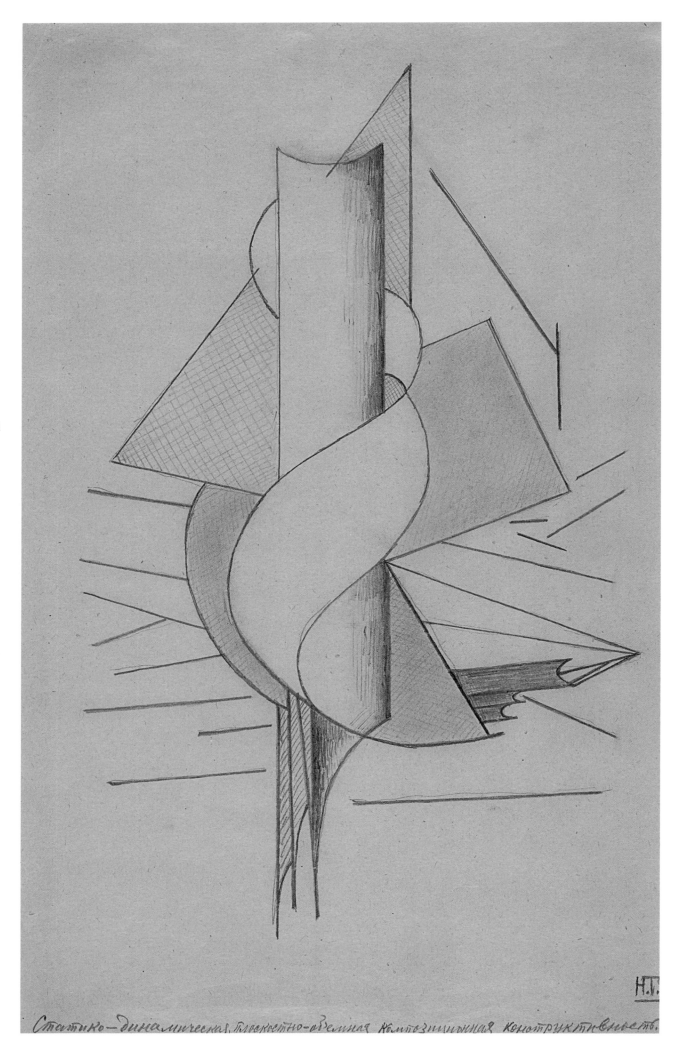

Статико—динамическая, плоскостно-объемная композиционная конструктивность.

Линейная композиция.   Н.Т.

Cat. 31 opposite
Nikolai Tarabukin
Static-dynamic, Planar and Volumetric
Compositional Constructivity, 1921
Pencil on paper, 358 x 222 mm

Cat. 32
Nikolai Tarabukin
Composition, 1921
Pencil on paper, 220 x 179 mm

64

Cat. 33
Vladimir Stenberg
Composition, 1920
Coloured pencil on paper, 210 x 139 mm

Cat. 34 opposite
Vladimir Stenberg
Constuction, 1920
Ink on paper, 254 x 193 mm

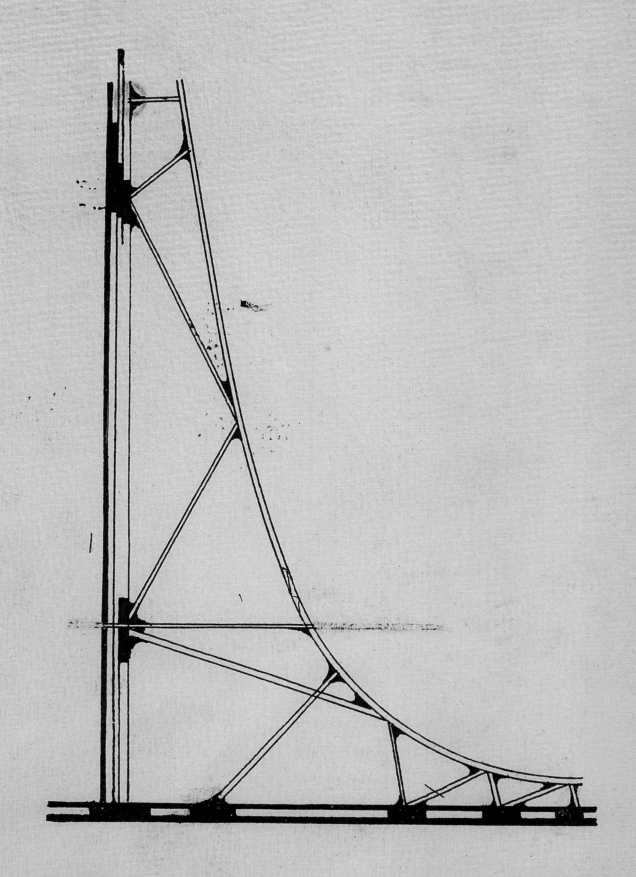

В. Стенберг.

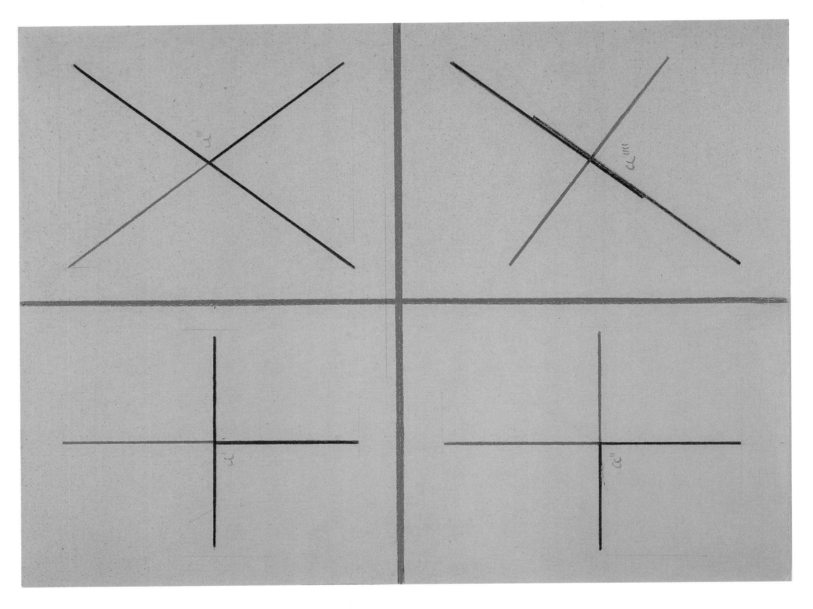

Cat. 35
Karel Ioganson
Construction, 7 April 1921
Pencil, coloured pencil and ink on paper,
243 x 318 mm

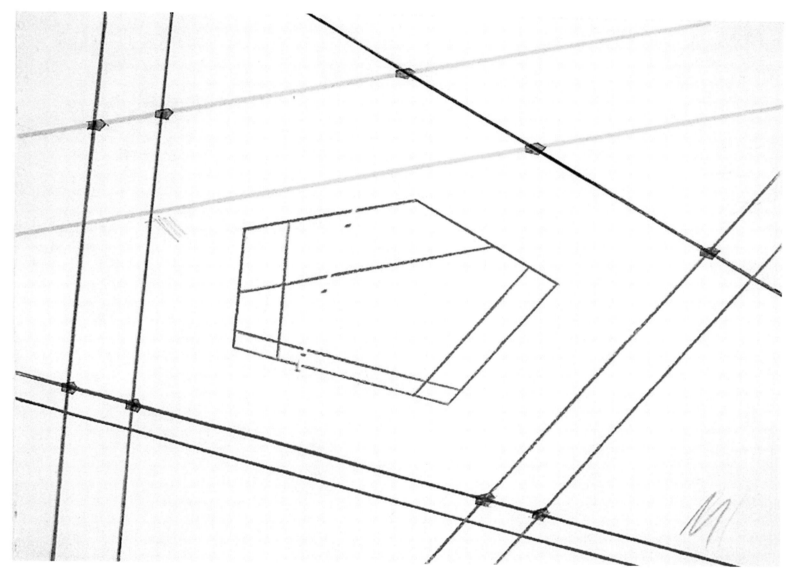

Cat. 36
Karel Ioganson
Composition, 7 April 1921
Pencil, coloured pencil and ink on paper,
242 x 323 mm

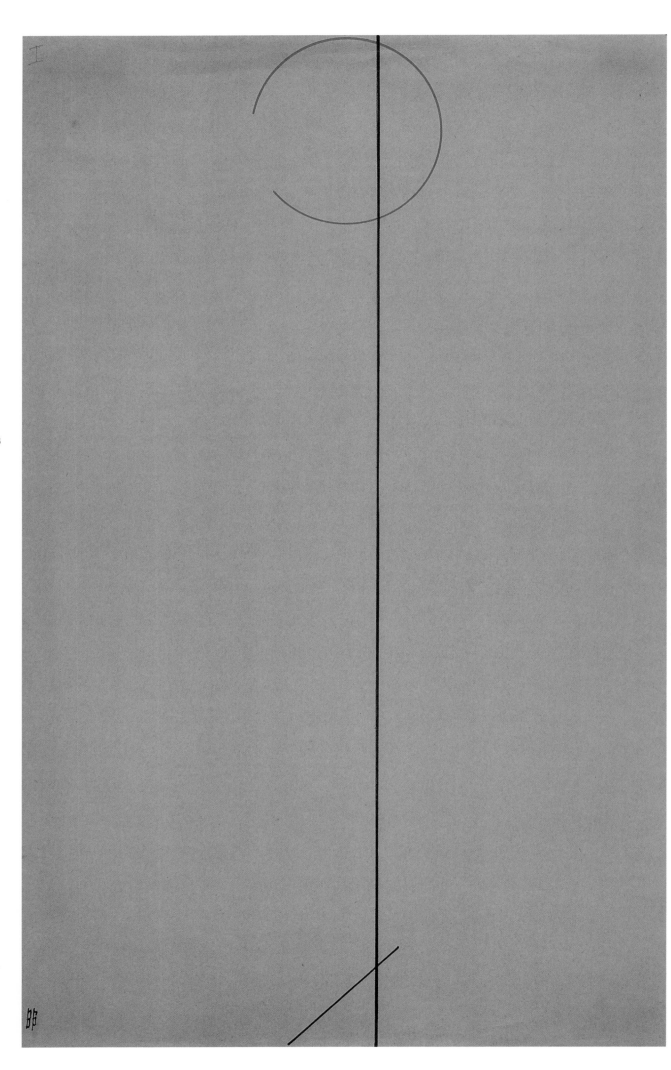

Cat. 37 opposite
Varvara Bubnova
Untitled, 1920–21
Ink on paper, 356 x 221 mm

Cat. 38
Varvara Stepanova
Construction, c. 1920
Collage on paper, 359 x 229 mm

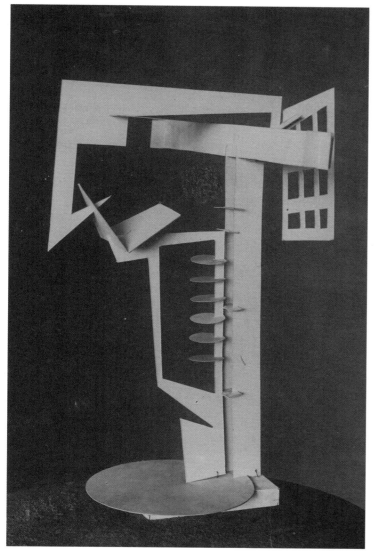

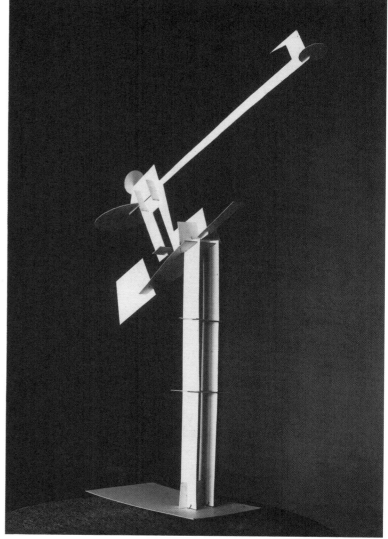

Cat. 39 opposite
Aleksandr Rodchenko
Untitled, 1921
Red and blue wax crayon on paper,
483 x 324 mm

Cat. 40.1 above left
Aleksandr Rodchenko
Photograph of *Spatial Construction No. 5*,
1918
155 x 105 mm

Cat. 40.2 above right
Aleksandr Rodchenko
Photograph of *Spatial Construction No. 6*,
1918
160 x 110 mm

Cat. 41
Liubov Popova
Part of the design for the stage set for
Earth in Turmoil, 1923
Photomontage on wood, 490 x 827 mm

Cat. 42 top
Anon.
Photograph of Liubov Popova's maquette
for *City of the Future*, 1921
168 x 242 mm

Cat. 43 bottom
Anon.
Photograph of Liubov Popova's maquette
for *Capitalist Fortress*, 1921
168 x 238 mm

Cat. 44.1
Konstantin Vialov
Design for the Construction of a Radio Tower,
1922
Pencil on paper, 205 x 91 mm

Cat. 44.2
Konstantin Vialov
Design for the Construction of a Radio Tower,
1922
Pencil on paper, 232 x 112 mm

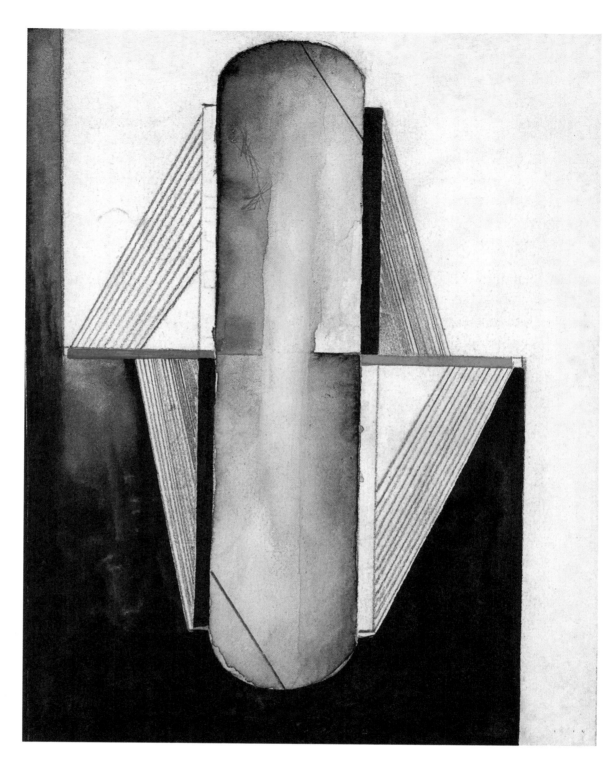

Cat. 45
Konstantin Vialov
Untitled, 1923
Pencil and gouache on paper,
212 x 163 mm

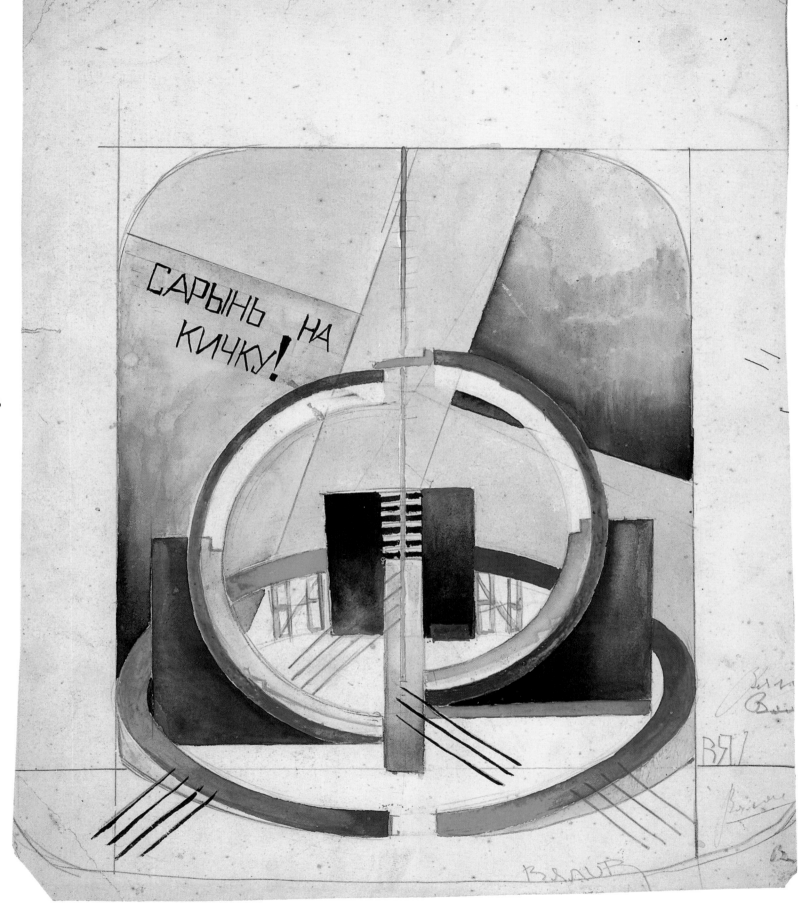

Cat. 46
Konstantin Vialov
Untitled, 1923–24
Pencil and gouache on paper,
284 x 238 mm

Cat. 47
Aleksei Babichev
*Metal Arches for a Projected Monument
to Sverdlov*, 1924
Metal, 395 x 700 x 470 mm

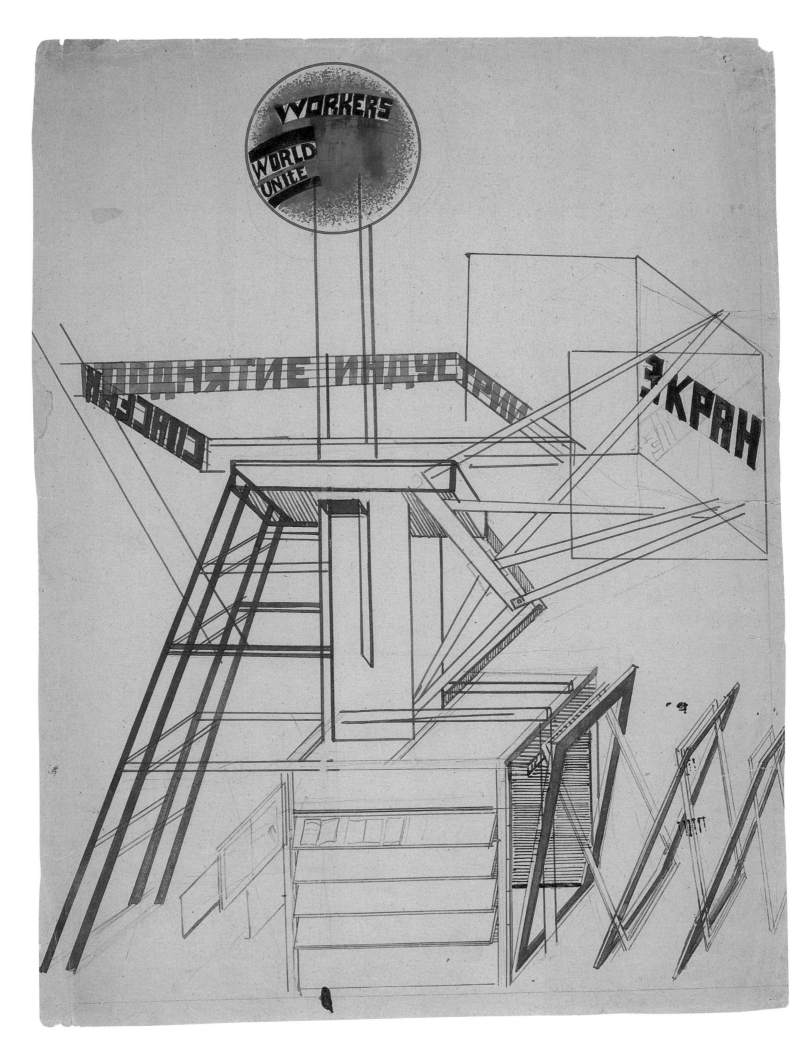

Cat. 48 opposite
Gustav Klutsis
Design for Propaganda Kiosk and
Loudspeaker Platform for the Fourth Congress
of the Comintern and the Fifth Anniversary of
the October Revolution, Moscow, 1922
Pencil, ink and watercolour on paper,
329 x 240 mm

Cat. 49
Gustav Klutsis
Design for Screen Rostrum Propaganda
Stand, 1922
Pencil, ink and watercolour on paper,
234 x 106 mm

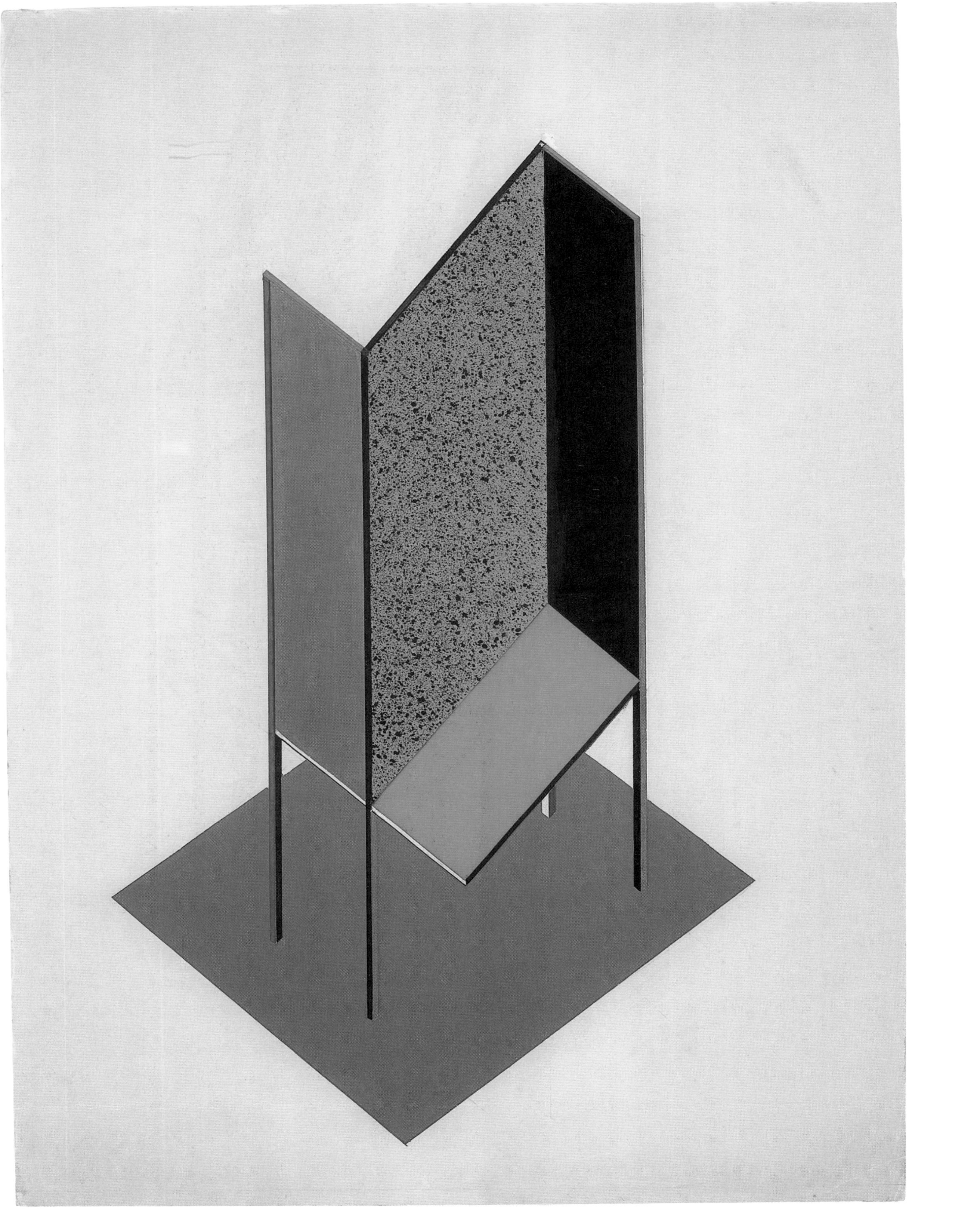

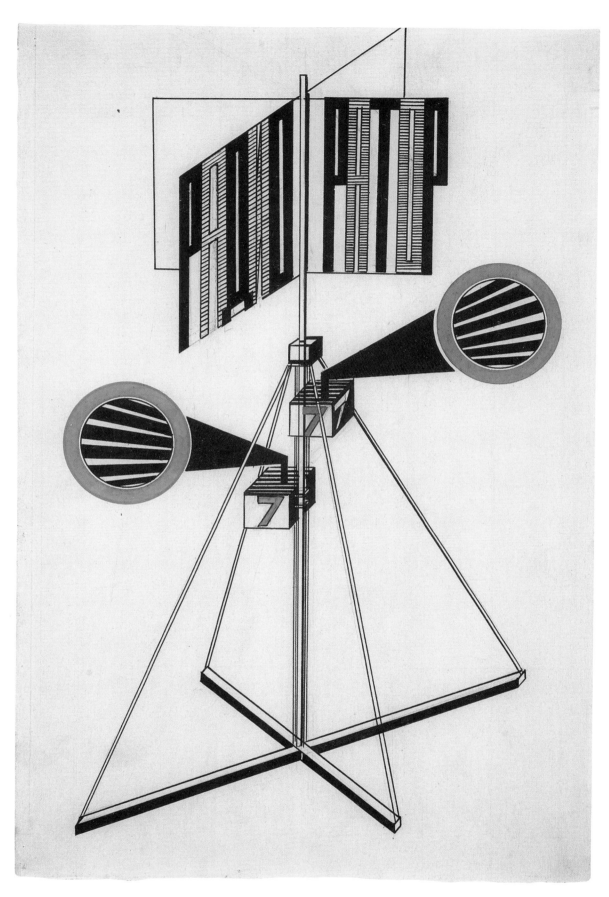

Cat. 50 opposite
Gustav Klutsis
Design for Exhibition Construction, 1924
Ink, gouache and paper collage on paper,
482 x 348 mm

Cat. 51
Gustav Klutsis
Design for Loudspeaker No. 7, 1922
Pencil, ink and gouache on paper,
269 x 177 mm

Cat. 52
Gustav Klutsis
Untitled, 1921–22
Pencil, ink and gouache on paper,
337 x 220 mm

Cat. 53
Gustav Klutsis
Design for Propaganda Kiosk, 1923
Linocut on paper, 230 x 131 mm

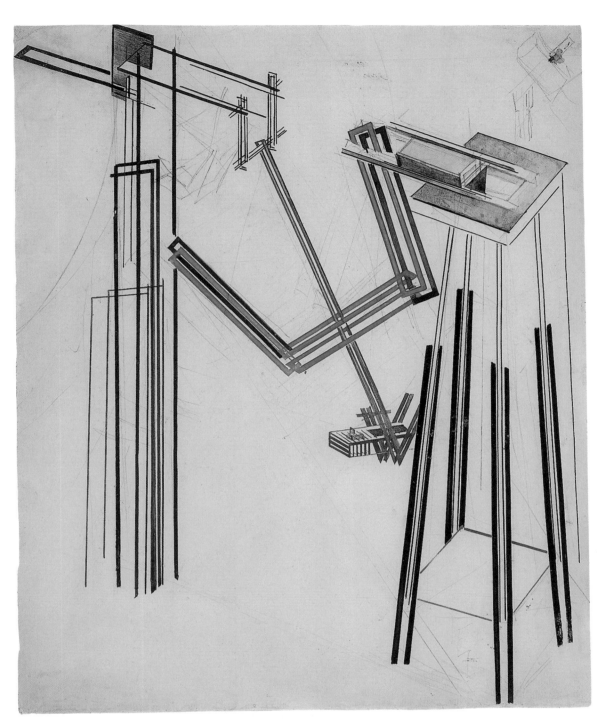

Cat. 54
Gustav Klutsis
Construction, 1921–22
Pencil, ink, watercolour and gouache
on paper, 268 x 213 mm

Cat. 55
Gustav Klutsis
Construction, 1922–23
Lithograph on paper, 155 x 221 mm

Cat. 56 opposite
Gustav Klutsis
Construction, 1921–22
Lithograph on paper, 228 x 147 mm

Cat. 57
Gustav Klutsis
Construction, c. 1920–21
Pencil, ink, watercolour and gouache
on paper, 285 x 237 mm

Cat. 58
Ivan Kudriashev
Linear Construction, 1922
Oil on canvas, 726 x 670 mm

Cat. 59
Ivan Kudriashev
Construction of a Rectilinear Motion, 1925
Oil on canvas, 663 x 707 mm

Cat. 60
Solomon Nikritin
Monument, 1930
Pencil and gouache on paper, 257 x 171 mm

Cat. 61
Ivan Kliun
Crematorium, 1930
Pencil on paper, 142 x 100 mm

PHOTOGRAPHS FROM THE SHCHUSEV STATE MUSEUM OF ARCHITECTURE
SOVIET ARCHITECTURE OF THE 1920s AND EARLY 1930s

Maria Ametova and Maria Rogozina

The Department of Photographs (specialist photo-archive section) is one of the most important departments of the Shchusev State Museum of Architecture in Moscow, holding more than 500,000 negatives and prints. It started life in 1934, the year the museum was founded, at that time as part of the Soviet Academy of Architecture. The current collection of documentary photographs, art and reportage offers the opportunity for a relatively detailed and thorough overview of Russian and international architecture. The oldest photographs date from the 1850s and the first negatives from 1880; the collection is continually being enriched with new items, both old and contemporary.

Architectural photography was born at almost the same moment as the invention of the photograph itself. In fact, the first photograph ever taken, by the Frenchman Joseph Nicéphore Niépce, can claim to belong to the genre: it is a sunlight exposure taken with a camera obscura from the window of the inventor's studio in St-Loup-de-Varennes in Burgundy in summer 1827, in which the outlines of the surrounding buildings are visible. The first dated photographs of Moscow were taken in the 1850s.

The Museum of Architecture has always sought to acquire photographs of new buildings. These images are of particular historical value since they convey the context within which the architect was working; photographers, as artists, are able to capture the spirit of the age. This is particularly so with the photographs of buildings from the 1920s and early 1930s.

The avant-garde movement of the 1920s made itself felt in all aspects of Soviet art. The art of photography was one of the first to answer its call, and the most widespread genre during these years was the journalistic photograph. To secure an expressive shot, photographers would adopt unusual angles and use photomontage. They showed a preference for such devices as distorting perspective through the choice of camera angle, diagonal framing of the composition and the stark contrast of light and shade. The social context meant industrial and urban themes dominated, with numerous images of such building types as workers' clubs, communal houses, sanatoriums, department stores and power stations.

The Constructivist artist Aleksandr Rodchenko, the leading figure in avant-garde photography, focused methodically on the architecture

of his period. The Moscow collection does not contain any original works by the artist, but there are negatives and prints by his students, the photographers of the period 1920 to 1950.

At this point we should mention the art historian Mikhail Ilyin, an expert on historic Russian architecture and for many years a member of the museum's scientific committee, who donated a collection of his photographs to the museum when it was founded. Ilyin was not a professional photographer but in his youth he had shown an interest in contemporary architecture and produced photographs of high artistic quality. He assimilated and exploited Rodchenko's compositional achievement. The camera angle in Ilyin's photographs tends to be acute, the camera is turned with some urgency on the subject, the composition is dynamic, and the particular characteristics of the new architecture are given prominence. The photographs, some of which are featured in this catalogue, include shots taken in 1931–32 in Moscow and Zaporozhye depicting major works of the avant-garde such as the Narkomfin Communal House by Moisei Ginzburg and Ignatii Milinis (Cat. 75.5), the Burevestnik, Kauchuk and Rusakov Workers' Clubs (Cats 85.1, 85.2, 85.7) and the Melnikov House (Cats 83.1, 83.5) by Konstantin Melnikov, the Zuev Workers' Club by Ilia Golosov (Cat. 87.1), the Mostorg Department Store by the Vesnin brothers, and the DneproGES Dam and Hydroelectric Power Station by Aleksandr Vesnin, Nikolai Kolli, Georgi Orlov and Sergei Andrievskii.

During the Stalin era many well-known photographers were commissioned to work for the museum, among them Petr Klepikov, Abram Sorkin and Sergei Shimanskii. The creative careers of Klepikov and Sorkin began in the decade from 1910, when they were honing their skills under the historian and archaeologist Ivan Barschevskii, the first Russian professional photographer to work in the genre of the architectural photograph. Barschevskii developed the principles of the classical representation of architectural monuments. Klepikov, in his photographs of buildings of the 1920s and early 1930s, used the expressive repertoire devised by the artists of the avant-garde, as in his photograph from 1954 showing the Tsentrosoyuz Building designed by Le Corbusier, Pierre Jeanneret and Nikolai Kolli (Figure 8).

Abram Sorkin was head of the photographic laboratories of the Palace of Soviets. His photographs are more straightforwardly structured and the shots are more monumental and stage-managed, closer to the

Figure 8 Tsentrosoyuz Building, Moscow: photograph by Petr Klepikov, 1954. Shchusev State Museum of Architecture, Moscow

Figure 9 Stepan Shaumian workers' settlement, Baku: photograph by Iacov Khalip, 1946. Shchusev State Museum of Architecture, Moscow

aesthetic of Socialist Realism. This is evident in a photograph of the Udarnik Cinema and the VTsIK Residential Complex for high-ranking officials of the Communist Party by architect Boris Iofan.

Sergei Shimanskii became involved with photography in the mid-1920s, while living in the Ukraine. During World War II he worked as a photo-journalist for the Soviet Navy and covered the Siege of Leningrad. In 1947, when he was recruited to the General Directorate for the Conservation of Architectural Monuments, Shimanskii returned to the subject of St Petersburg, photographing the architecture of the city and its suburban villas, both for archival documentation and for specialist architectural publications. Shimanskii's work conveys the splendour of the city's urban complexes. Many façades were in poor condition after the war, but he devised ingenious solutions, shooting from a considerable distance or exploiting the possibilities of light and shade. These are works of substance and grandeur that might even be described as baroque. The same epithet would suit his series of photographs of avant-garde St Petersburg architecture, such as the S.M. Kirov Palace of Culture by the architect Noi Trotskii.

From its earliest days the museum has been acquiring work by the country's most eminent practitioners of reportage or art photography with architecture as its subject. These include Naim Granovskii, Andrei Tartakovskii, Boris Ignatovich and Yurii Eremin. Granovskii began work in Moscow in the 1920s but his talent did not really become apparent until the 1950s, when interest in the avant-garde had faded. The country's capital had changed in appearance and the dominant architectural mode was the so-called Imperial Stalinist style. In photography, realism prevaled, with academically rigorous compositions, harmony of light and shade and a deliberate emotional distancing from the subject. Granovskii preferred the official view of Moscow and frequently used general shots from elevated positions. So it is interesting to see a photograph from 1950 taken with a 1920s aesthetic that offers an oblique view of Mytnaia ulitsa, with rows of new standardised prefabricated buildings stretching towards the interior of the settlement and Vladimir Shukhov's vertical Shabolovka Radio Tower on the left-hand side of the composition (Cat. 62.2). The image has an acute camera angle and intensified perspective, characteristics of Rodchenko. It demonstrates that when the subject required it Granovskii could draw on great skill.

The collection also contains negatives and prints by Iakov Khalip, the foremost Soviet photo-journalist of the period 1930–60. Khalip was a student of Rodchenko and in the late 1930s the two men collaborated on the journal *USSR in Construction*, the most ambitious illustrated publication of the inter-war period. A photograph of 1947 (Figure 9), probably taken for the magazine *Ogonek*, for which Khalip worked from 1946 to 1954, shows a workers' settlement in Baku designed by A. Samoilov and A. Ivanitskii. It is not so much a photograph of a specific subject as an exercise in lyricism, where the composition shows traces of the old avant-garde methods, with the street shot from an acute angle and a stark contrast of light and shade.

Two remarkable prints from the 1920s are the work of photographers from outside Moscow. The first is by Leonid Andrievskii, who in 1927 photographed the completion of the Traktornaia ulitsa Workers' Housing in St Petersburg's Kirovskii district by the architects Aleksandr Gegello, Aleksandr Nikolskii and Grigorii Simonov. Among the series are images showing Traktornaia ulitsa with the communal apartment blocks still uninhabited and the surrounding area looking abandoned. However, the subject is treated with such knowledge of, and fidelity to, the Constructivist aesthetic that the buildings' muted tones acquire a scale and epic character they cannot have had in reality.

The second photograph is the work of Semen Khabibulin, a photo-journalist from the city of Tambov, who was born in Sochi in 1928. It shows a new hotel by the architect Aleksei Shchusev in the summer resort suburb of Matsesta. To photograph the central section of this Constructivist building Khabibulin used a low-angle perspective pioneered by Rodchenko. A photograph of the turbine chamber of DneproGES, dating from the 1950s, uses a more standard camera angle. It was taken by the architect Vladimir Krinskii, a devotee of realism within Soviet avant-garde architecture.

The archive of the Museum of Architecture also contains a number of exceptional works whose photographers are, sadly, unknown. Some of these, too, are published here.

THE PAINTER AS ARCHITECT
EXPLORATIONS TOWARDS A CONSTRUCTIVIST ARCHITECTURE

Christina Lodder

The relationship between painting, sculpture and architecture in Russia's immediate post-Revolutionary period was extremely close. The movement towards synthesising the arts was given added impetus by the October Revolution, the practical demands of designs for propaganda and mass festivals, and the aspiration to reconstruct the country's material environment in line with its social and political transformation. The notion that Russia stood at the dawn of a new era inspired creative figures to contribute their expertise to articulating a radically different style that would reflect and promote the values of this changed world. Constructivism epitomised these innovative creative concepts and political idealism.

One of the first manifestations of this original approach was Vladimir Tatlin's *Model for a Monument to the Third International*, which was unveiled in November 1920 in St Petersburg as part of the festivities celebrating the third anniversary of the Revolution. The model linked avant-garde art with Revolutionary politics, proclaiming a new style of architecture, a new type of art and a new kind of artist. Tatlin celebrated the link between art and technology with his banner exhorting 'Engineers and bridge-builders do your calculations and invent a new form'.[1] He declared that he had combined 'purely artistic forms with utilitarian intentions' and had restored the connection between 'painting, sculpture and architecture'.[2]

Tatlin exemplified this novel fusion of the arts: he was a painter who had become a sculptor in 1914 when he had started making his relief constructions (Cats 2, 3), and he had subsequently become involved with architecture when he designed his *Monument* – a gargantuan skeletal structure, a third higher than the Eiffel Tower, that was to act as the headquarters for the Communist body responsible for fostering world revolution. Tatlin's nine-metre

model was a paradigm of utopian possibilities, demonstrating how the arts of painting, sculpture and architecture could be synthesised. It appeared at a crucial moment, acting both as a summation of artistic achievements and a stimulus for future experimentation, leading directly to the emergence of Constructivism in early 1921.

Tatlin's Tower, as it came to be called, was one of the few large-scale three-dimensional structures actually produced at a time when only 'paper architecture' was possible, for it was 'only in 1923 that building awoke again after almost ten years sleep.'[3] Not surprisingly, when Moisei Ginzburg, the leading theoretician of the emergent architectural Constructivism, wrote *Style and Epoch*, his important 1924 treatise on the new style, he prefaced the chapter on 'Construction and Form in Architecture' with a drawing of the Tower. For architects, faced with the task of creating an appropriate environment for Communism, experimentation by Tatlin and others associated with Constructivism acted as a valuable source of inspiration.

In spring 1921 the Tower was on display in Moscow, and its technological, architectural and functional qualities sharpened the 'composition and construction' debate, then being conducted at INKhUK. Some artists thought that construction could exist as a purely aesthetic principle within a two-dimensional artwork. For others, the concept only referred to real, three-dimensional, material structures, demonstrating 'the most efficient use of material' and 'the absence of all superfluous elements', in which the lines and planes acted as 'a system of forces', defining form.[4] This was the position adopted by those artists who subsequently became Constructivists, such as Konstantin Medunetskii and Vladimir Stenberg, whose construction drawings showed spatial structures (Cats 27, 31) while their compositions focused on

1 See the photograph of Tatlin's *Monument* on display in the Academy of Arts, St Petersburg, November 1920, reproduced in L.A. Zhadova (ed.), *Tatlin*, London, 1988, plate 177.
2 V.E. Tatlin, T. Shapiro, I. Meerzon, P. Vinogradov, 'Nasha predstoyashchaya rabota' ('Our forthcoming work'), in *VIII Sezd Sovetov: Ezhednevnyi byulleten sezda* (*VIII Soviet Congress: Daily Bulletin*), No. 13, Moscow, 1 January 1921, p. 11; English translation in Zhadova, *ibid*, p. 239.
3 I.B. Shub, 'Stroitelstvo v gody vosstanovitelnogo protsessa 1923/4–1926/7' ('Construction in the years of rehabilitation 1923/4–1926/7', in *Plannovoe khoziaistvo* (*Planned Economy*), No. 10, 1926, pp. 43–56.
4 See C. Lodder, *Russian Constructivism*, New Haven and London, 1983, pp. 83ff; and M. Gough, *The Artist as Producer: Russian Constructivism in Revolution*, Berkeley, Los Angeles and London, 2005, pp. 21–59.

Figure 10 Vladimir Tatlin and his assistants
S. Dymshits-Tolstaia, T.M. Shapiro and
I.A. Meerzon constructing the first model
for the *Monument to the Third International*,
St Petersburg, between March and
7 November 1920.
Collection Centre Canadien d'Architecture/
Canadian Centre for Architecture, Montréal

decorative visual effects (Cats 28, 33). Aleksandr Rodchenko demonstrated his concern for structure in his drawing investigating the organisational potential of line, which he had explored earlier in his painting (Cats 9, 11). This attitude was also adopted by the sculptor Aleksei Babichev and the theoretician Nikolai Tarabukin, although their constructions depict solid rather than skeletal forms and have a less technological resonance (Cats 29, 30, 34). The only architect involved, Nikolai Ladovskii, presented two identical cubes: his drawing of a composition repeats the shape of the essential structure (Cat. 24.2), whereas his inscription explains that the constructive drawing 'reveals both the angle and inherent properties of each of the planes' (Cat. 24.1).

Having clarified their notion of construction, Rodchenko, Medunetskii, the Stenberg brothers (Georgii and Vladimir), Varvara Stepanova and Karel Ioganson established the Working Group of Constructivists (*Rabochaia gruppa konstruktivistov*) within INKhUK in March 1921. They decided to relegate their purely artistic explorations to the role of 'laboratory work' and to extend their experiments with manipulating three-dimensional, abstract forms into everyday life by participating in the industrial manufacture of useful objects. They called this new activity 'intellectual production' and asserted that their ultimate goal was the 'communistic expression of material structures', which they hoped to attain by organising their material according to the three principles of *tektonika* ('tectonics', or the socially and politically appropriate use of industrial material), construction (the organisation of such material for a particular purpose), and *faktura* (the conscious handling and manipulation of this material).[5] That May, the group exhibited their 'laboratory works' of paintings and numerous large openwork constructed sculptures in Mocow. Rodchenko's hanging constructions based on a sequence of

similar geometric forms were produced by cutting concentric shapes from a sheet of plywood and rotating them into space. The structural rigour of these works and of the other constructions on display differs radically from earlier sculptural experiments.

Among the first practical demonstrations of the Constructivist method were Gustav Klutsis' designs for a series of propaganda stands. A committed Communist, Klutsis had belonged to the Latvian Red Rifles and fought for the Revolution. He subsequently trained as an artist in Moscow, producing *Dynamic City* (Cat. 12) around 1920, on a painstakingly prepared icon board, explicitly imbuing his utopian image with a metaphysical resonance. The articulation of the circle implies a spherical volume, evoking the Earth and a world transformed. A shifting, layered structure of transparent and textured planes extends through and beyond the circular element, suggesting motion through space. The architectural qualities of the composition possess strong affinities with El Lissitzky's *Proun* compositions, which also project visions of new spatial environments (Cats 14, 15). For El Lissitzky, the *Proun* (*Proekt utverzhdeniya novogo* – Project for the Affirmation of the New) represented an 'interchange station between painting and architecture', a constructive entity that went beyond painting 'and advances to the construction of space, divides it by elements of all dimensions, and creates a new, multi-faceted unity.'[6] For both artists, the Suprematist vocabulary of geometric forms on white grounds provided the language for envisaging new material structures, but both deviated from Suprematism by adding textures to their images to reinforce their materiality and potential relationship to reality. Klutsis added sand and concrete to the pigments in *Dynamic City*, calling it 'a painting-object' (*kartina-veshch*).[7] Embracing the material and structural emphasis

5   See S.O. Khan-Magomedov, *Rodchenko: The Complete Work*, London and Cambridge, Mass., 1986, p. 290; and Lodder, *ibid*, pp. 94ff.

6   El Lissitzky, 'Proun: Not World Vision, but – World Reality', 1920, in S. Lissitzky-Küppers, *El Lissitzky: Life, Letters, Texts*, London, 1968, p. 344.

7   M. Tupitsyn, *Gustav Klutsis and Valentina Kulagina: Photography and Photomontage After Constructivism*, New York, 2004, p. 17.

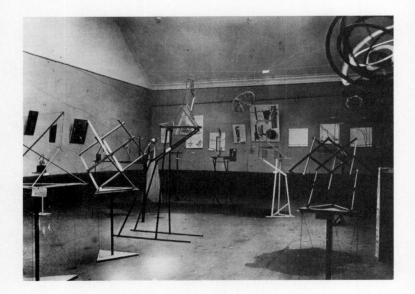

Figure 11 Installation photograph of the Constructivist display at the Second Spring Exhibition of OBMOKhU in Moscow, 1921. Shchusev State Museum of Architecture, Moscow

Figure 12 Aleksandr and Viktor Vesnin, competition entry for the Leningradskaia Pravda Building, 1924

of Constructivism, Klutsis began to explore the structural potential of geometric form in a succession of openwork constructions, drawings and prints (Cats 52–57).

Klutsis' series of propaganda stands for the Fourth Congress of the Comintern, held in Moscow in November 1922 (Cats 48, 49, 53), were conceived to display visual material (texts or posters), give spatial presence to Revolutionary slogans (such as 'Workers of the World Unite'), transmit Revolutionary speeches through loudspeakers, or project films. Sometimes they performed several tasks, like Screen Rostrum Propaganda Stand (Cat. 49), which combines a film screen, bookshelves and a speaker's platform. Using canvas, cables and wooden rods of uniform thickness, Klutsis reduced the stands' components to a few essential elements, revealing the structure of each item and providing stability through a multiplicity of vertical, diagonal and horizontal supports. He coloured the components red, black and white (the colour code of the Revolution) to minimise the natural texture of the wood and give the stands an ideological and industrial gloss. The compression of several functions into a small compact unit, as well as economy of space, materials and manufacture, became established principles of Constructivist design.

Throughout, Klutsis developed a modular system, exploring a variety of structural frameworks made from essentially similar elements. This systematic approach recalls Ivan Kliun's Suprematist designs for constructions, which comprise numerous permutations combining similar geometrical shapes in space (Cat. 4). Yet Suprematism and Constructivism were different. The Constructivists were concerned to explore the internal structure of geometry (for example, Aleksei Babichev's glass and metal openwork arch for his monument to the

revolutionary Iakov Sverdlov, Cat. 47). By contrast, the Suprematists used the plane as the primary means of orchestrating form. This is evident in the decorative schemes that Ivan Kudriashev devised for the First Soviet Theatre in Orenburg of 1920 (Cats 18–20) and in the proposals that were probably produced by a member of UNOVIS, the group established by Kazimir Malevich in Vitebsk in late 1919 (Cat. 17). In these, doors and windows are marked, suggesting that the designs were intended for a specific building. In both projects the language of Suprematist painting was applied to existing structures, enhancing them rather than totally reorganising them. By 1923, however, Malevich had begun to explore the possibilities of a Suprematist architecture, making drawings and three-dimensional white plaster models which he called *Architectons* (*arkhitektony*, Cat. 21).[8]

For the Constructivists, the theatre played an important role in providing a forum for concrete experimentation, acting as a bridge between visions of a new reality (on paper or in model form) and the materialisation of those visions on a large scale. Konstantin Vialov, for instance, used his drawings of constructions to transform the conventional space of the stage (Cats 44–46). Liubov Popova likewise explored structural concerns. Her early canvases in a Suprematist idiom (Cat. 5) were followed by paintings that focused on dynamically intersecting forms (Cats 6, 7) and a series of works on wood in which the lines and planes interact to create energetic 'spatial force' constructions (Cats 8, 10). In 1921 she collaborated with Aleksandr Vesnin and the director Vsevolod Meyerhold on the design for a mass festival to take place that summer on Khodyn Field, Moscow, in honour of the Third Congress of the Comintern. This was to include a 'cast of thousands' who would move from the fortress of capitalism, with its massive and imposing buildings, to the city of the future, with its skeletal and semi-

8 See C. Douglas, C. Lodder (eds), *Rethinking Malevich*, London, 2007, pp. 172–202.

transparent structures (Cats 42, 43).[9] The parade never took place, but Popova used this experience and that of her paintings when she designed a multi-level skeletal apparatus as the set for *The Magnanimous Cuckold* (1922) and a gantry-crane-like structure for *Earth in Turmoil* (1923); this could be wheeled to any site, and various elements could be hung from it, including a screen for showing film footage of the 1918–20 Civil War (Cat. 41).

The creative importance of these theatrical environments was demonstrated admirably by the fact that among the first Constructivist architectural designs was Aleksandr and Viktor Vesnin's scheme for the Leningradskaia Pravda Building of 1924, which used a skeletal frame, recalling the Khodyn Field designs, Popova's theatre sets, and the urban scaffolding structure that Aleksandr had devised for the play *The Man Who Was Thursday* (1923). For Vesnin, 'every object, created by artists today, must enter into life as an active force, organising man's consciousness, acting on him psychologically, and generating within him an upsurge of energy.'[10] The new style also drew on his experience of painting. He had started studying Cubism in 1912 and joined Tatlin's studio in Moscow, subsequently exhibiting as a professional artist and contributing to the Constructivist *5x5=25* show in autumn 1921. He shared a studio with Popova and developed an abstract style that was similar to hers, in which precisely defined geometric planes of colour intersect to generate sensations of movement and translucency. These paintings encouraged him to develop transparency, dynamism, asymmetry and contrasting forms in his architecture, as well as giving him the confidence to define the spatial and functional components of a building as distinct geometric elements and to intensify the sensations of fluidity between interior and exterior. These concerns continued to characterise the Vesnins' architecture (se Cats 68 , 86) and also

influenced other Constructivist architects, notably Ilia Golosov, who designed the Zuev Workers' Club in 1926 (Cat. 87). Aleksandr Vesnin subsequently concentrated on architecture, but like Tatlin he epitomised Constructivism's synthesis of the arts; he was an architect–painter, as well as a painter–architect.

By the late 1920s Constructivist architects had developed the functional method (which systematically defined a building's spatial requirements), while adopting the white walls of the International Style. The Narkomfin Communal House, designed by Moisei Ginzburg and Ignatii Milinis in 1930, exemplified this new idiom (Cat. 75). In developing their approach, the architects had drawn on a wealth of small-scale Constructivist experimentation, in both two and three dimensions. As Ginzburg acknowledged, 'Constructivism, as one of the facets of a modern aesthetic... is unquestionably one of the characteristic aspects of the new style, avidly accepting modernity.'[11] By fervently rejecting the past and celebrating the present, Constructivism embraced a utopian vision, and by encompassing all the arts it generated specific structures and pointed the way towards a new architecture.

9 See R. Fülop-Miller, *The Mind and Face of Bolshevism: An Examination of Cultural Life in Soviet Russia*, London, 1927, pp. 145, 148–49.

10 A. Vesnin, 'Kredo', 1922, reprinted in *Mastera sovetskoi arkhitektury ob arkhitekture: Izbrannye otrivki iz pisem, statei, vystuplenii i traktatov* (*Masters of Soviet Architecture on Architecture*), Vol. 2, Moscow, 1975, p. 14; English translation in S.O. Khan-Magomedov, *Alexander Vesnin and Russian Constructivism*, London, 1986, p. 88.

11 M. Ginzburg, *Stil i epokha*; English translation, *Style and Epoch*, Cambridge, Mass., and London, 1982, p. 102.

SPREADING THE WORD

Richard Pare
interviewed by Tim Tower

Tim Tower: You have a deep sympathy for Soviet Modernism. Would you explain how that developed?

Richard Pare: This goes back to the early impressions of a schoolboy listening to the Dean of Canterbury, an ardent Socialist and great fan of the Soviet regime. He was completely bamboozled by the Stalinists, but his panegyrics about building factory chimneys in five days and the Five Year Plan did leave a lasting impression.

Later I had a very fine art teacher who took his own slides and, as part of his course, gave lectures on Le Corbusier, Mies van der Rohe and the Bauhaus. But there were no Russians. That work was unavailable. Also, my father was an artist, a painter and a teacher. I was familiar with the works of Mondrian, Picasso and Braque among others from a very early age. The idea of Modernism as a way of thinking and an aesthetic was instilled in me. It is something I have admired for a very long time.

I eventually ended up with an office in the Seagram Building [the Modernist high-rise by Mies van der Rohe in New York City], working on photographic history and building the photography collection that became one of the cornerstones of the Canadian Centre for Architecture. Some years later still, in 1993, in the gallery of a friend, I ran across a picture of Vladimir Tatlin and his assistants building the model of the *Monument to the Third International* (Figure 10). Of course the photograph entered the CCA collection and as a result of my interest my friend invited me to join him on a trip to Moscow. That was the beginning.

I found there was a lot more surviving construction than anybody thought existed, in varying degrees of preservation and decay. I set about acquiring a network of contacts and friends, who have been unbelievably supportive. The generosity with which people went out of their way to help me was exemplary.

The European Modernists have been known in detail for decades, but the correspondence between European Modernism and the Soviet experiment was virtually unknown. The chance to record the range and brilliance of that work, even 70 years after the fact, was an extraordinary opportunity.

EMERGENCE OF A NEW STYLE

TT: There was an exceptional flowering of creative work. Where did it come from? There had been some development of Modernism in Russia before the Revolution. Architects, painters and writers found support among merchants, even among the nobility. But it took on a different character in the aftermath of the Revolution.

RP: I believe it did. Some of the early steel-frame buildings in Moscow provided the seed from which the later and more radical Modernist works developed. But there was also a very conscious desire to get away from the architecture of the regime that had gone before.

Architecture under state patronage in the Tsarist period had looked backwards to produce bankrupt works in a rigid, proto-medieval style. The prime example is a church in St Petersburg that was built [in 1883–1907] on the spot where the assassination of Alexander II took place. The classical line of the canal bank of the original town plan was even broken to accommodate it. The result was an extraordinarily vulgar concoction of church architecture. It's called 'The Church of Our Saviour on the Spilled Blood'.

To me, the whole generative force of the avant-garde in Russia was an attempt to move as far in the opposite direction as possible. Which is not to say that there were no Modernist antecedents. There were some extraordinarily fine Style Moderne and Art Deco buildings constructed in Russia in the late nineteenth and early twentieth centuries.

TT: Regarding the character of the new work, let me quote a little of what you wrote:

'Wandering in the empty silence of the abandoned Vasileostrovskii district factory kitchen [1930–31] in St Petersburg late one afternoon, in the surrounding desolation I felt as though the structure had returned to the essence of the architects' intention; all superfluity had been torn away and what remained was the bare bones of the structure, peeling and crumbling until it revealed the ancient techniques that had been employed in its construction.'

In general terms, how would you describe the architects' underlying intention?

RP: It was the idea of reinventing architecture for a new age. The paradigms were the communal house and the factory instead of the mansion and the cathedral. Architects were responding to the opportunities presented by the Revolution in the early years, before it became suborned all too swiftly.

The roof pavilion of the big factory kitchen looks as if it were built of steel but the trusses are actually made of wood. Steel was so scarce it had to be used with the greatest economy so the only steel components are plates bolted on to reinforce the joints. Really, it was a subterfuge. They were trying to use the vocabulary of steel but with wood. Behind the trusses you can see the array of wood lath that once supported the pristine plaster surfaces of the interior.

TT: A technique which is a thousand years old.

RP: Exactly. They were deploying medieval construction techniques to fulfil the requirements of a modern vocabulary, which I think is fascinating in the way it was worked out.

THE CHARACTER OF RUSSIAN MODERNISM

TT: Many different tendencies are represented in the structures you documented. How would you characterise what they hold in common?

RP: Consider Konstantin Melnikov, who was a maverick. He rarely collaborated with anybody, though I have seen it suggested that Vladimir Shukhov may have been responsible for engineering the cantilevers in the Rusakov Workers' Club (Cat. 85). It does make sense: the two men worked together on garages, with Shukhov making the plans for the lightweight steel roofs.

Still, Melnikov was no mean engineer himself. He was able to devise unsupported floors for his own house (Cat. 83). Short pieces of timber were laid in such a way as to make a grid, then the boards were put on in opposing directions. But there is no supporting beam from one side to the other.

The whole house was built remarkably cheaply. There is no waste at all. Materials are never highly finished; he used what he could get. It was the same problem for everybody, and that's another condition

that drove the movement. The very stripped-down, Modernist style came to seem completely in tune with the times. In a sense the vocabulary of Modernism was enforced by the availability, or rather the scarcity, of materials. There is no excess and nothing superfluous. The whole concentration on efficiency, clarity and transparency was driven at least in part by necessity.

There was also the exchange with the Europeans. Le Corbusier came to Moscow and met and shared ideas with a number of architects including Moisei Ginzburg, the founder of the Constructivist movement and its chief theoretician. His 1924 treatise *Style and Epoch* was the most influential document of the Constructivist movement. Because he was Jewish, he was prevented from undertaking his architectural training in Russia and went to the École des Beaux-Arts in Paris and the Accademia di Belle Arti in Milan. Aleksandr Rodchenko travelled to Paris with Melnikov, who built the Soviet Pavilion at the 1925 *Exposition Internationale des Arts Décoratifs et Industriels Modernes* in Paris. They were all very well versed in European culture of the time.

Ginzburg's *Style and Epoch* responds to Le Corbusier's *Vers une architecture* of the previous year, but Ginzburg takes the warship and the communal house rather than the luxury liner and the private villa as his examples.

TT: While they represented different tendencies, they all seemed to be striving to express something that was common between them. That coherence gives the work a certain power. It was no accident.

RP: Far from it. There was a lot of lower-level Modernist construction using a similar vocabulary in and around Moscow at that time – you see it as you travel around the city once you become attuned to the idea. But it's like the developers who built things along Sixth Avenue in New York after Gordon Bunshaft built Lever House and Mies van der Rohe built the Seagram Building. It's in the manner of, but it doesn't rise to great heights. It's dull, usable space. It doesn't have the intellectual spine that gives the key works a quality that is magical.

Take MoGES, for example (Cat. 69). The side that faces away from the Kremlin is far more radical than the river façade, which is more Classical, deploying what its architect Ivan Zholtovskii called Neo-Palladianism.

TT: It has the little Renaissance palazzo in the middle.

RP: Exactly. But it's the same architect. In the interior court, with the structure that houses the turbines, which is visible only from within the compound and can't be seen from anywhere else, he flung caution to the winds. He saw what he could do. He was never so radical again. It was an experiment and unique in his output.

TT: The Revolution placed the social programme at the forefront of cultural life. This must have played an enormous role for architecture. The building types for the initial period included the radio tower, different forms of housing, factories, factory kitchens, workers' clubs that were cultural centres, power stations and sports facilities. Still, an analysis that stops at the level of the building programme leaves out the richness of the aesthetic, intellectual and cultural currents that found expression. A new style must be motivated by a living complex of moods and sentiments, of psychological needs; that which had been the status quo before the Revolution could no longer satisfy the needs of post-Revolutionary Russia. Would you say this could characterise early Russian Modernism?

RP: From one example to another there is an enquiring creativity at work offering considerable variations on the basic typologies. There were experiments with prefabrication which were totally different from Ginzburg's experiments. For example, the Vesnins did prefabricated housing in Ivanovo which is very advanced, really intelligent and well thought out [First Workers' Settlement, 1924–26: architects Leonid Vesnin and others]. It is so different in emphasis from the Ginzburg approach.

The eye is drawn to the boards laid into the stucco, which I initially thought were demonstrations of joints between the units. Actually they are not, which is a little disappointing, shall we say. They are not structural at all, just planks laid on as a decorative scheme. But the architects did articulate the unit system very carefully, which becomes apparent in the variable form of the footprint of the different types and the way the windows are laid out. Everything was coming off a production line and yet everything could be put together in different configurations. It was an early example of that kind of prefabricated approach to housing.

INTERNATIONAL CONNECTIONS

TT: What attracted leading architects from Europe and America, men like Erich Mendelsohn and Le Corbusier, to work in the USSR?

RP: Both of them were ardent supporters of the Revolution, so there was an effort to respond and participate. A number of the major architects in Moscow literally stepped aside, removing themselves from competition and issuing a statement in favour of the Tsentrosoyuz project (Cat. 64) being awarded to Le Corbusier. It was the biggest project he had ever built, and he was very committed to it. There were all kinds of difficulties in funding, political opposition, and the shortages of materials we have already discussed; nothing was easy to come by. The work was overseen in Moscow by Nikolai Kolli. Le Corbusier never saw it completed.

In spite of everything, it came out very well. Le Corbusier eventually sent a photographer, Lucien Hervé, to record it in the 1950s. But as far as we know, the view of the ramps had never been published until I took the picture (Cat. 64.7), which is remarkable when you think about it. That is one of the great Corbusian spaces; perhaps technical limitations prevented Hervé from making such an encompassing image.

With Mendelsohn it was the same. He had travelled in Russia and written a book, *Russland–Europa–Amerika*, published in 1929, as a pendant to his *Amerika* of 1926, which is about the Modernist experiment. He went there with the commission to build the Red Banner Textile Factory (Cat. 71), but withdrew his name from it ultimately because he was dissatisfied. He had designed it for steel, but they had to build it with wood and other materials.

It's still there – a singularly original building, what's left of it. It took me a long time to find it because the drawing I had was a section through one of the factory floors, which was probably destroyed in the war. The main factory spaces for the looms had big vents on the sharply upswept roof. Presumably, if you opened the windows at the bottom there would be an up-draft that would take all the fibre and fluff out of the atmosphere to improve working conditions. That was what I was looking for, and that was the bit that did not survive.

TT: You have written about the near-miraculous results achieved by the peasant workforce. Would you explain what you meant?

RP: During fallow periods, in winter, and at the time between seedtime and harvest, peasants went into the cities to do construction work in what was an ongoing tradition long before the Revolution. Contemporary photographs show scaffolding made up of great baulks of timber that is so cumbersome, yet quite beautiful in its simplicity (see, for example, Cats 64.1, 69.2, 83.2, 92.5). What they achieved with such primitive means is remarkable.

There is frequently considerable roughness in the detailing. The architectural vocabulary required absolute simplicity of decoration. Beyond a slight articulation in the façade, the way window mouldings were cut and the frame handled, there is none. There was a perfect fit between the scarcity of resources and a minimal aesthetic.

If you look carefully at details in the ramps of Ivan Nikolaev's Textile Institute Student Housing (Cat. 78.6), for example, the round columns at the acute angles of the triangles that constitute each ascending level do not quite match up. But it doesn't matter because the intentionality was so strong that the message comes across very clearly anyway.

This is actually quite exceptional. When I was in India some years ago, I went to see some of Le Corbusier's buildings at Ahmedabad. He built a museum there with similarly unskilled labourers and the concrete beam at the roof line is not quite straight. It is jarring; and the necessary connection between intention and execution is lost.

Somehow the Russians got away with it. The buildings are vibrant with a kind of earthy dynamic that was not present in the more politely refined version of European Modernism.

ARCHITECTURE AND SOCIETY

TT: Leon Trotsky wrote the following passage in 1924:

'There is no doubt that, in the future – and the farther we go, the more true it will be – such monumental tasks as the planning of city gardens, of model houses, of railroads, and of ports, will interest vitally not only engineering architects, participators in competitions, but the large popular masses as well. The imperceptible, ant-like piling up of quarters and streets, brick by brick, from generation to generation, will give way to titanic constructions of city–villages, with map and compass in hand. Around this compass will be formed true peoples' parties, the parties of the future for special technology and construction, which will agitate passionately, hold meetings and vote. In this struggle, architecture will again be filled with the spirit of mass feelings and moods, only on a much higher plane, and mankind will educate itself plastically, it will become accustomed to look at the world as submissive clay for sculpting the most perfect forms of life. The wall between art and industry will come down.' (*Literature and Revolution*)

This notion has suffered in the years since then. What would you say? Can architecture contribute to the development of a better society?

RP: One would like to think so. It is one of the major catastrophes of the history of architecture in the twentieth century that in Russia they were never given the opportunity to develop their ideas fully and work them out. Even within that short period of time, the physical discourse, the ferment of ideas and the effort to construct represent a heroic achievement, considering the small number of contributing architects. They were striving to create an ideal way of living, but I think they also realised very quickly that they were leaning into the wind. It was becoming more and more difficult, and they were conducting a kind of rearguard action.

It was the most radical experiment ever attempted. It did not succeed, but it was not from lack of will. The regime became ultimately so repressive; it was impossible to deviate from the Stalinist norm. You can feel the sense of optimism seeping out of the work around 1932. After that the heavy catechism of the Stalinist regime imposed itself.

In looking at the work of the Russian Modernists, my aim was to get beneath the surface, to attempt to fathom their intentions and render that intent through the filter of time. The idea was to articulate the poetic vocabulary of Modernism and also to allow the accumulation of time to have a part in the dialogue, to give a depth and richness to the subject that it might not have had when it was built.

For me, perhaps the most emblematic photograph of the whole series is the blue interior of Moisei Ginzburg and Ignatii Milinis' Narkomfin Communal House (Cat. 75.8). It is actually less about architecture than most of the pictures. It's about the way life is being lived in that space, and more, because it spans two or three generations.

Narkomfin, designed for the workers of the Commissariat of Finance, is a very successful building – one of the masterpieces of the century. Let us hope it survives. It came at a key moment and had a vast influence on the further development of architecture: Le Corbusier borrowed heavily from it and deployed what he had learned in his Unité d'habitation in Marseille, though almost 20 years elapsed before he had the chance.

It was assembled with such intelligence – the transparency of it, the possibility to walk underneath it. The roof garden was beautifully thought out, though not completely realised, and there was a communal refectory, a laundry and a nursery for children. All the necessities of existence were gathered together in one place.

In spite of all the difficulties under which it was built, it rose to the level of an extraordinarily humane building. It has places for single people, places for married couples without children and places for families. The use of natural light and easy access to the ribbons of the exterior window boxes, inviting plant growth to be incorporated into the principal façade and thus softening the rigour of its composition, is beautifully done. Everything is brought together with a sense of community; it really is a communal house.

TT: It seems this building concentrated many of the fundamental characteristics of early Modernism. You mention 'transparency'. In studying the photographs, one begins to appreciate that this term has literal, figurative and conceptual significance. You also call it 'extraordinarily humane'. Perhaps you could explain these ideas a bit more.

RP: The entry level is now so corrupted that it's difficult to get any sense of what it was once like. The whole idea of the building floating on pilotis has been eliminated by it having been enclosed in the shoddiest construction imaginable. So the open character of the entry level as planned has been replaced by a dour and cave-like gloom.

However, as soon as you ascend, the powerful original character of the building begins to assert itself. The whole trajectory seems to be towards lightness; the landings are suspended and free of the glass curtain wall, allowing you to see all the way up and down the full height of the building. The glass is old, cracked and dirty, but it is still possible to understand the intention.

TT: In a number of images there is bright sun, suggesting something special about how the building was oriented.

RP: Upon entering the interior street levels, on the eastern side and catching the morning sun, the proportions of the corridor do not seem cramped. It is open and airy. With the light from the windows, and radiators to warm it in winter, it must have been a congenial place to pass the time of day with your neighbours.

The plan appears effortless when you are passing through it but is actually characterised by great ingenuity and a masterly arrangement of space. The degree of variability in the different apartment types, still accompanied by formal rigour in the way they are arranged, provides every unit with well-lit space. Some of the apartments have a clear connection with both sides of the building, allowing exposure to the sun in both the morning and afternoon.

The westerly façade is characterised by large expanses of double glazing, further enhancing the lightness and transparency of the interior. This was a time when fresh air and sunlight were thought of as highly therapeutic. This aspect reached its apogee in Alvar Aalto's sanatorium at Paimio, which was being constructed at the same time.

Ginzburg equipped Narkomfin with similar facilities – places to exercise and sunbathe on the roof. There is a coherence and free-flowing character to the whole scheme and a clear sense of idealism in the search for new patterns of existence to shape communal life.

TT: Jean-Louis Cohen has written about the way Russian industry of the time combined relatively new materials and techniques with truly ancient methods. Ginzburg seems to use glass and steel in a bold and straightforward way that challenges the technical limitations he encountered.

RP: The building was very advanced technically, a factor that has had an effect on its present condition. There was little time to test the materials and there were problems from the beginning with some of the components. The blocks tended to be permeable and thus, compounded by official neglect, the surface stucco is continually being forced off in the harsh winters. However, the core frame in cast reinforced concrete was so well constructed that it remains uncompromised. Other elements of the construction were ancient, however. Behind the stucco of the rooftop apartment for Commissar of Finance Nikolai Miliutin, for example, you can see that the insulation was chopped straw.

RECENT PHOTOGRAPHS

TT: The catalogue includes two photographs from your recent work at the Ordzhonikidze Sanatorium and annex at Kislovodsk (Cat. 91). Construction of the complex occurred in two phases, the first part from 1934 to 1937, with the annex begun in 1947, the year after the principal architect, Moisei Ginzburg, had died. Would you comment on the significance of the complex and the difference between the two phases?

RP: Towards the end, the sense of optimism was rapidly being extinguished. At that moment, in 1934, Ginzburg was commissioned by G.K. Ordzhonikidze, one of Stalin's oldest collaborators, to lead a team of architects to build the Narkomtyazhprom sanatorium (sanatorium for workers in the Commissariat for Heavy Industry). The predicament of the Modernist architects working at this critical moment is expressed in this building. I sense a will to confound the arbiters of Stalin's historicist taste by using ancient motifs of which they were no doubt entirely ignorant. The political climate was in flux once more but the regulatory oversight had not yet become completely ossified.

The plan for the sanatorium makes compromises, but with finesse, and still looking for a workable solution within the strictures handed down from above. The central therapy block which stands at the focus of the development is still highly innovative in its construction, filled with flying stairs, bridges and large expanses of glass, and with a strong linearity in the sweeping arc of its plan. For the bathing establishment behind and above the treatment section, Ginzburg repeats the circular plan that had been used for public baths throughout the Modernist period. But here the idea is elaborated with a colonnade surrounding a central atrium and with finely executed mosaics let into the floor.

The interior of the therapy block represented a major change in Ginzburg's use of space. It begins to take on attributes of the 'palaces for the people' exemplified in the lavishly appointed Metro stations in Moscow. Leonidov's stairs, which define the main axis of the whole complex, are a part of this effort to create a dramatic processional programme.

Ginzburg's Narkomfin has a more intimate attitude toward space than the much more imperial Kislovodsk sanatorium. The later project is elegant in its distribution of form and space, but what is missing is the sense of radical experimentation that was so distinctive in the earlier masterpiece.

In the later annex all hope has been extinguished. I was told by the current librarian that the architect had a falling out with his collaborators. By the time the project went forward, he was dead. His grandson confirmed, however, that he had been involved with the design. The exaggerated rustication of the ground-floor stonework and the huge arches and oculi are almost preposterous in their gigantism. The whole structure is uncharacteristic; full of gloomy halls and corridors. I found it impossible to believe it was the work of Ginzburg, the architect of transparency and light. There is a cruel irony in that when Le Corbusier was planning the Unité d'habitation in Marseille, using Narkomfin as his source of inspiration, Ginzburg was compelled to produce a structure he must have considered anachronistic.

CONTEMPORARY PRACTICE AND PRESERVATION

TT: Can you tell us something about the relation of this work to current practice and the motive for preserving it?

RP: There is always an unease between architects having to fulfil a brief from the client, cost, and architectural intent. I think the Russian Modernists were trying to break free from those kinds of constraints. In spite of the difficulties, there was an underlying optimism and vigour. Visionaries saw possibilities and, against all the odds, found ways to produce some canonic buildings that define Modernism in the early years of the Soviet regime.

That is why I, and an ever-increasing number of others, are intent on securing the future of some of the most significant structures. I am aware, at the same time, of the perils arising from ending up with a few token 'masterpieces' divorced from the urban context.

There is a catastrophe unfolding in Moscow at present. They are tearing down listed buildings from before 1812. The texture of the city is being erased. Such an indiscriminate wave of destruction and unbridled speculative construction is unbearable. The city has altered beyond recognition in the years since my own first trip in 1993. When they do make decisions to retain part of the legacy, the results are as often as not a fiasco. The Hotel Moskva [1932–38], one of Aleksei Shchusev's late works, was knocked down completely to build a huge underground shopping mall and garage and then rebuilt as a concrete facsimile on top. The mentality appears to be that it must be better now because it has air-conditioning and a concrete structure. But all the original detail and atmosphere have been swept away.

TT: What about the preservationist movement? Where is it coming from and who supports it?

RP: It seems to be coming up from the bottom. This is not just about the Modernist legacy but about the whole fabric of the city. The city government has looked on while developers have torn down buildings that officially were protected, by the same government. People are paid to look the other way.

TT: Allowing these monuments to decay seems to have another motive beyond money. There must be a real fear of the history these buildings represent. Some people would just as soon they were forgotten. The experiment had failed and the record held no particular interest. History would carry on as if the Russian Revolution were really an aberration. But the ideas have refused to fade.

RP: I think the tide is turning. Since the collapse of the Soviet regime there has been a tendency to see all the works created during those years, in architecture especially, as being bad by definition. I don't think it is fear so much as blindness, an inability to accept the

transformative intention of the visionaries who conceived the radical buildings of the Modernist period. But now there are moves afoot to draw attention to the legacy of the Russian Modernists, with the emergence within the last decade of the Moscow Architecture Preservation Society. It has highlighted the plight of the entire Modernist canon.

TT: What are your plans in the near future?

RP: There is still work to do to finish this project. There are cities I have still not been able to reach. Even in Moscow there are buildings which are closed and inaccessible. I intend to record as many of these structures as I am able, running a race to make the study as complete as possible before too much more is swept away.

Putting these pictures together as an exhibition has been a revelation. Even a subject as familiar as Aleksei Shchusev's Lenin Mausoleum on Red Square in Moscow took people by surprise (Cat. 92). When you go through it as a visitor, being hurried through the tomb chamber, you are so dominated by the body lying there that you pay little attention to the space. It is Shchusev's masterpiece, symbolising that moment of historical change and the focus of the regime on the relics of Lenin. The main ceremonial event of the Soviet calendar, the May Day parade, passed in front of the assembled leaders, who took the salute literally standing on Lenin's body (92.9).

The exhibition opens with a very different image, Vladimir Shukhov's Shabolovka Radio Tower, which was about transparency, openness and spreading the word, the dawn of the Socialist state (Cat. 62). And the mausoleum, at the other end of the sequence, is the heart of darkness.

NOTE

Tim Tower spoke with Richard Pare on several occasions during February and March 2008 following the publication of *The Lost Vanguard: Russian Modernist Architecture 1922–1932* and the exhibition based on it at the Museum of Modern Art in New York (both 2007). They discussed the work again recently to update the piece for the current volume. A shortened version of this interview appeared on the World Socialist Web Site (www.wsws.org).

ART

ARCHITECTURE

STATE
COMMUNICATIONS
INDUSTRY
HOUSING
EDUCATION
HEALTH
RECREATION
LENIN
MAUSOLEUM

SHABOLOVKA RADIO TOWER

**SHABOLOVKA ULITSA
MOSCOW, RUSSIA
Vladimir Shukhov, 1922**

Shukhov's radio tower was
the first permanent industrial
structure to be built after the
Revolution. It is constructed from
a series of six stacked steel-lattice
hyperboloids, with each section
built on the ground inside the
lowest segment and then raised
into place. This system was
invented by Shukhov for water
towers in 1896. The innovative
design uses straight steel
members arranged to act as
trusses to reduce the tendency
to buckle. The tower was
intended to be taller than
the Eiffel Tower, rising over
350 metres, but because of a
shortage of steel at the time
its height was restricted to
150 metres.

Since its construction the tower
has functioned as a symbol of
the Revolution and of industrial
progress. During the early
post-Revolutionary years it was
included on several propaganda
posters extolling the virtues
of Soviet communications.
The patterns created by the
latticework appealed to avant-
garde artists, who reproduced
its image in photographs,
photomontage, lithographs,
films and paintings; it was
photographed by Aleksandr

Rodchenko as a symbol of
modernity and reappeared on
posters as an emblem of Soviet
progress during the first Five
Year Plan. The tower's skeletal
form and function as a
radio transmitter also relate
it to Vladimir Tatlin's unrealised
1919 *Monument to the Third
International* (Figures 1 and 10).

Although the Shabolovka tower
remains the tallest of them,
Shukhov built several other
towers in Soviet Russia using
the same system of construction.
It remains an important feature
of the Moscow skyline and is still
used as a radio and television
transmitter. MC

Cat. 62.1 above
Havsko-Shabolovskii residential block
and Shabolovka Radio Tower viewed
from Sepukhovskii Val ulitsa
Photographer unknown, 1929
115 x 169 mm

Cat. 62.2 top right
Shabolovka Radio Tower: view
from Mytnaia ulitsa
N.S. Granovskii, 1950
115 x 169 mm

Cat. 62.3 opposite
Shabolovka Radio Tower
Richard Pare, 1998
154.8 x 121.9 cm

Cat. 62.5
Shabolovka Radio Tower:
detail of structure
Richard Pare, 1998
60.5 x 60.5 cm

GOSPROM BUILDING

SVOBODY PLOSHCHAD
(FORMERLY DZERZHINSKII
PLOSHCHAD)
KHARKOV, UKRAINE
Samuil Kravets with Sergei
Serafimov, Mark Felger, 1929

The Gosprom Building (Palace of
Industry) was constructed as the
central government office for the
new Ukrainian capital of Kharkov.
The building was to be not only
a political, social and economic
centre but also the city's
visual focal point. Based on a
competition entry led by Kravets,
it reflects major contemporary
town-planning initiatives,
especially the principles of
the Garden City movement, in
which cities were to be developed
in radiating bands organised
by function. Kravets and his
assistants intended to construct
a complete circle from which
new buildings could radiate as
the town expanded. Though only

four blocks, making a semi-circle,
were completed, the scale of the
project ensured it became one
of the city's key features.

The Gosprom Building united
more than 25 government
institutions in a series of
interlocking blocks linked
by covered skywalks. Each
of the four blocks had its own
entrance hall, though they were
connected internally and shared
a library, conference centre and
dining hall.

The use of skywalks created
a new architectural language
for communal life while the
juxtaposition of horizontal
and vertical forms provided
a visual dynamism that recalls
developments in Suprematist
and Constructivist art. Different
treatments for the fenestration
distinguished transitional spaces
from office areas and added to

the grid-like pattern of the
building forms. While the
overall effect is of asymmetrical
intersections of different forms,
the plans for each block are in
fact symmetrical, a symmetry
that can only be perceived
from particular points within
Svobody ploshchad.

One of the blocks was badly
damaged during World War II.
A radio tower was added in
the 1990s. Since the pictures
reproduced in this catalogue
were taken the main façade has
been painted and many of the
windows have been replaced,
altering the effect of scale and
the balance of the composition.
MC

Cat. 63.1 above
Gosprom Building: panoramic view
across Svobody (formerly Dzerzhinskii)
ploshchad
Photographer unknown, 1930s
144 x 612 mm

Cat. 63.2 left
Gosprom Building: part of the complex
looking across Svobody ploshchad
Richard Pare, 1999
60.5 x 83.8 cm

Cat. 63.3
Gosprom Building: aerial view
Photographer unknown, 1930s
163 x 238 mm

Cat. 63.4
Gosprom Building: detail of fenestration
Richard Pare, 1999
70 x 70 cm

Cat. 63.5
Gosprom Building: detail with
covered skywalk
Richard Pare, 1999
121.9 x 120.1 cm

TSENTROSOYUZ BUILDING

39 MIASNITSKAIA ULITSA
MOSCOW, RUSSIA
Le Corbusier, Pierre Jeanneret,
Nikolai Kolli, 1929–36

The cooperative movement had been suppressed by the Bolsheviks after the Revolution, but its right to operate was restored under the New Economic Policy and in the 1920s it again became a powerful force in retailing, banking and food production and distribution. As the private sector contracted, consumer cooperatives gained a large share of the retail market.

In 1926 Tsentrosoyuz (the Central Union of Consumer Cooperatives) was allocated a prominent site on Miasnitskaia ulitsa to construct a headquarters for its 2,000 office workers, an undertaking that would express the importance and power of the movement. An open competition was launched, eliciting proposals from 32 Soviet architects; Le Corbusier was one of three foreign architects invited to submit. By the time the scheme was completed, however, cooperatives had again fallen into disfavour and the building was occupied by the Commissariat for Light Industry (Narkomlegprom).

Le Corbusier's final design was for three glass-faced rectangular blocks for the offices and a block with a semi-circular end for the workers' club and auditoriums. The longest block faces Miasnitskaia ulitsa, set back from the street. At each side is the blank end-wall of one of the other blocks, which run back into the site, angled slightly towards the centre. The club is behind the central block.

The Moscow Plan of the time anticipated that two further sides of the site would face on to newly formed streets, and Le Corbusier envisaged that the second long office block would have an entrance from the street. The failure to implement the plan limited the scheme's frontage to a single street, considerably reducing its impact.

Tsentrosoyuz pioneered important innovations in office design. The plan, with its freestanding but linked rectangular blocks, introduced a flexibility previously lacking in courtyard plans for office complexes. The narrowness of the blocks maximised interior natural light and the raising of the buildings on pilotis to create an open ground floor – subsequently largely filled in – allowed space for vehicle access. The use of internal ramps as well as stairs facilitated the passage of large numbers of people at the beginning and end of the working

Cat. 64.1
Tsentrosoyuz Building: under construction
M.A. Ilyin, 1930
104 x 77 mm

day. But some of Le Corbusier's innovations proved impossible to realise, notably his proposal for temperature control by airflow into the double-glazed façades.

Completed in 1936, at a time when avant-garde architecture had come under attack in the Soviet Union, the building provoked predictable criticism. But Aleksandr Vesnin praised the clarity of its architectural thought, the precision of the construction of masses and volumes, and its success in combining lightness and monumentality. NDBdeM

Cat. 64.2
Tsentrosoyuz Building: perspective view of office block
Photographer unknown, 1930s
112 x 169 mm

Cat. 64.3
Tsentrosoyuz Building: under construction
M.A. Ilyin, 1930
106 x 77 mm

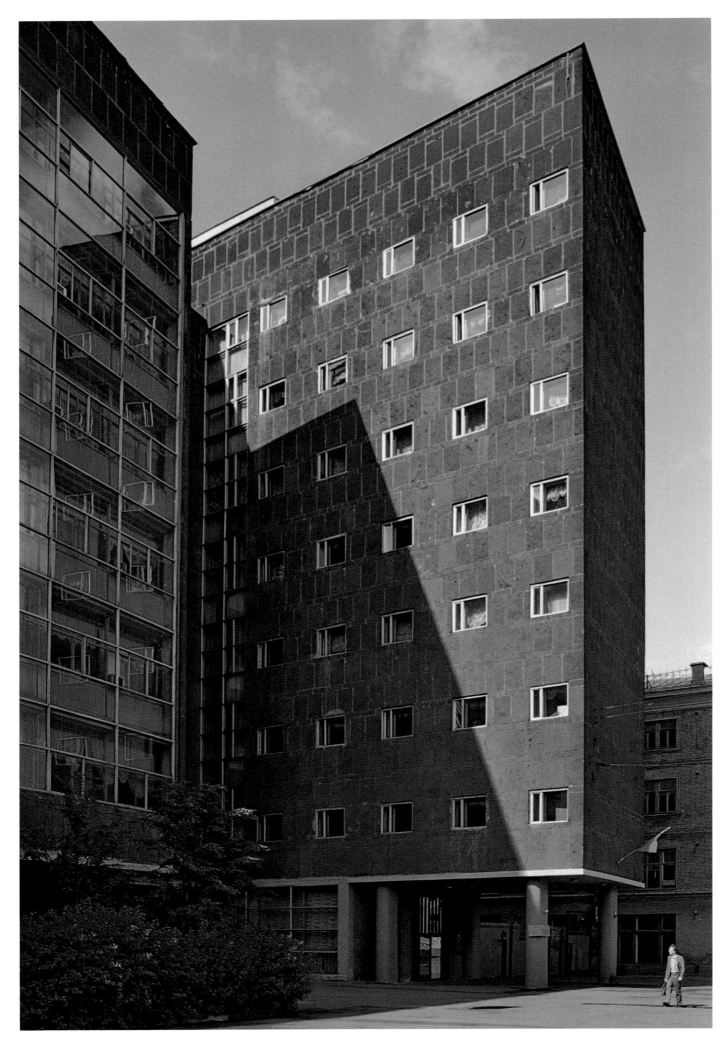

Cat. 64.5 above
Tsentrosoyuz Building: the block
accommodating the workers' club
and auditorium
Richard Pare, 1995
75.7 x 113.8 cm

Cat. 64.6 right
Tsentrosoyuz Building: the block
accommodating the workers' club
and auditorium
Photographer unknown, 1950
120 x 175 mm

Cat. 64.4 opposite
Tsentrosoyuz Building: narrow
rectangular blocks raised on pilotis
Richard Pare, 1995
75.7 x 50.3 mm

Cat. 64.7
**Tsentrosoyuz Building: interior circulation
with ramps to auditorium**
Richard Pare, 1999
121.9 x 154.9 cm

126

IZVESTIA BUILDING

5 PUSHKINSKAIA PLOSHCHAD
MOSCOW, RUSSIA
Grigorii Barkhin, Mikhail Barkhin,
1925–27

Positioned on a prominent site, this was one of the first major buildings to be erected in Moscow after the 1918–20 Civil War. Unambiguously avant-garde in design, the new building can be seen in an early photograph (Cat. 65.1) towering assertively above its Classically inspired neighbour. The Strastnoi Monastery and its church, which were originally in front of the Izvestia Building, were demolished in the 1930s to clear the centre of the square.

The building was designed to house the offices and printing presses of *Izvestia*, which, like *Pravda*, was an official organ of the Bolshevik party. The Barkhins' initial proposal had incorporated a twelve-storey tower inspired by Walter Gropius and Hannes Meyer's entry for the 1922 *Chicago Tribune* competition but the introduction of height restrictions in central Moscow obliged the architects to abandon this idea. The liveliness of the façade owes much to the complex rhythms of its irregular grid form. The building was attacked at the time in the pages of *SA* because the distribution of balconies and the use of circular windows, resembling portholes, seemed decorative rather than functional.

The façade is now hidden by advertising and the ground floor is occupied by fast-food outlets.
NDBdeM

Cat. 65.1
Izvestia Building
A. Teleshev, 1930s
76 x 80 mm

Cat. 65.2 right
Izvestia Building: stairs to roof pavilion
Richard Pare, 1999
45.7 x 30.5 cm

Cat. 65.3 below
Izvestia Building: detail
Richard Pare, 1994
27.5 x 38.9 cm

130

Cat. 65.4
Izvestia Building: view across
Pushkinskaia ploshchad
Richard Pare, 1999
75.5 x 60.5 cm

PALACE OF THE PRESS

NIZAMI PLOSHCHAD
BAKU, AZERBAIJAN
Semen Pen, 1932

Before the construction of
the Palace of the Press, new
architecture in Azerbaijan tended
to incorporate elements of the
local vernacular. Pen's design
rejects this aesthetic in favour
of a Modernist building that
includes both international
and Soviet vocabulary.

The printing and office complex
displays the influence of
Le Corbusier, with its pilotis,
roof terraces, ribbon windows
and wraparound balconies, all
elements that were appropriate
for the warm climate, allowing
maximum air flow. Although the
overall appearance is of simplicity
and refined geometry, the
building is eclectic in its use of
avant-garde vocabulary drawn
from a variety of sources. Such
elements include intersecting
perpendicular blocks, long
corridors, round windows, and
circular, semi-circular and
straight uninterrupted balconies.

The protruding balconies
exaggerate and enhance the
curved form that cuts through the
otherwise rectangular block to
create a visual dynamism. This
juxtaposition is reminiscent of
both the Textile Institute Student
Housing in Moscow (Cat. 78)

and Erich Mendelsohn's Red
Banner Textile Factory in
St Petersburg (Cat. 71). Probably
because the techniques and
materials necessary for banded
fenestration were not available in
Baku at the time, Pen attempted
to create the same effect using
traditional windows.

The plan shows a large, open,
rectangular printing hall in
the central building with office
spaces in a smaller building
perpendicular to it. The complex
was built during the year of the
official declaration of a return
to historicism in Soviet art and
architecture and Pen's choice
of a Modernist aesthetic may be
explained by its location beyond
any important political centre. It is
also possible that it was designed
in the mid-1920s but was not built
until 1932 because of shortages of
funds and materials.

The Palace of the Press is now
a bank. It has been renovated
and painted in a semi-gloss finish
while new windows have been
installed throughout, destroying
the balance of the façade. MC

Cat. 66.1
Palace of the Press: printing hall
Richard Pare, 1999
91.4 x 74.4 cm

134

Cat. 66.2
Palace of the Press: rectangular blocks containing the editorial and printing functions
I.O. Sosfenov (?), 1930s
105 x 160 mm

Cat. 66.3
Palace of the Press: view from Nizami ploshchad
Photographer unknown, 1930s
83 x 143 mm

Cat. 66.4 above
Palace of the Press: view showing
balconies and roof terrace
Richard Pare, 1999
39.2 x 50.3 cm

Cat. 66.5 left
Palace of the Press: curved balconies
Richard Pare, 1999
61 x 61 cm

STATE
COMMUNICATIONS
INDUSTRY
HOUSING
EDUCATION
HEALTH
RECREATION
LENIN
MAUSOLEUM

BAKERY

2 KHODYNSKAIA ULITSA
MOSCOW, RUSSIA
Engineer: Georgii Marsakov, 1931

Industrial bakeries, like industrial kitchens (see the Narvskii Factory Kitchen, Cat. 72), freed women from time-consuming domestic chores. The construction of mass bakeries began in 1924, initially using German or American equipment. Subsequently the engineer Georgii Marsakov designed equipment that could be manufactured in Russia.

Operating 24 hours a day, the bakery used a mass-production process with a different stage – mixing, proving the dough, baking, packing – implemented on each of its four floors. The plan makes effective use of residual heat from the oven, which provides warmth for the proving process on the floor above. Production on this scale both reduced the cost of bread and allowed architects to install stoves without a baking facility in the kitchens of new housing schemes.

The building stopped functioning as a bakery in 2007. Now gutted, it appears to be in the process of conversion fors use as a cultural centre and condominiums. Two other examples remain in use in St Petersburg. NDBdeM

138

Cat. 67.1
Bakery: exterior showing the four production levels
Photographer unknown, 1938
93 x 146 mm

Cat. 67.2
Bakery: interior showing industrialised
baking using mass-production techniques
Richard Pare, 1999
121.9 x 308.4 cm

DNEPROGES, DAM AND HYDROELECTRIC POWER STATION

**ZAPOROZHYE
DNEPR RIVER, UKRAINE
Aleksandr Vesnin, Nikolai Kolli,
Georgii Orlov, Sergei Andrievskii,
1927–32**

DneproGES was the earliest and most extensive industrial installation created as part of Stalin's First Five Year Plan. As such, it was widely used as visual propaganda to communicate the magnitude of the plan and its objectives. Begun in 1927 and officially opened with the completion of the power station and turbine hall on 10 October 1932, it was the largest hydroelectric dam in the world at the time of its construction. Once completed, the dam consisted of 47 sluice gates mounted between piers, and nine turbines and generators produced 16.7 million kilowatts, enough to power the numerous industrial plants near the site as well as the new workers' town of Zaporozhye and its surroundings. The scheme was lauded as the fulfilment of the goal of building Socialism and the establishment of the Soviet Union as a modern industrial state. As the first of many major projects realised under the plan, the dam and its role in increasing electrical power throughout the USSR were symbols of the triumph of Stalin's vision.

The design for the power station, turbine hall and the gates of the dam resulted from an architectural competition. The Vesnin team's winning entry reveals a Constructivist emphasis on functionalism in architecture. It features a flat roof, banded fenestration and a machine-like simplicity devoid of ornament. In line with their functionalist interest in a machine-based aesthetic and desire to unite design and technology, the architects made extensive use of modern techniques and materials such as reinforced concrete, plate glass and exposed metalwork.

With its geometric form and machine aesthetic, the design is appropriate for an industrial project aimed at modernising society. But though the dam set a precedent, the design did not become a standard one and its formal vocabulary was not employed in subsequent schemes.

The installation was damaged during World War II and rebuilt between 1944 and 1946 with slight adjustments to the power station: the exterior stucco was replaced with local granite, and the band of upper windows was replaced by octagonal ones set within porthole openings. It still functions as a power station. MC

Cat. 68.1 above
DneproGES: sluice gates under construction
Photographer unknown, 1930s
111 x 750 mm approx.
(four prints: left to right 110 x 180, 111 x 190, 111 x 180, 111 x 200 mm)

Cat. 68.2 opposite top
DneproGES: turbine hall exterior with granite replacing the original stucco and octagonal windows replacing the original banded fenestration
Richard Pare, 1999
50.8 x 64.5 cm

Cat. 68.3 opposite bottom left
DneproGES: dam under construction
Photographer unknown, 1931
123 x 173 mm

Cat. 68.4 opposite bottom right
DneproGES: turbine hall and sluice gates
Photographer unknown, 1930s
106 x 163 mm

Cat. 68.5
DneproGES: turbine hall
Richard Pare, 1999
121.9 x 154.4 cm

MOGES

**1 OSIPENKO ULITSA
MOSCOW, RUSSIA
Ivan Zholtovskii, 1926**

MoGES (Moscow City Electric Power Station), situated in central Moscow east of the Kremlin on the Moskva River, is the oldest power plant in the city still in operation. The dramatic contrast between the Modernist interior courtyard and the Classically inspired river façade demonstrates Zholtovskii's application of Classical principles of proportion and composition to industrial architecture.

The inner façade, which is only visible from the facility's courtyard, is an exercise in avant-garde geometry and modern materials. Four pairs of tall and angular glazed bays stand directly below the upper-level windows, which have a narrow balcony, and protrude from an otherwise flat façade. The extensive use of glass and the geometric volumes point to the influence of Constructivism, while the symmetry and reference to pilasters supporting a frieze convey Zholtovskii's preference for Classical and Renaissance architecture. Though this façade gives the impression of an innovative use of glass and concrete, photographs recording its construction reveal it to have been built using traditional methods and materials.

This inner façade is in stark contrast to the river frontage, where a series of arches set between pilasters is clearly Classically inspired. But while the front and back are stylistically different, they share a symmetry and absence of ornament.

Zholtovskii's design demonstrates how Classically trained architects responded to the demand to produce new building types to meet industrial needs. MC

Cat. 69.1
MoGES: the Classically inspired façade
on the Moskva River
Richard Pare, 1998
40.2 x 108.1 cm

Cat. 69.2
MoGES: under construction
Photographer unknown, c. 1924
228 x 164 mm

Cat. 69.3
MoGES: angular glazed bays
of the inner façade
Richard Pare, 1998
121.9 x 154.7 cm

WATER TOWER FOR THE SOCIALIST CITY OF URALMASH

1 KULTURY BULVAR
EKATERINBURG, RUSSIA
Moisei Reisher, 1929

The tower was built to provide water to the Uralmash plant, a production facility for heavy machinery, and the surrounding district. Its construction coincided with the development of Uralmash Sotsgorod, a Socialist city for workers from a production facility in Ekaterinburg.

Situated at the end of one of three main boulevards that radiate from the city centre, the tower was intended as a visual feature, striking not only because of its height and location but also because of its novel form. One of the first structures in Ekaterinburg to use ferro-concrete, it rose above the surrounding buildings on six stilt-like pilotis that support

the cylindrical water tank. The form of the cylinder is articulated by a lower ring of small circular windows and an upper ring of banded fenestration. Though the effect of the upper ring is of a continuous ribbon, the windows are in fact constructed traditionally with small panes enclosed in rectangular frames.

The tower's status as a landmark has earned it the nickname White Tower (*Belaya Bashnina*). In the 1970s the House of Culture was built, obstructing the view to the tower along the main axis of Kultury bulvar.

While the machinery and water tank have been removed, the building is still considered an important symbol, used unofficially as a viewing tower and lending its name and image to a local insurance company. Debate over ownership has

stalled attempts at renovation and preservation, though the structure remains in fairly good condition. MC

Cat. 70.1
Water Tower: panorama of Ekaterinburg with the water tower at the end of Kultury bulvar
Photographer unknown, 1948
111 x 647 mm (four prints, each 105 x 165 mm)

Cat. 70.2
Water Tower: a ferro-concrete
structure raised on pilotis
Richard Pare, 1999
121.9 x 154.2 cm

Cat. 70.3
Water Tower: inside the now empty drum
Richard Pare, 1999
75.7 x 50.3 cm

RED BANNER
TEXTILE FACTORY

53 PIONERSKAIA ULITSA
ST PETERSBURG, RUSSIA
Erich Mendelsohn, 1925–37

In 1925 the Leningrad Trust for Textile Production invited the German architect Erich Mendelsohn to submit designs for a factory on a large site. Mendelsohn noted that the scheme would include '3 dye works, 5-storey buildings with staircase towers, a dispatch centre with administration… coal yard, workshops and power plant'.

Mendelsohn's proposal for the entire site was initially accepted. Once construction started, however, changes were made by the Soviet engineers supervising the work and Mendelsohn was later to disown the final design altogether.

The power station (Cat. 71.3), which provided energy for the entire project, was the one major element constructed largely to Mendelsohn's plans and is the visible face of the factory to the outside world. Its core is the huge main plant hall, one side of which faces the street with the apsidal structure at its northern end dominating a crossroads. The power station has been seen as a cathedral dedicated to heavy industry – a reference in part to the windows, which extend almost the full height of the plant hall. It has also been described as a ship towing the rest of the plant behind it, a metaphor for its role in mobilising the productive capacity of the factory.

From the time of its construction the building was controversial. It was naturally subject to attack by opponents of Modernism but it was also criticised by parts of the avant-garde. The OSA group, through their journal *SA*, objected to the award of the contract without the usual tendering procedure and Moisei Ginzburg suggested that Mendelsohn's architecture, specifically his use of curved surfaces, was calculated to evoke emotion rather than to ensure functionality. Nevertheless, in the 1930s Mendelsohn's power station would appear on the cover of a guidebook to Leningrad, indicating its status as a symbol of a new modern, industrial city.

It is disused, although there are plans to convert it into a cultural centre. NDBdeM

Cat. 71.1 top
Red Banner Textile Factory: view of the power plant
Photographer unknown, first half of 1930s
108 x 162 mm

Cat. 71.2 above
Red Banner Textile Factory: detail of the curved upper structure for water tanks
Richard Pare, 2000
61 x 61 cm

Cat. 71.3 opposite
Red Banner Textile Factory: view of the power plant
Richard Pare, 1999
101.6 x 78.7 cm

152

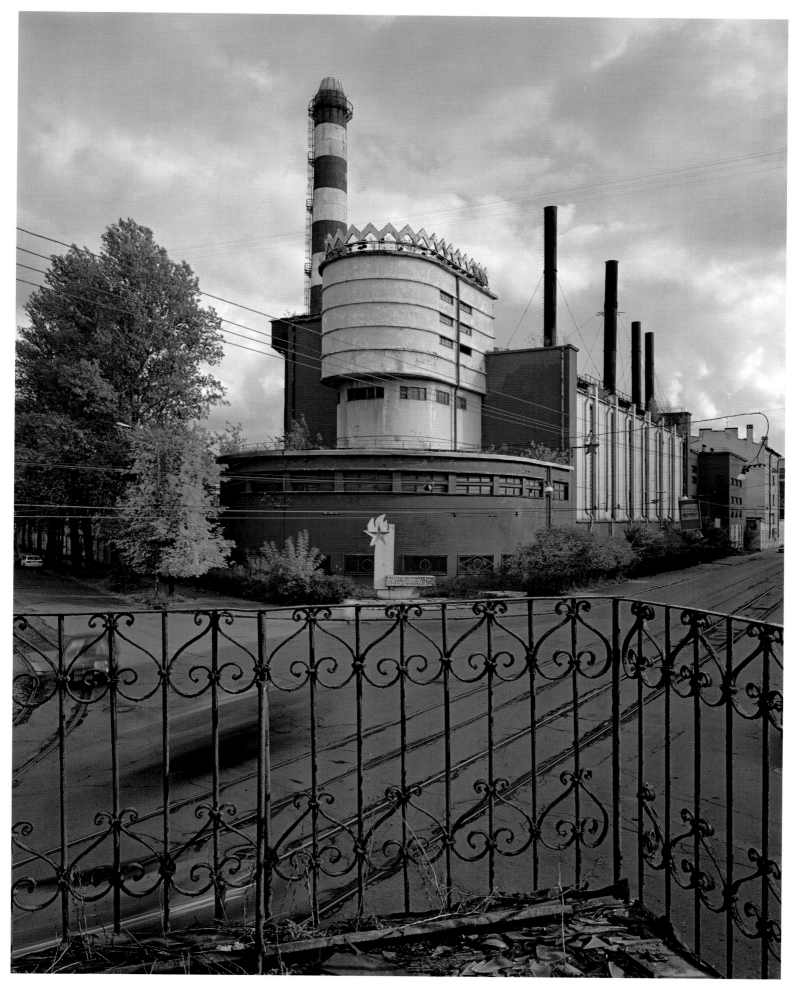

Cat. 71.4
Red Banner Textile Factory: power-plant control room
Richard Pare, 1999
60.5 x 76.5 cm

Cat. 71.5 left
Red Banner Textile Factory: inside
the power plant
Richard Pare, 1999
121.9 x 153.9 cm

Cat. 71.6 above
Red Banner Textile Factory: façade detail
Photographer unknown, 1930s
109 x 160 mm

NARVSKII FACTORY KITCHEN AND DEPARTMENT STORE

Lenin followed Friedrich Engels' assertion that the liberation of women was impossible as long as they were bound to the domestic sphere. He argued that although the Revolution had established equal political rights for women, true economic and social equality could be delivered only if they were drawn fully into active participation in the productive activities of the nation.

Thus the 1920s saw a range of initiatives to relieve women of the task of preparing food in the home. In St Petersburg large factory kitchens like the Narvskii provided meals for entire districts. In communal-housing schemes residents were served by smaller communal kitchens and there were also plans for labour-saving domestic kitchens like those installed in the Narkomfin Communal House (Cat. 75).

The Narvskii Factory Kitchen was one of four schemes in St Petersburg all designed by the same group of architects in the late 1920s and early 1930s. The kitchens were scaled for the mass throughput of materials and diners; all had extensive food-preparation areas, a canteen and a shopping area.

Close attention was paid to the efficient functioning of these multi-purpose buildings. The Narvskii scheme is organised around an internal courtyard. The side facing the street, with its long glass frontage, houses the shopping area, with the canteen to one side. On the other two sides of the courtyard are the food-preparation area and the interface with the canteen. This arrangement ensured that the flows of people and goods to the different activities were separated, while facilitating the delivery of prepared food to the diners. Steel and concrete structural elements were used to provide large spans in both the processing areas and the canteen.

The long horizontal of the third floor unifies the asymmetrical street frontage. The contrasts between the fenestration of the shop front and the upper floor, and the emphatic curve near one end, all serve to animate the long street façade. The use of modern materials, the careful consideration of the building's functionality and the overall aesthetic reflect the most avant-garde thinking among St Petersburg architects of the late 1920s.

The top floor, originally a terrace with seating for canteen users, has now been enclosed. NDBdeM

Cat. 72.1
Narvskii Factory Kitchen and Department
Store: shop window detail
Richard Pare, 1995
41.4 x 27.5 cm

Cat. 72.2 left
Narvskii Factory Kitchen and Department
Store: general view
Photographer unknown, 1930–33
75 x 109 mm

Cat. 72.3 below
Narvskii Factory Kitchen and Department
Store: glazed street frontage; the top
floor was originally a terrace but is
now enclosed
Richard Pare, 1995
40.2 x 51.6 cm

GOSPLAN GARAGE

63 AVIAMOTORNAIA ULITSA
MOSCOW, RUSSIA
Konstantin Melnikov with
V.I. Kurochkin, 1936

The development of motor
transport in the 1920s created
new opportunities for architects:
Melnikov, for instance, was invited
to design a garage for a thousand
vehicles in Paris. He responded
with a remarkable multi-storey
cantilevered structure to be
raised over the River Seine.
The authorities no doubt thought
this too daring.

In Moscow, however, he was
to build four garages over the
following decade. The interiors
are in general soberly functional:
spaces are based on an analysis
of vehicle movements and have
undecorated brickwork walls with
metal roof structures to provide
the wide spans required.

The exteriors are much less
restrained. The white fluting on
the office block of the Gosplan
Garage is perhaps related to the
surrounds of the large doors of
his earlier Bakhmetevskaia ulitsa
garage but it also resembles
a vehicle's radiator grille. The
vigorously sculpted decoration
around the circular window
seems to set it in motion and is
perhaps a reference to a wheel.
Such emphatic decorative motifs
are unusual in 1920s avant-garde
architecture.

The Gosplan Garage is still in use
as a workshop. NDBdeM

Cat. 73.1
Gosplan Garage: detail of sculpted
decoration around the circular window
Richard Pare, 1993
61 x 51 cm

Cat. 73.2 opposite
Gosplan Garage: side elevation
Photographer unknown, c. 1936
180 x 132 mm

Cat. 73.3
Gosplan Garage: general view
Photographer unknown, c. 1936
136 x 200 mm

Cat. 73.4 opposite
**Gosplan Garage: circular window
dominating one façade**
Richard Pare, 1993
75.5 x 60.5 cm

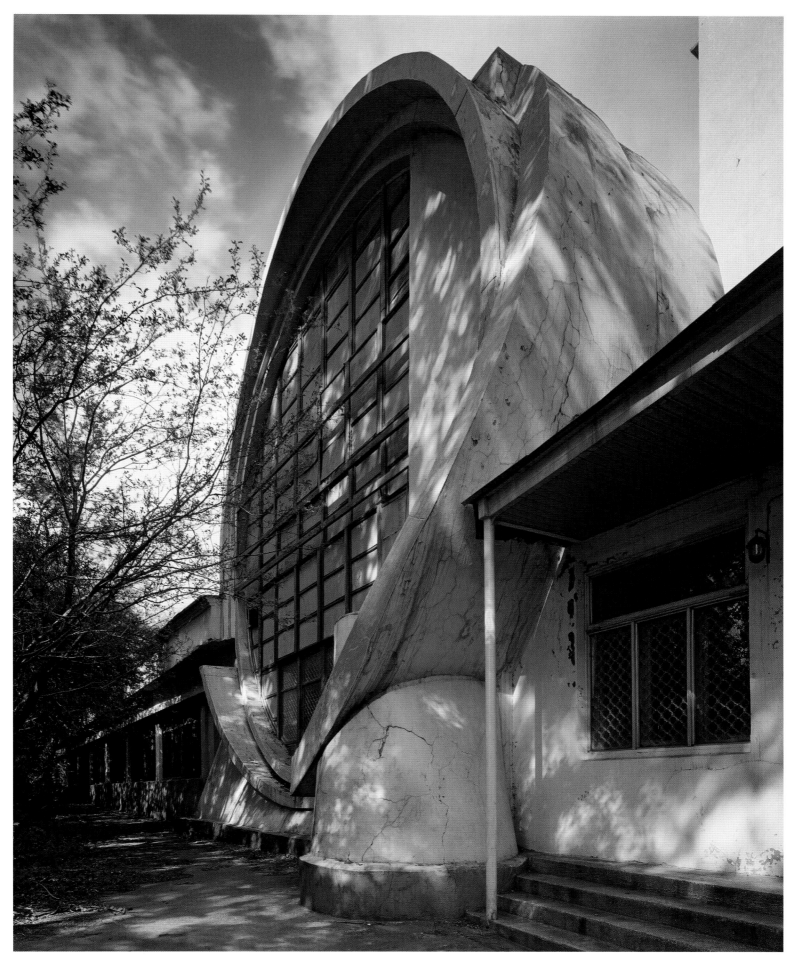

CENTRAL INSTITUTE OF AERODYNAMICS AND HYDRODYNAMICS

16 RADIO ULITSA
MOSCOW, RUSSIA
Aleksandr Kuznetsov with
Boris Gladkov, Ivan Nikolaev,
Gennadi Movchan,
Anatoli Fisenko, 1924–28

The Central Institute of
Aerodynamics and Hydrodynamics
(TsAGI) was founded in 1918 as
a research and development
centre. The design of its
headquarters is characteristic
of the work of graduates of
MVTU in its combination of
explorative engineering, quality
and creativity. New architectural
elements such as the geometric
articulation of volumes and
combinations of blind and
glazed walls and rectangular and
semi-circular forms in a dynamic
spatial composition convey the
architects' desire to experiment
with form and articulate the
building's function as a centre
for innovation. The use of a

traditional and durable material
such as brick both reflects an
emphasis on quality and provides
an interesting counterpoint to the
building's streamlined Modernist
lines, as well as demonstrating
that modern materials such
as concrete were not readily
available. A combination of
innovative forms and traditional
materials was also employed in
the fenestration.

TsAGI still uses the building and
a museum of Soviet aviation and
marine engineering has been
added to the complex. MC

Cat. 74.1
Central Institute of Aerodynamics
and Hydrodynamics: exterior
Richard Pare, 1994
61 x 51 cm

Cat. 74.2
Central Institute of Aerodynamics
and Hydrodynamics: innovative forms
and traditional materials combined
Richard Pare, 1998
75.7 x 101.1 cm

STATE
COMMUNICATIONS
INDUSTRY
HOUSING
EDUCATION
HEALTH
RECREATION
LENIN
MAUSOLEUM

NARKOMFIN COMMUNAL HOUSE

**25 NOVINSKII BULVAR
MOSCOW, RUSSIA
Moisei Ginzburg, Ignatii Milinis,
1930**

Whereas with the early
St Petersburg developments
communal facilities were
provided by the municipality
(see the Workers' Housing on
Traktornaia ulitsa, Cat. 79), in
later housing schemes, especially
in Moscow, such facilities were
often attached to the dwelling
block or complex. In part this
may reflect a 1924 law which,
in keeping with the greater
liberalisation of the New
Economic Policy, had encouraged
the creation of cooperatives
to construct housing for their
members.

The Narkomfin Communal
House, commissioned by the
first Commissar of Finance,
Nikolai Miliutin, was designed
for the staff of his ministry.
It was originally conceived as
four units: an accommodation
block; a communal block with
a sports hall and a mezzanine
space for rest on its lower floors
and a communal dining hall
with a kitchen and mezzanine
reading room above; a laundry
block at some distance from
the other two buildings; and a
block for children, which was
never built, though the roof
of the accommodation block

had a dormitory and recreation
area apparently designed
for children.

There were 42 dwelling
units when the building was
completed. Of these, 24 consisted
of a sleeping area with a small
study area and shower, designed
for participants in the communal
life of the block who would eat
in the dining hall and, if they
had children, lodge them in the
children's block. Eighteen larger
units had kitchens, bathrooms
and a separate bedroom for
children, suitable for families
not wishing to participate in
communal life. When financial
limitations meant that space
for mechanical plant in the
roof became superfluous,
Miliutin converted it for use
as living quarters for his
family, designing much of
the interior himself.

The plans were based on
earlier studies by a group led
by Ginzburg to produce designs
for living units that optimised
use of space, economy of
construction and efficient
patterns of living. The units
were open plan, thus eliminating
the need for internal corridors,
and the kitchen size was reduced
to minimise the amount of
movement necessary for food
preparation. Access corridors
were on alternate floors, so the

flats, which almost all extend over
two levels, have windows on both
sides to ensure the circulation
of fresh air, access to light, and
views over the wooded grounds,
which were formerly the park
of an aristocratic dwelling.

Ginzburg described the
Narkomfin Communal House
as 'transitional', intended to
accommodate those still choosing
traditional family life and those
who had advanced to living
communally. The building's
design, however, was expected
to persuade its traditional families
to convert to communal living.

The building clearly shows
the influence of Le Corbusier,
whose 'five points' Ginzburg had
embraced: a free plan without
structural internal walls; a free
façade; horizontal banded
fenestration; a roof garden; and
the use of pilotis (now partially
hidden by the later addition
of a ground floor). The wide
access corridors, designed for
social interaction, are reminiscent
of the decks of ocean liners,
which were illustrated by
Le Corbusier in *Vers une
architecture* (1923). It should
be noted that Le Corbusier
was not to construct a building
on the scale of Narkomfin
until his post-1945 Unités
d'habitation, which owe much
to Ginzburg's scheme.

The social experimentation of
the 1920s gave way to a more
conservative stance in the
1930s and the building's
communal programme was
never implemented. The building
has been badly maintained and is
now in very poor condition, with
no solution for its conservation or
future function. NDBdeM

Cat. 75.1 opposite left
Narkomfin Communal House:
detail of communal block interior
Photographer unknown, 1930s
120 x 185 mm

Cat. 75.2 opposite right
Narkomfin Communal House:
detail of communal block interior
Photographer unknown, 1930s
181 x 118 mm

Cat. 75.3 right
Narkomfin Communal House:
walkway connecting residential
and communal blocks
Photographer unknown, 1930s
184 x 120 mm

Cat. 75.4 below
Narkomfin Communal House:
façade detail
Photographer unknown, 1930s
121 x 182 mm

170

Cat. 75.5 opposite
Narkomfin Communal House:
corner detail of residential block
M.A. Ilyin, 1931
116 x 80 mm

Cat. 75.6 right
Narkomfin Communal House: exterior
Richard Pare, 1998
75.7 x 50.3 cm

Cat. 75.7 below
Narkomfin Communal House: banded
windows giving views over the grounds
Richard Pare, 1994
50.8 x 70 cm

171

Cat. 75.9 opposite top
Narkomfín Communal House: roof with
'penthouse'; a projected rooftop garden
was not realised
Richard Pare, 1994
75.7 x 95.7 cm

Cat. 75.10 opposite bottom
Narkomfín Communal House:
wide corridors intended to promote
social interaction
Richard Pare, 1994
50.3 x 75.7 cm

Cat. 75.8 above
Narkomfín Communal House: interior
Richard Pare, 1995
121.9 x 154.2 cm

SOVIET DOCTORS' HOUSING COOPERATIVE

KIEV, UKRAINE
Pavel Aleshin, 1927–30

This housing complex was built
in the late 1920s at a time when
cooperative groups, in particular
those from a single workplace
or profession, were encouraged
to construct apartment buildings.
In this case, Aleshin himself
occupied one of the flats.

Aleshin was trained as an
architect before 1914 and his
principal pre-1914 building in
Kiev was in the city's Classical
tradition. However, extensive
travel in Central and Western
Europe may have inspired him to
create the exuberant, curvaceous
façade with its concave centre
flanked by two protruding bays.
These may reflect his observation
of buildings of the 1900s in
Budapest, Vienna, Hamburg
or Brussels. The richness of
the front is augmented by two
contrasting colours of brick.
NDBdeM

Cat. 76.1
Soviet Doctors' Housing Cooperative:
brick balcony detail
Richard Pare, 2000
60.5 x 60.5 cm

Cat. 76.2 above
Soviet Doctors' Housing Cooperative:
view of façade
Richard Pare, 2000
40.2 x 59.8 cm

Cat. 76.3 right
Soviet Doctors' Housing Cooperative:
exterior detail
Photographer unknown, c. 1930
124 x 85 mm

CHEKIST HOUSING SCHEME

69 LENIN PROSPEKT
EKATERINBURG, RUSSIA
Ivan Antonov, Veniamin Sokolov,
Arsenii Tumbasov, 1929–36

Constructed for the officers of
the Cheka, the security force later
known as the KGB, this is one
of a large number of residential
buildings for the administrative
and military elite built from the
end of the 1920s (see also the
Lensovet Communal House, Cat.
81, and the VTsIK Residential
Complex, Cat. 82).

The ten-storey building with
its semi-circular plan – one of
a number of schemes from the
period referring to the form of
the hammer and sickle – contains
single-room units for individuals
or small families with the access
corridors on the inside of the
semi-circle. Other five-storey
blocks house larger flats of two,
three or four rooms.

The complex also contained
amenities including a
kindergarten with play areas,
a canteen, shops and hairdressers,
a club, a library and study area,
medical services and a pharmacy,
and exercise facilities.

This kind of large complex
incorporating a wide range
of services differed from the
experiments in the St Petersburg
districts such as the Traktornaia
ulitsa Workers' Housing (Cat. 79)
in its greater density. It would
evolve to form a model for future
high-density housing. NDBdeM

Cat. 77.1 above
Chekist Housing Scheme: panoramic view
Photographer unknown, 1947
93 x 280 mm (two prints, each 93 x 170 mm)

Cat. 77.2 opposite
Chekist Housing Scheme: general view
Richard Pare, 1999
41 x 41 cm

178

Cat. 77.3 top
Chekist Housing Scheme: view down
through stairwell to entrance
Richard Pare, 1999
50.8 x 40.6 cm

Cat. 77.4 right
Chekist Housing Scheme: view up
through stairwell
Richard Pare, 1999
91.4 x 61 cm

Cat. 77.5 opposite
Chekist Housing Scheme: stairwell
Richard Pare, 1999
60.5 x 40.2 cm

STUDENT HOUSING, TEXTILE INSTITUTE

8/9 ORDZHONIKIDZE ULITSA MOSCOW, RUSSIA
Ivan Nikolaev, 1929–31

This complex belongs to a unique category of communal housing intended specifically for youth. Many young adults attended training colleges and institutes of higher education, creating a new need for a particular housing type. Since these students were often away from home, communal life was deemed practical. It was also thought that as young people tended to associate with their peers, sharing value systems and social outlooks, they should be housed together to ensure that they were effectively instilled with the new values of Socialist society.

Nikolaev's design consists of a long, narrow eight-storey block housing 2,000 students in double bedrooms, each just six square metres in area. This block was connected by the sanitation block to a shorter three-storey building that contained a sports centre, assembly hall, dining hall, reading room, large study centre and several study cubicles for individual use. While this layout follows the plans for previous housing schemes, Nikolaev's proposal was in fact more radical since the dormitory spaces were intended only for sleeping and the students were to use the communal spaces for all other activities. The original proposal reduced the sleeping space for each student to a small cubicle but this was considered too extreme and the spaces were expanded to their current size. They did, however, maintain their function as strictly for sleeping and the dormitory block features a triangular ramp that ascends to each level to link the bedrooms with spaces for changing and

bathing, as well as a laundry and sun terrace.

In both form and function the complex is reminiscent of the Narkomfin Communal House (Cat. 75) with its separation of communal and living spaces into two blocks. The plan differed, however, in that the two main blocks were positioned parallel to one another with the linking ramp intersecting them. By the end of the 1920s the use of covered walkways or corridors to connect larger buildings had become a convention in communal housing. Other formal features, including pilotis and continuous banded fenestration, were also associated with the visual language of communal living, as well as with international Modernist designs.

The Student Housing ramp recalls Le Corbusier's use of ramps in buildings such as the Tsentrosoyuz Building (Cat. 64) in Moscow and the Villa Savoye near Paris. In Nikolaev's building, however, the ramp is triangular rather than curved as in the Tsentrosoyuz Building and is expressed in the rounded form that projects from the end of the sanitation block closest to the communal-activities block.

The dormitory block is now abandoned and derelict. In 2003 the winged entrance portico was radically truncated at each end, destroying the elegant aerodynamic form. The entire complex continues to deteriorate though the communal-activities block is still at least partially occupied. MC

Cat. 78.1 top
Student Housing, Textile Institute:
dormitory block under construction
M.A. Ilyin, 1931
83 x 115 mm

Cat. 78.2 bottom
Student Housing, Textile Institute: detail
of pilotis and banded windows
Photographer unknown, 1934
120 x 212 mm

Cat. 78.3 above
Student Housing, Textile Institute:
exterior view
Photographer unknown, 1930s
136 x 198 mm

Cat. 78.4 left
Student Housing, Textile Institute:
communal dining hall
Photographer unknown, 1930s
93 x 130 mm

Cat. 78.5 above
Student Housing, Textile Institute:
ramp linking bedrooms with spaces
for changing and washing in the
dormitory block
Richard Pare, 1994
26.8 x 40.1 cm

Cat. 78.6 right
Student Housing, Textile Institute:
dormitory block, ramp detail
Richard Pare, 1994
75.7 x 60.5 cm

Cat. 78.7
Student Housing, Textile Institute:
dormitory block
Richard Pare, 1994
40.1 x 51.1 cm

WORKERS' HOUSING

TRAKTORNAIA ULITSA
KIROVSKII DISTRICT
ST PETERSBURG, RUSSIA
Aleksandr Nikolskii with
Aleksandr Gegello and
Grigorii Simonov, 1927

Provision of homes for the urban working class was one of the pressing problems confronting the Bolsheviks after their victory in the 1918–20 Civil War. The significant role of factory workers from the Narvskaia Zastava area of St Petersburg in the 1917 Revolution gave them an important claim to priority for new housing. Furthermore, unrest in St Petersburg and other cities following shortages in early 1921 showed the need to consolidate working-class support. The Traktornaia ulitsa Workers' Housing would be the authorities' reward and incentive to the workers of the Narvskaia Zastava area.

With the nationalisation of most land and property by the Bolsheviks in 1918, housing became the responsibility of the local Soviets. Migration from the countryside before 1914 had produced rapid growth in urban populations and concomitant housing shortages. A 1914 enquiry revealed that the average number of occupants per room in St Petersburg was six. A common unit for rental

in working-class tenements was not a room, but 'a corner of a room'.

In the early 1920s housing design and urban planning were also regarded as instruments of social change. Contemporary intellectual ferment gave rise to a wide variety of visions for the society of the future and the kind of social change needed to realise it. A number of solutions for workers' housing were formulated, ranging from plots that were large enough to support self-sufficient occupants to strictly communal schemes.

The solution developed by the Leningrad Soviet centred on large housing estates supported by communal facilities provided by the municipality. Traktornaia ulitsa was within walking distance of the Narvskii Factory Kitchen and Department Store (Cat. 72), providing a canteen for the entire community, and the A.M. Gorky Palace of Culture (designed by Gegello and David Krichevskii), which offered a library, sporting facilities, clubs and theatrical performances. A school faces the Traktornaia ulitsa estate across a broad highway. Municipal trams, prominent in the early photograph (Cat. 79.2), link the area to other parts of the city.

There is an evocation of imperial St Petersburg in the axial central street, the segmented arches, the cornices supporting the roofs and the stucco finish. Such aristocratic references invited the city's proletariat to see itself as a new aristocracy. However, by replacing elaborate Classical decoration with plain travertine door surrounds and unadorned stucco walls the designers also evolved a distinctly new, proletarian language of architecture.

The architects also sought to provide a healthier living environment, using balconies to give access to fresh air. Living areas were oriented to the south to take advantage of natural light and staircases were placed to the north.

There is evidence too of foreign stylistic and planning influences. Simonov had made a trip to Germany during the preparatory phase of the design and the solution to place flats in three- or four-storey blocks is similar to that being developed for contemporary German mass-housing estates (*Siedlungen*).

The housing at Traktornaia ulitsa is still in use. NDBdeM

Cat. 79.1 above
Workers' Housing: view from
Traktornaia ulitsa
Photographer unknown, 1930–33
114 x 162 mm

Cat. 79.2 opposite top left
Workers' Housing: general view
Photographer unknown, c. 1947
114 x 170 mm

Cat. 79.3 opposite top right
Workers' Housing: detail of
segmented arch
Photographer unknown, 1930–33
161 x 114 mm

Cat. 79.4 opposite
Workers' Housing: segmented arches
Richard Pare, 1995
40.2 x 59.9 cm

Cat. 79.5
Workers' Housing: an entry
Richard Pare, 1999
27.5 x 41.4 cm

Cat. 79.6 opposite
Workers' Housing: balcony detail
Richard Pare, 1999
41.4 x 27.5 cm

COMMUNAL HOUSING

**21 MALYSHEV ULITSA
EKATERINBURG, RUSSIA
Moisei Ginzburg, Aleksandr
Pasternak, 1929–31**

Ginzburg would be involved in
the construction of two further
housing schemes after the
completion of the Narkomfin
Communal House (Cat. 75).
One (with Solomon Lisagor)
was at Rostokino in the Moscow
suburbs and the other was this
communal housing project
in Ekaterinburg.

The complex consists of four
blocks arranged in a square
around a courtyard. The block
facing on to Malyshev ulitsa was
designed as a student hostel
with accommodation consisting
entirely of small units with
sleeping and study areas like
the Narkomfin units for those
wishing to live communally. As
in Narkomfin, each unit is on two
levels with windows on both sides
and access from corridors on
the third and sixth floors. On the
top floor was a dining hall that
originally had a terrace running
the length of the street frontage.

The other three buildings contain
flats with kitchen and bathroom
facilities designed for families
not living communally. The roof
level of one of the buildings was
equipped as a kindergarten.

Towards the end of the 1920s
studies of communal living
began to suggest that the most
successful experiments were
those designed for student
communities. The fact that this
complex provided communal
living arrangements only in the
student hostel seems to reflect
this evaluation. NDBdeM

Cat. 80.1 top
Communal Housing: general view
D.A. Egorov, 1940s
88 x 118 mm

Cat. 80.2 bottom
Communal Housing: general view
D.A. Egorov, 1940s
89 x 118 mm

Cat. 80.3
Communal Housing: view of two
of four blocks
Richard Pare, 1999
34.7 x 91.5 cm

Cat. 80.4
Communal Housing: view within
the courtyard
Richard Pare, 1999
29 x 51 cm

LENSOVET COMMUNAL HOUSE

**13 KARPOVKA NABEREZHNAIA
ST PETERSBURG, RUSSIA
Evgenii Levinson, Igor Fomin, 1934**

The Lensovet Communal House was one of many residential buildings constructed for elite members of the administration and the military in the late 1920s and early 1930s. Built to a high specification, it contains large apartments of between three and six rooms, some arranged over two floors, and a nursery.

The building sits on the embankment of the Karpovka River; its long central section is gently concave to the river side and convex to the rear. Rectangular blocks at each end run back at right angles to the river and at the rear the three elements enclose a garden court. The concave frontage may have been designed to echo the convex facade of the nearby Polygrafmash factory.

Apparently designed to express the power and prestige of its occupants, the concave frontage, faced in stone and set back slightly from the river, makes it easy for the visitor to survey the entire symmetrical façade. Height is emphasised by raising the main body of the building on columns.

Yet the desire to impress is mixed with a degree of architectural exuberance. The open stairways that spring up the front and rear express the liberating potential of reinforced concrete, disregarding the inappropriateness of uncovered stairs in a northern climate. Parts of the building and its surrounding walls are embellished with carved decorative details and the concave form and deep window recesses create a play of light and shade.

The scheme marks a clear break with St Petersburg buildings of the late 1920s such as the Narvskii Factory Kitchen and Department Store (Cat. 72) by abandoning asymmetry, a horizontal emphasis and flat undecorated surfaces. The Lensovet Communal House, however, retained the austerity of these earlier buildings. This too would be abandoned as the city's architects moved in the later 1930s towards a more explicit and rhetorical Classicism.
NDBdeM

Cat. 81.1 above left
Lensovet Communal House: river façade
Photographer unknown, 1930s
99 x 140 mm

Cat. 81.2 above right
Lensovet Communal House:
open stairways and balconies
Photographer unknown, 1930s
110 x 162 mm

Cat. 81.3
Lensovet Communal House: river façade
Richard Pare, 1999
60.5 x 76.5 cm

Cat. 81.4
Lensovet Communal House:
exterior detail
H.D. Koveshnikov, 1966
107 x 147 mm

Cat. 81.5 left
Lensovet Communal House:
street boundary detail
Richard Pare, 1999
41.1 x 27.5 cm

Cat. 81.6 opposite
Lensovet Communal House:
detail of river façade
Richard Pare, 1999
41.9 x 27.5 cm

VTSIK RESIDENTIAL COMPLEX

**2 SERAFIMOVICH ULITSA
BERSENEVSKAIA NABEREZHNAIA
MOSCOW, RUSSIA**
<u>Boris Iofan, 1928–31</u>

Built as a communal house
for high-ranking officials of the
Communist Party, the VTsIK
(All-Russian Executive
Committee) Residential Complex
was more luxurious than most
buildings of its type. It is an
example of the way early
experiments in communal
housing developed into the idea
of creating units for specific
professional groups or unions.
The complex also represents a
departure from the experiments
of the early 1920s because
the communal spaces are not
attached to the dwelling unit
as they are in the Narkomfin
Communal House (Cat. 75) and
Textile Institute Student Housing
(Cat. 78). Rather, the public
spaces, which include a cinema,
kindergarten, crèche, dining hall
and shop, adjoin the dwelling
area but are clearly contained
in a separate structure. This is
reflected in the different formal
treatment of each building.

Ten floors high and made up
of three connected blocks, the
complex is the largest project
of its kind in Moscow to use the
formal vocabulary of the avant-
garde. The ground plan, which
is almost square, takes up an

entire city block, while the
position of the complex on
the river opposite the Kremlin
ensures it is a prominent
landmark. Its imposing geometric
massing and large scale also
serve to communicate the high
social standing of the residents
for whom it was intended.

Iofan used different types of
fenestration to break up the mass
of the residential block and to
create an interesting visual
pattern. This also conveys the
internal organisation of the space.
The stepped formation at the end
of the cinema roof anticipates
the architect's design for the
Soviet Pavilion at the 1937 Paris
*Exposition Internationale des
Arts et Techniques dans la Vie
Moderne*. The roof was intended
to retract to create an open-air
theatre in summer but it proved
too expensive and technically
challenging and was never
realised.

The building is known colloquially
as both the House on the River
and the House of Ghosts, the
latter because many residents
disappeared during Stalin's
purges. Its prominence and
location mean it is still a highly
sought-after place to live – it is no
longer a communal dwelling. MC

Cat. 82.1 top
VTsIK Residential Complex: view between
elongated piers
Photographer unknown, 1930s
145 x 187 mm

Cat. 82.2 bottom
VTsIK Residential Complex: general view
Richard Pare, 1994
60.5 x 76.5 cm

Cat. 82.3 left
VTsIK Residential Complex: view
across the Moskva River
Photographer unknown, after 1930
82 x 114 mm

Cat. 82.4 below
VTsIK Residential Complex: view
across the Moskva River
Richard Pare, 1994
60.5 x 76.5 cm

Cat. 82.5 above
VTsIK Residential Complex: view from the
Kadashevskoi embankment towards the
Udarnik cinema and residential complex
I.O. Sosfenov (?), early 1930s
104 x 162 mm

Cat. 82.6 right
VTsIK Residential Complex: view
of the roof of the theatre, originally
intended to retract to form an open-air
performance space
Richard Pare, 1995
121.9 x 154.9 cm

MELNIKOV HOUSE

17 KRIVARBATSKII PEREULOK MOSCOW, RUSSIA
Konstantin Melnikov, 1927–31

Following the success of his Soviet Pavilion for the 1925 Paris *Exposition Internationale des Arts Décoratifs et Industriels Modernes*, the authorities made a plot in the centre of Moscow available to Melnikov. Here he constructed the building that would be both a home for his family and his architectural studio. The white exterior, cylindrical forms and setting in a garden offer the visitor a startling contrast to the dense urban surroundings.

Melnikov's notes describe the building as consisting of two cylinders, one eleven metres high, the other eight metres high, intersecting for one third of their ten-metre diameters. The interlocking cylinders have been likened to the grain silos that Le Corbusier had illustrated in *Vers une architecture* (1923) but Melnikov's use of this device was unique at the time and is one of several highly original features of the design.

The internal plan is largely allocated to three near-circular spaces that serve respectively for sleeping, living and working. The upper part of each cylinder, one for living and one for working, is double height and the living

space in the front cylinder has full-height windows that fill the room with light. At the rear is the architect's studio.

Below the studio is a single-height sleeping area that was originally fitted with screens separating parents' and children's spaces. Melnikov believed that an airy, dust-free environment was important for sleep and this room was without traditional furnishings. Reinforcing the ritualistic and symbolic aspects of the house, the beds were treated as elaborate altar-like plinths stained a golden shade. Later removed, the beds can be seen in paintings made during the early years of the house's existence. The multiple hexagonal windows cast a light that is at the same time intense and even and the interior reflects the architect's belief that human well-being depends on ideal sleeping conditions and the quality and amount of available light.

The exterior walls, made of brick clad in stucco, are pierced with hexagonal openings at regular intervals. When not required as windows, the openings were filled with rubble to allow window positions to be changed if the internal plan was altered. The floors use a timber grid. Melnikov's choice of traditional materials exploited the skills of the existing labour force and

saved on concrete and steel, which were needed for the country's industrialisation programme.

Critics attacked Melnikov's house in part for the ideas that its architect seemed to be embracing. At a time when progressive thought was championing communal living, a house designed to support all the needs of a family appeared retrograde. Both the allocation of space to his personal studio and his prominent signature at the top of the entrance façade evoked an image of a solitary creative artist at a moment when architects were increasingly working in teams, often as part of local administrations. Some commentators understood that the use of the cylinder and of traditional materials could find wider application in housing schemes, but Melnikov's estrangement from the rest of the profession and the originality of his ideas probably made it inevitable that his house would remain an isolated masterpiece.

Melnikov, his family and descendants have lived in the house continuously since it was completed. It is still occupied by a granddaughter of the architect, but its future is precarious. DBdeM

Cat. 83.1
Melnikov House: entrance façade
M.A. Ilyin, 1931
117 x 90 mm

Cat. 83.2 opposite
Melnikov House: under construction, showing the method of laying bricks to create hexagonal openings
Photographer unknown, 1920s
153 x 108 mm

Cat. 83.3
Melnikov House: external view
showing interlocking cylinders
Richard Pare, 1998
50.3 x 49.1 cm

Cat. 83.4 above
Melnikov House: entrance hall and stairs
Richard Pare, 1994
60.5 x 76.5 cm

Cat. 83.5 far left
Melnikov House: interior detail showing
stairwell enclosure in the salon
M.A. Ilyin, 1931
107 x 95 mm

Cat. 83.6 left
Melnikov House: full-height window
in the salon
Photographer unknown, 1970
92 x 90 mm

Cat. 83.7
Melnikov House: salon
Richard Pare, 1998
121.9 x 154.5 cm and 121.9 x 153.9 cm

STATE
COMMUNICATIONS
INDUSTRY
HOUSING
EDUCATION
HEALTH
RECREATION
LENIN
MAUSOLEUM

SCHOOL

Cat. 84.1
School on Tkachei ulitsa: general view
Photographer unknown, 1930s
112 x 176 mm

9 TKACHEI ULITSA
NEVSKII DISTRICT
ST PETERSBURG, RUSSIA
Grigorii Simonov, 1927–29

This school, planned for 1,500 pupils, is formed of three blocks of different lengths and heights. A gallery at first-floor level contains libraries and dining halls and carries a wide passage that links the blocks. The senior school is at the northern end of the gallery in a four- and five-storey building with an observatory on the top floor. The junior school is in a long three-storey block at the southern end and between the two classroom blocks is a building for sports and cultural activities.

The dispersal of the blocks ensures excellent access to light for all parts of the school, allowing the classrooms to face south and giving a sense of airiness and space. The loose-knit plan reflected an OSA preference for designs to grow naturally from a study of the requirements arising from the building's different functions.

The remarkable geometry of the end wall of the sports hall, however, seems to indicate a Suprematist influence. It has been suggested that Lasar Khidekel, who had worked with the leading Suprematist artist Kazimir Malevich to translate his ideas into architectural forms (Cat. 21), may have assisted in the design.

The school is largely in its original condition and is still in use.
NDBdeM

Cat. 84.2
School on Tkachei ulitsa:
wide passage linking blocks
Richard Pare, 1999
40.2 x 60.5 cm

210

Cat. 84.3
School on Tkachei ulitsa: end wall
of the sports hall
Richard Pare, 1999
60.5 x 76.5 cm

RUSAKOV WORKERS' CLUB

6 STROMYNKA ULITSA
MOSCOW, RUSSIA
Konstantin Melnikov, 1927

Centres for cultural and educational activity for the working classes existed before the Revolution, but after 1917 the Bolsheviks created a large number of workers' clubs as platforms for the inculcation of Marxist values. This narrow programme was criticised in 1924 by Leon Trotsky, writing in *Pravda*, who complained that the 2,500 clubs in the Soviet Union received an average of only thirteen visitors per day.

The clubs' objectives were subsequently broadened to include educational, sporting and cultural activities, though propaganda remained a key part of their role. Alfred Barr, the future director of New York's Museum of Modern Art, visiting the Moscow Transportation Workers' Club in 1927, admired the 'wall newspaper' and enjoyed a performance by the Blue Blouses, whose song-and-dance version of the news he described as 'sugar-coated propaganda'.

Clubs were established by municipalities, industrial combines, residents of housing schemes and trades unions. Melnikov's five completed clubs, all in Moscow, were built for trades unions, in the case of Rusakov for the Union of Municipal Workers.

To accommodate the range of activities, Melnikov devised a flexible space for the upper two levels. This could serve as a single auditorium for 1,200 people but could also be divided into three independent segments using a system of soundproof panels designed by the architect. For still smaller rooms, the lower and balcony level of each segment could be subdivided.

The external form seems to move dynamically outwards and upwards from a point at the rear entrance through the building and into the three cantilevered prisms that contain the segments of the auditorium. The internal form is thus directly expressed in the striking and original exterior.

In each of his completed clubs Melnikov sought a solution based on a large flexible internal space that was echoed in the sculptural external form. As he would never content himself with recycling a previous solution, his five clubs present a remarkable range of arresting forms.

Although badly degraded, the building still functions as a theatre. NDBdeM

Cat. 85.1
Rusakov Workers' Club: detail of cantilevered auditorium segment
M.A. Ilyin, 1929
97 x 77 mm

Cat. 85.2
Rusakov Workers' Club: general view
M.A. Ilyin, 1929
79 x 107 mm

214

Cat. 85.3
Rusakov Workers' Club: general view
H.Ia. Epanechnikov, 1938
105 x 162 mm

216

Cat. 85.4
Rusakov Workers' Club: general view
showing the three auditorium segments
Richard Pare, 1995
50.8 x 61 cm

Cat. 85.6 top
Rusakov Workers' Club: rear wall of stage
Richard Pare, 1993
50.3 x 75.7 cm

Cat. 85.5 opposite
Rusakov Workers' Club: detail of
cantilevered auditorium segment
Richard Pare, 1993
60.5 x 47.8 cm

Cat. 85.7 above
Rusakov Workers' Club: general view
from the back
M.A. Ilyin, 1929
106 x 176 mm

PALACE OF CULTURE, SURAKHANI DISTRICT

BAKU, AZERBAIJAN
Leonid Vesnin, 1929

This is one of two near-identical theatre buildings designed by Vesnin as part of a series of workers' clubs constructed in Baku during the late 1920s. The title 'Palace of Culture' brings to mind Soviet architectural competitions from the first half of the decade which aimed to reinforce the concept of a palace as a place for the masses rather than the elite, in which a range of communal activities to promote Socialist ideology could take place.

The back of the theatre conveys a sense of austerity. The simple design encompasses the stage flies and allows internal functions to be expressed on the exterior. The two staircases running up each side of the backstage give access to the stage equipment and gantries above.

Including a large auditorium in a club suggests that theatre was an important activity for encouraging both creativity and the dissemination of the Socialist programme. The radical design points to the importance of culture in the growth of Socialism.

The stage was designed to accommodate both indoor and outdoor performances, the rear wall featuring another proscenium arch that was later filled in; a line above the back door probably marks where the extended cover was originally attached. The club is no longer used for its original purpose but the building has recently been renovated. MC

221

Cat. 86.1 opposite top
Palace of Culture, Surakhani District:
entrance façade
H.D. Koveshnikov, 1967
166 x 223 mm

Cat. 86.2 opposite bottom
Palace of Culture, Surakhani District:
side detail
M.M. Tsurakov, 1975
151 x 108 mm

Cat. 86.3 above
Palace of Culture, Surakhani District:
rear of the theatre with staircases in
both half towers
Richard Pare, 1999
121.9 x 156.5 cm

ZUEV WORKERS' CLUB

Cat. 87.1
Zuev Workers' Club: interior detail
M.A. Ilyin, 1931
75 x 103 mm

**18 LESNAIA ULITSA
MOSCOW, RUSSIA
Ilia Golosov, 1926**

As with most Moscow workers' clubs, Golosov's design resulted from a competition, in this case attracting architects including Konstantin Melnikov. The expressive form is characteristic not only of the innovation fostered by architectural competitions in the early 1920s but also of Golosov's tendency to develop his buildings around a single external formal element.

A large glazed cylinder within an otherwise rectilinear building provided the basis for the scheme. The cylinder dominates the corner of the facility and contains a staircase that links multi-purpose spaces adaptable to changing needs. An experimental vocabulary had to be employed since there was no architectural precedent for the building type, and the novel form expresses its function as a centre for propaganda and for the creative and educational development of the working class.

While many clubs were associated with housing units, industrial plants or specific economic groups, the Zuev Workers' Club was for all workers who lived within the municipality.

It contains meeting rooms, an 850-seat theatre and several reading rooms. The intersecting rectangular masses of the exterior articulate interior spaces devoted to different activities.

The glass cylinder became a motif for Golosov and was employed in several other designs for public buildings. The dramatic form and interest created by the intersection of the angled and curved volumes combined with the reflective qualities of the glass made the Zuev building a popular subject for photographers, including Aleksandr Rodchenko.

The building still functions as a theatre and conference centre. Most of the exterior has remained intact, although the removal of the lower-level overhang has reduced the sensation of the cylinder being enclosed by the rectangle and the disappearance of balconies along the side has eliminated some of the spatial dynamism. MC

Cat. 87.2 left
Zuev Workers' Club: the glazed
cylinder dominating the corner
Richard Pare, 1993
60.5 x 47.8 cm

Cat. 87.3 below
Zuev Workers' Club: general view
Photographer unknown, 1930s
136 x 213 mm

Cat. 87.4 opposite
Zuev Workers' Club: view from
inside the glazed cylinder
Richard Pare, 1993
91.4 x 61.7 cm

Cat. 87.5
Zuev Workers' Club: detail of
the glazed cylinder
Richard Pare, 1993
61 x 76.2 cm

PISHCHEVIK CLUB

**10 KONTRAKTOVAIA PLOSHCHAD
KIEV, UKRAINE
Nikolai Shekhonin, 1931–33**

Sited on a prominent corner
in the centre of the city next to
a library, the Pishchevik (Food
Industry Workers) Club is one of
a number of facilities designed for
specific economic groups. It was
intended to provide entertainment
and leisure activities as well as
to function as a dissemination
point for propaganda and
educational materials.

The most prominent feature
is the central exhibition space,
a rotunda with a domed roof.
This Classically derived form
is very rare in Soviet Modernist
architecture, though Shekhonin
used other Classical forms on the
main entrance and in the interior.
The Classical references end
here, however, as the rotunda
is flanked by rectangular blocks
that extend along the roads that
flank the site and lead to the
square. These blocks frame
the exhibition space, creating
an asymmetrical frontage
enhanced by the addition of
a staircase tower on the left of
the entrance.

As in previous schemes,
Shekhonin's combination of
different volumetric forms
indicates the range of social
and leisure functions available
in the club as well as the
importance of its role in the new
Soviet society. This is underscored
by the scale of the building.

Shekhonin's innovative formal
vocabulary is in marked contrast
to the symmetry of the adjacent
early-nineteenth-century
Neoclassical library. An aerial
photograph of Kiev (Cat. 88.1)
shows his club's unique design
and impressive scale in
comparison with the surrounding
architecture.

The club is still in use as a
performing-arts centre. MC

Cat. 88.1 above
Pishchevik Club: panoramic view of
Kiev with the Pishchevik Club at
extreme left
V.A. Martynov, 1957
97 x 398 mm (three prints: left to right
97 x 156, 97 x 168, 97 x 136 mm)

Cat. 88.2 opposite top
Pishchevik Club: interior detail
Richard Pare, 2000
50.8 x 61 cm

Cat. 88.3 opposite bottom
Pishchevik Club: view across
Kontraktovaia ploshchad
Richard Pare, 2000
76.2 x 121.2 cm

DIVING BOARD, DINAMO SPORTS CLUB

KIROVA BULVAR
KIEV, UKRAINE
Vasilii Osmak, 1935

The Dinamo Sports Club was a society formed in 1923 to provide sports training and facilities for the Soviet people. Healthy, active citizens were equated with strong, productive workers while exercise was seen as a form of communal activity that would strengthen society as well as providing physical benefits. Hence involvement in sport became an important government target for both health and culture. During the First Five Year Plan physical fitness was lauded as an essential characteristic of the well-rounded worker and several Dinamo stadiums and clubs with athletic tracks, sports fields, gymnasiums and swimming pools were built throughout the Soviet Union in the late 1920s and 1930s.

Osmak's diving board and pool in Kiev are constructed in reinforced concrete. The arched form, based on a catenary arc and supporting diving boards set at different heights, still appears modern and dramatic. The two longest boards are set on rails and are retractable. The creative design is indicative of the enthusiasm that went into planning new sports centres, and versions of the diving board also appear in Moscow. One example was even constructed in a Stalinist Neoclassical sports complex, indicating that despite its Modernist aesthetic it had become a standard design by the late 1930s.

Both this example and its exact replica in Moscow have now been destroyed. A third, less elegant example, also in Moscow, survives. MC

Cat. 89.1 above
Diving Board, Moscow: general view
V.M. Mastiokov, B.C. Trepetov, 1960
155 x 230 mm

Cat. 89.2 right
Diving Board, Dinamo Sports Club,
Kiev: general view
Richard Pare, 2000
101.6 x 103.4 cm

VOROSHILOV SANATORIUM

MATSESTA
SOCHI, RUSSIA
Miron Merzhanov, 1930–34

Before the Revolution holiday resorts were accessible only to the wealthy elite but from the very beginning of Soviet power they were made available to all workers. Like workers' clubs, sanatoriums and resorts were developed for trades unions, ministries and other large organisations, with their prices often heavily subsidised by the state. Since planned leisure time for workers was an important priority, there was a need to create new spaces where they could find respite from often overcrowded communal homes and from work. Sanatoriums provided health and recreational facilities as well as another channel for the transmission of Socialist culture.

At first former palaces and country homes were requisitioned, but as demand grew, notably in popular vacation spots such as Sochi, new buildings were required. The Voroshilov Sanatorium, sponsored by Commissar of Defence Kliment Voroshilov,

was designed for members of the Red Army, whose high status ensured that the facilities were luxurious.

Set among a garden of palm and pine trees and accessed by a funicular railway, the symmetrically planned buildings exploit several 1920s avant-garde conventions. The extensive use of glass and large balconies allowed the maximum amount of light and air to pass into the rooms. As in the Palace of the Press in Baku (Cat. 66), rectangular buildings end in curved terraces and balconies, providing panoramic views and signifying the latest in design and building technology. The sanatorium has a separate complex for entertainment and dining and was cleverly planned with each bedroom facing the ocean.

Although the structure employs the language of the avant-garde, its setting and symmetry and the quality of detailing link it to the Stalinist architecture that emerged in the mid-1930s. Classical elements such as a colonnaded promenade at the base of the funicular signal a move towards historicism. MC

Cat. 90.1
Voroshilov Sanatorium: panoramic view of the gardens
A.A. Aleksandrov, 1949
101 x 293 mm

Cat. 90.2
Voroshilov Sanatorium: view of complex
Photographer unknown, 1937
205 x 151 mm

Cat. 90.3 top
Voroshilov Sanatorium: panoramic view
Photographer unknown, 1941
145 x 394 mm

Cat. 90.4 above
Voroshilov Sanatorium: view with funicular
Richard Pare, 1999
121.9 x 154.5 cm

Cat. 90.5
Voroshilov Sanatorium: curved
balconies
Richard Pare, 1999
121.9 x 123.7 cm

Cat. 90.6
Voroshilov Sanatorium: terrace
Richard Pare, 1999
75.7 x 50.3 cm

ORDZHONIKIDZE SANATORIUM

KISLOVODSK, RUSSIA
Moisei Ginzburg, Ivan Leonidov,
Evgenii Popov, Nikolai Paliudov,
1934–37

The Ordzhonikidze (formerly
Narkomtyazhprom) Sanatorium
was commissioned in 1934 by
Grigorii Ordzhonikidze, one of
Stalin's chief lieutenants and
since 1912 a member of the
Central Committee of the Russian
Social Democratic Workers'
Party. He became head of the
Commissariat for Heavy Industry
(Narkomtyazhprom) in 1934 but
committed suicide in the year of
the sanatorium's completion
after falling out with Stalin.

Constructed for members
of the Union for Workers in
Heavy Industry with a generous
budget of 33 million rubles, this,
the largest and most lavishly
appointed of all Ginzburg's
buildings (see also Cats 75, 80),
was the result of a collaboration
that included the visionary
architect Ivan Leonidov. The
perfectly pitched stairway is
Leonidov's only major completed
work; it ascends from the valley
below, approaching along the
main axis of the complex from
the southwest.

Though more imperial in its
architectural gestures than
Ginzburg's earlier works, the
building makes only minor
concessions to Stalinist
Neoclassicism. Ginzburg appears
to have adapted his designs to
suggest a continuum reaching
far further back into historical
sources than the Stalinist
tastemakers were capable
of undertaking. Its richness
manifests itself in the quality
of the materials, particularly the
warm, fine-grained sandstone
of the exterior walls, the elegantly
slender steel framing of the large
curtain walls, and such things
as the fine glass tiles lining the
indoor mineral-water swimming
pool and the subtle mosaics of
watery fauna set in the floor of
the circular therapy block.

Certain design elements, some of
which may be securely attributed
to Leonidov, suggest that sources
include the work of Frank Lloyd
Wright (Midway Gardens) and the
works of the earliest architects in
Assyria and Ancient Egypt.

Still operating as a therapy
centre, the sanatorium is the
best preserved of all the buildings
from the Soviet Modernist period.
Many original features – windows,
lamps and light fixtures, and
some furniture – survive and the
complex also retains some of its
original colour scheme. RP

Cat. 91.1 opposite
Ordzhonikidze Sanatorium: façade
Richard Pare, 2010

Cat. 91.2 below
Ordzhonikidze Sanatorium: the stairway,
Leonidov's only completed work
Richard Pare, 2010

STATE
COMMUNICATIONS
INDUSTRY
HOUSING
EDUCATION
HEALTH
RECREATION
LENIN
MAUSOLEUM

LENIN
MAUSOLEUM

KRASNAYA PLOSHCHAD
MOSCOW, RUSSIA
Aleksei Shchusev, 1924–30

Immediately after Lenin's death
on 24 January 1924, Shchusev
was commissioned to design
a temporary wooden mausoleum
to house his embalmed body.
It was to stand beneath the walls
of the Kremlin on Red Square
(Krasnaya ploshchad). The
geometric form consisted of
three simple rectangular boxes,
the central one providing the
mortuary chamber and the two
outer ones giving covered access
and egress for visitors.

The initial structure was
quickly deemed too small to
accommodate the hundreds
of thousands of pilgrims who
flocked to the tomb and a larger
and more permanent version was
commissioned. For this version,
also in wood and completed in
1924, Shchusev redesigned the
mortuary chamber in a more
Classical language of stepped
cubes, pared-down pilasters
and in one plan placed a pyramid
at the apex, echoing the Tomb
of Mausolus at Halicarnassus
(350 BC). He also discarded the
side entrance and exit buildings
and provided official viewing
platforms accessed by screened
staircases. The mausoleum
acquired a more permanent and
stately character, with references

to both Ancient Egyptian and
Classical traditions. By 1929 a
decision was made to preserve
Lenin's body permanently and
to keep it on display for the public
so Shchusev was commissioned
to create a structure in stone.

The final design takes the same
form as the second version but
stripped of all Classical ornament.
It is constructed in dark red
granite, marble, porphyry and
labradorite and its polished
surfaces reflect its surroundings
in Red Square. The changes
in texture and colour produce
a composition that enhances
the form of the whole. The
unornamented simplicity and
emphasis on formal qualities
demonstrate Shchusev's ability
to incorporate Constructivist
principles into his pre-
Revolutionary historicist style.

Lenin's status as the father of
the Russian Revolution was
perpetuated throughout the
Soviet Union until its collapse
in 1991. His mausoleum remains
in excellent condition and is still
open to the public. MC

Cat. 92.1
Lenin Mausoleum: general view
on Red Square
Richard Pare, 1998
45.2 x 61 cm

Cat. 92.2 top
Lenin Mausoleum: panorama of
Red Square
A.A. Sorkin, 1954
151 x 416 mm

Cat. 92.3 centre
Lenin Mausoleum: first mausoleum
under construction
N.N. Lebedev, 1924
115 x 175 mm

Cat. 92.4 left
Lenin Mausoleum: first mausoleum
with wreaths
Photographer unknown, 1924
113 x 176 mm

Cat. 92.5 top
Lenin Mausoleum: second
mausoleum
N.N. Lebedev, mid-1920s
149 x 210 mm

Cat. 92.6 right
Lenin Mausoleum: full-scale
plywood maquette for the final
version erected in situ
Photographer unknown, c. 1930
153 x 226 mm

242

Cat. 92.7 top
Lenin Mausoleum: representatives
of the state and party leadership
with the builders of the mausoleum
Photographer unknown, 1930
163 x 216 mm

Cat. 92.8 above
Lenin Mausoleum: workers
Photographer unknown, 1930
164 x 225 mm

Cat. 92.9
Lenin Mausoleum: Red Square with
May Day parade
Photographer unknown, 1946
168 x 258 mm approx.

244

Cat. 92.10
Lenin Mausoleum: north corner detail
Richard Pare, 1998
50.3 x 50.3 cm

Cat. 92.11
Lenin Mausoleum: exterior detail
Richard Pare, 1998
122.4 x 152.4 cm

Cat. 92.12
Lenin Mausoleum: tomb chamber
Richard Pare, 1998
121.9 x 152.4 cm

GLOSSARY

ARU
(Association of Architect-Planners)
Assotsiatsiia arkhitektorov urbanistov

Founded in 1928, with Nikolai Ladovskii as chairman, ARU was based in Moscow but also had a branch in St Petersburg. Along with other architectural associations it was dissolved in 1932. The establishment of ARU coincided with the launch of the First Five Year Plan and the association's first declaration reflected on the need to respond to the impact of industrialisation within the Socialist context through large-scale urban-planning solutions rather than schemes for individual buildings. In contrast to the Disurbanists (qv), ARU favoured a realistic acceptance of the importance of large towns.

ASNOVA
(Association of New Architects)
Assotsiatsiia novykh arkhitektorov

An association of architects established in 1923 and active until it was dissolved, along with other groupings of architects, in 1932. The founders included Nikolai Ladovskii, Nikolai Dokuchaev and Vladimir Krinskii. As the first such grouping it attracted many members of the avant-garde, though some transferred their allegiance to OSA (qv) after 1925. From its first constitution ASNOVA aligned itself with the Rationalism (qv) developed primarily by Ladovskii.

Constructivism

The example of Vladimir Tatlin's 'counter reliefs' and his project for a colossal tower to house the operations of the Comintern, the *Monument to the Third International*, provoked a vigorous debate within INKhUK (qv) about the distinction between 'composition' and 'construction' that led, in 1921, to the establishment of the First Working Group of Constructivists. This group mostly renounced two-dimensional geometric painting such as that of the Suprematists (qv) in favour of three-dimensional work in which materials and geometric factors determined construction. Adherents tended also to favour the ideas of Production Art (qv). Constructivist works were presented at the third OBMOKhU (qv) exhibition of 1921. In Russia the term was also applied to the architecture of the OSA group (qv). Constructivist groups subsequently emerged outside Russia; these lacked a political dimension but used its forms.

Cubofuturism

A term applied to Russian avant-garde painting integrating elements of the visual languages of Italian Futurism and French Cubism. From around 1912 the work of painters including Kazimir Malevich, Liubov Popova, Natalia Goncharova and Mikhail Larionov began to include elements drawn from the Futurists' work, in particular their interest in machines and devices indicating trajectories of movement. At the same time the Russian artists also began to deploy the fractured planes of Cubism.

Disurbanisation

Soviet town planning of the early 1920s, stimulated by the abolition of the private ownership of land, was much influenced by Ebenezer Howard's idea of the garden city, combining aspects of town and country life in small settlements surrounded by countryside. When the First Five Year Plan (1928) proposed the creation of 200 industrial towns and 1000 rural settlements, it stimulated the development of large-scale planning schemes, many of them confirming the anti-urban bias of earlier town-planning theory. The sociologist Mikhail Okhitovich's concept of Disurbanisation envisaged low-density housing accompanied by social services to be developed in strips along roads linking them to industrial nodes. Opponents of these ideas, associated with the concept of the *Sotsgorod* (Socialist town), envisaged small towns, also often in linear formation and emphasising the importance of green areas, but with high-density communal housing and services.

INKhUK
(Institute of Artistic Culture)
Institut khudozhe stvennoi kultury

A state-sponsored research institution, active between 1920 and 1924, INKhUK brought together painters, sculptors, architects, art historians and theoreticians and was an important forum for avant-garde research and debate. It was established on the initiative of Wassily Kandinsky to study the relationship between formal artistic means and viewer experience. However, this psychological approach was soon challenged by members proposing that the study of the 'object' and of its material construction should be the principal focus (see Constructivism). Subsequently this group was in turn challenged by those wishing to subordinate artistic activity to the needs of industrial production and of the new society (see Production Art). The debates within INKhUK involved the leading figures of the avant-garde and represented the main currents of artistic opinion of the early 1920s.

IZO
(Visual Arts Section)
Otdel izobrazitelnykh iskusstv

Established in 1918 within Narkompros (the Commissariat for Education), which was concerned with education and cultural policy, IZO was responsible in the immediate post-Revolutionary years for the staging of art exhibitions, for art and monumental propaganda and for the organisation of the art and architecture schools. IZO also established provincial art galleries and purchased avant-garde work. IZO's administrators consisted mainly of avant-garde artists although the architectural sub-section, created under the leadership of Ivan Zholtovskii, held more conservative views.

LEF
(Left Front of the Arts)
Levyi front iskusstva

LEF was a journal published from 1923 to 1925 and as *Novyi LEF* from 1927 to 1928. The editors were Vladimir Mayakovskii and Osip Brik. According to Mayakovskii's application for permission to publish, the journal was concerned with 'extreme Revolutionary movements in art'. The editors sought to reconcile their enthusiasm for the Revolution with their engagement with an artistic avant-garde whose roots lay in the pre-Revolutionary world. The magazine gave considerable support to the ideas of Production Art (qv).

MAO
(Moscow Architectural Society)
Moskovskoe arkhitekturnoe obshchestvo

A professional association of architects founded in 1867. It was revived after 1917 and played an important part in the organisation of competitions until it was abolished in 1932.

(MVTU)
Moscow Higher Technical Institute
Moskovoskoe vysshee tekhnicheskoe uchilishche

Tracing its origins back to the College of Artisans, MVTU retained a more technical orientation in its architectural training than VKhUTEMAS (*qv*), with faculties of architecture and construction-engineering and a particular strength in the area of industrial building.

OBMOKhU
(Society of Young Artists)
Obshchestvo molodykh khudozhnikov

A group of young artists established in 1919 initially from students at the SVOMAS (Free Art Studios) set up after the Revolution. They were probably brought together by their participation in the creation of propaganda works for the Moscow streets, which were the main subject of their first and second exhibitions (1919 and 1920). Their third exhibition (1921) was dedicated entirely to three-dimensional constructions in wood or metal and other materials. They described these exhibits as 'laboratory work' – art developed in relation to work, geometry and engineering, and contributing to the design of useful artefacts or buildings.

OSA
(Union of Contemporary Architects)
Obedinenie sovremennykh arkhitektorov

Founded in 1925 with Aleksandr Vesnin as chairman and Moisei Ginzburg and Viktor Vesnin as deputy chairmen, OSA drew into its orbit many of the avant-garde architects of the 1920s but was absorbed into other associations after 1930. OSA distinguished itself from ASNOVA (*qv*) in its focus on functionality and construction. For OSA architects, the priority was to derive form from purpose, in particular for new building types such as communal housing, to meet the needs of Socialist development. The group also studied the use of appropriate modern construction methods and materials and followed attentively the development of avant-garde architecture in the rest of Europe.

Production Art
(Productivism)

Productivists advocated the deployment of materials and technology by artists in the creation of politicised and socially useful artefacts. These ideas were injected into the debates within INKhUK (*qv*) by thinkers such as Aleksei Gan and Boris Arvatov and were embraced by Constructivist artists (*qv*), many of whom subsequently became active in furniture, textile and theatre design. Interpretations of the role of the Productivist artist ranged from the creation of abstract designs applicable to industrial products to a total involvement in the process of industrial design, with the disappearance of autonomous artistic activity. In Arvatov's analysis, the alienation of the world of art from that of industry and work brought about by bourgeois hegemony would be healed by reinserting the artist into the world of industrial activity and by creating objects whose utilitarian values would render them pleasing to proletarian users.

Rationalism

The name adopted by a movement in architecture developed under the leadership of Nikolai Ladovskii from the early 1920s and particularly promoted by ASNOVA (*qv*). The Rationalist view was that the architect's main concern was the manipulation of space and its impact on the psychology of the user. Ladovskii believed it was possible to develop a reasoned approach to the manipulation of space through an understanding of the viewer's responses to different spatial configurations. For the Rationalists, construction technology and materials were important but secondary issues.

SA
(Contemporary Architecture)
Sovremennaia Arkhitektura

A journal founded in 1926, *SA* published six issues a year until 1930. Edited by Aleksandr Vesnin and Moisei Ginzburg, the journal constituted an effective platform for the views of OSA (*qv*).

Socialist Realism

A methodology and style largely dictated by the state authorities of the Soviet Union from the early 1930s. The theorists of Socialist Realism valued art that they saw as having a strong relationship to proletarian ideas and subjects and which reflected the class awareness and Party loyalty of the artist. They repudiated the avant-garde work of the 1920s. Much Socialist Realist painting and sculpture deploys elements of the artistic language of Russia's nineteenth-century realists to represent idealised visions of the heroic present or the bright future envisaged in Bolshevik propaganda. Socialist Realist architecture drew on Classical and other historical models applied to monumental ensembles often decorated with elaborate sculpture glorifying the past or future achievements of the regime.

Suprematism

A term applied by Kazimir Malevich at *The Last Exhibition of Futurist Painting: 0.10* (1915) to the display of his paintings, below which he hung a roughly painted sign with the words '*suprematizm zhivopisi*' (suprematism of painting). These paintings, with geometrical forms floating on white backgrounds, reflected his vision of the supremacy of a new art concerned entirely with form and supposedly free of political or social meaning. Malevich's Suprematism influenced many progressive artists in subsequent years and would constitute a fundamental element of the artistic language of the 1920s avant-garde.

VKhUTEMAS/VKhUTEIN
(Higher State Artistic and Technical Workshops/Higher State Artistic and Technical Institute)
Vysshii gosudarstvennie khudozhestvenno-tekhnicheski masterskie/Vysshii gosudarstvennii khudozhestvenno-tekhnicheskii institut

In 1918 the Moscow Institute for Painting, Sculpture and Architecture and the Stroganov Institute of Industrial Art were reformed and became the Free Art Studios (SVOMAS). Entry was granted to all irrespective of previous training and students were given a free choice of teachers and courses. In 1920 the two schools were merged into VKhUTEMAS, which became VKhUTEIN in 1927. The school was closed in 1930 and its disciplines reintegrated into specialised academies. Faculties included architecture, metalwork, wood, textiles, ceramics, painting and sculpture. Teaching staff included leading avant-garde figures. Moving away from traditional academic training, the school instituted foundation courses on formal topics important to avant-garde art, such as space, volume, colour and graphics.

UNOVIS
(Affirmers of the New Art)
Utverditeli novogo iskusstva

An association of artists and students at the Vitebsk School of Art, UNOVIS was founded in late 1919 by Kazimir Malevich, who replaced Marc Chagall as head of the school. The group's objectives were research, study and the application of new theories of art, specifically of Suprematism (*qv*), with the aim of using art in the development of a new Socialist society. El Lissitzky, Ilia Chashnik, Nikolai Suetin and Ievgenia Magaril were some of Malevich's closest colleagues at UNOVIS. The group published a journal of the same name and established branches in provincial cities such as Orenburg and Smolensk. The group was dissolved in summer 1922, when its first students graduated. AC

VOPRA
(All-Union Society of Proletarian Architects)
Vesoiuznoe obedinenie proletarskikh arkhitektorov

Established in 1929 and active until 1932, VOPRA was one of several cultural organisations engaged in the late 1920s in reacting against the avant-garde. VOPRA attacked OSA (*qv*) and ASNOVA (*qv*) as reflections of bourgeois ideology and Western influence, claiming that VOPRA alone was the source of proletarian architecture.

ZhivSkulptArkh
(Collective for the Synthesis of Painting, Sculpture and Architecture)
Kollectiv zhivopisno-skulpturno-arkhitekturnogo sinteza

SinKkulptArkh (Collective for the Synthesis of Sculpture and Architecture), founded early in 1919 as a group of seven architects and the Cubist sculptor Boris Korolev, had sought to break with Classical models and develop innovative architectural forms. It became ZhivSkulptArkh at the end of 1919 when the painters Aleksandr Rodchenko and Taras Shevchenko joined the group, exploring the application of the forms of avant-garde painting to architectural design. The group dissolved in 1920 but its experimental debates continued within INKhUK (*qv*).

BIOGRAPHIES: ARTISTS

Babichev, Aleksei Vasilievich (1887–1963)

Born in Moscow, Babichev studied mathematics at Moscow University (1905–06) before attending the private studios of Ivan Dudin and Konstantin Iuon and the Moscow Institute for Painting, Sculpture and Architecture (1907–13).

He took part in the *World of Art* exhibition in 1913 and in 1915 he established his own studio in Moscow. After the Revolution he taught at SVOMAS (1918–20) and VKhUTEMAS (1920–21). A member of the Monolith group (1919–20), he worked with other sculptors making propaganda monuments and he later became a significant member of the Constructivists' group at the Moscow INKhUK. He was appointed head of the Workers' Faculty at VKhUTEMAS and between 1926 and 1929 he took part in exhibitions with the Association of Artists of the Revolution (AKhRR).

He returned to figurative painting in a recognisably Cézannesque manner and continued to teach at the Moscow Architectural Institute from 1944 to 1963.

Bubnova, Varvara Dmitrievna (1886–1983)

Born in St Petersburg, Bubnova trained at the School of the Society for the Encouragement of the Arts (1903–06) before attending Jacob Goldblat and Ivan Tsioglinskii's private studios (1906–07), the Imperial Academy of Art (1907–14) and the Institute for Archaeology (1913–15).

In the 1910s she took part in exhibitions with the Union of Youth. In 1911 she travelled with Matvei and Anastasia Ukhanova to Italy; in 1913 to Scandinavia, Holland, Belgium, France and Germany; and in 1915 to the ancient Russian cities on the Volga River. In 1917 she moved to Moscow, where she worked in the Historical Museum. A member of INKhUK (1920–21), she was a friend of Liubov Popova, Aleksandr Rodchenko and Varvara Stepanova. From 1922 to 1958 she lived in Japan and later in Sukhumi, Abkhazia.

- I.P. Kozhevnikova, *Varvara Bubnova – Russkii Khudozhnik v Iaponii i Apkhazii* (*Varvara Bubnova – A Russian Artist in Japan and Abkhazia*), Moscow, 2009.

Ioganson, Karel Valdemarovich (1890–1929)

Born in Sweden, Ioganson attended Riga School of Art in the mid-1910s, Penza School of Art (1915–16), and SVOMAS and VKhUTEMAS in Moscow.

A member of the Moscow INKhUK (1920) and of the First Working Group of Constructivists (1921), he contributed to the OBMOKhU exhibition in 1921 and in March 1922 he submitted his paper 'From Construction to Technology and Invention' to INKhUK. In the same year he took part in the *First Russian Art Exhibition* in Berlin. In the mid-1920s he was working in a rolling-stock mill.

Kliun, Ivan Vasilievich (1873–1943)

Born in Bolshiye Gorkii, Vladimir province, Kliun attended the School of the Society for the Encouragement of the Arts in Warsaw (1896) and Fyodor Rerberg's private studio in Moscow.

A friend and colleague of Kazimir Malevich, he moved from Symbolism to Cubofuturism, created a series of reliefs and constructions in space (1914–19) and went on to support Suprematism, taking part in avant-garde exhibitions including *Tramway V: The First Exhibition of Futurist Painting* and *The Last Exhibition of Futurist Painting: 0.10* in St Petersburg (both 1915), and *The Store* and *Jack of Diamonds* shows in Moscow (1916). He was appointed head of the Central Exhibition Bureau of the Commissariat for Education in 1918 and contributed works to the *Fifth State Exhibition: From Impressionism to Non-objective Art* and the *Tenth State Exhibition: Non-objective Creation and Suprematism* (both 1919) as well as to the *First Russian Art Exhibition* in Berlin (1922). He was a member of INKhUK (1920) and taught at SVOMAS and VKhUTEMAS (1918–21).

In 1925 Kliun turned to Purism. During 1936–38 he created a monumental composition for the All-Soviet Research Institute of Fishery and Oceanography.

- *Ivan Kliun v Tretiakovskoi Galleree* (*Ivan Kliun in the Tretyakov Gallery*), N. Avtonomova (ed.), exh. cat., State Tretyakov Gallery, Moscow, 1999.
- I. Kliun, *Moi Put v Iskusstve: Vospominania, Stati, Dnevniki* (*Ivan Kluin, My Way in Art: Reminiscences, Articles, Diaries*), A. Sarabianov (ed.), Moscow, 1999.

Klutsis, Gustav Gustavovich (1895–1938)

Born in Volmar, Latvia, Klutsis (Latvian Gustavs Klucis) attended Riga School of Art (1913–15), the School of the Society for the Encouragement of the Arts (1915–17) and SVOMAS and VKhUTEMAS in Moscow (1918–21).

A member of UNOVIS and later of INKhUK, he collaborated with Kazimir Malevich, Naum Gabo and Antoine Pevsner. In 1922 he created a series of agitprop stands and 'radio orators' for the fifth anniversary of the Revolution and the Fourth Congress of the Comintern. His activities included graphic design, posters, typography, photography, photomontage and constructions, as well as producing Revolutionary festivals.

From 1923 to 1925 he worked for the journal *LEF*. From 1924 to 1930 he taught at VKhUTEMAS, where he proposed the creation of a 'Studio of the Revolution' which aimed to educate artists in propaganda production. In 1928 he became a co-founder of the October group and he was one of the designers of the Soviet Pavilion at the Paris *Exposition Internationale des Arts et Techniques dans la Vie Moderne* in 1937. He was arrested and executed in 1938.

- *Gustav Klucis: Retrospektive*, H. Gassner, R. Nachtigaller (eds), exh. cat., Kunsthalle Fridericianum, Kassel, 1991.
- *Gustav Klutsis and Valentina Kulagina: Photography and Montage After Constructivism*, M. Tupitsyn, exh. cat., International Center of Photography, New York, 2004.
- *Gustav Klucis: Collection du Musée National des Beaux-Arts de Lettonie*, E. Guigon (ed.), exh. cat., Musée de Strasbourg, 2005.
- *Gustavs Klucis: On the Constructivist Art Front. Works from the Latvian National Museum of Art and Other Collections*, I. Derkusova, C. Lodder *et al*, exh. cat., Cajasol Obra Social, Seville, and Viviendas Municipales de Córdoba, Córdoba, 2009.

Korolev, Boris Danilovich (1885–1963)

Born in Moscow, Korolev studied physics and mathematics at Moscow University from 1902 until he was expelled in 1905. He then trained in private studios from 1907 to 1910 and at the Moscow Institute for Painting, Sculpture and Architecture from 1910 to 1915 before returning to Moscow University to study archaeology and art history.

He was a co-founder of the Union of Professional Artists and Sculptors of Moscow (1917), a member of the Monolith group of sculptors, of ZhivSkulptArkh (1919–20), of INKhUK (1920–21) and of the Society of Russian Sculptors (1926). He taught at VKhUTEMAS in Moscow (1920–21) and St Petersburg (1929–30) and took part in the Venice *Biennales* of 1924, 1928 and 1930.

- S.O. Khan-Magomedov, *Boris Korolev*, Moscow, 2007.

Kudriashev, Ivan Alekseevich (1896–1972)

Born in Kaluga in western Russia, Kudriashev attended the Moscow Institute for Painting, Sculpture and Architecture (1913–17) and then SVOMAS.

He painted his first abstract compositions in 1917. In 1919 he was sent to Orenburg to establish a branch of SVOMAS. He took part in the *First State Exhibition* in Orenburg, where he showed his designs for the mural decorations of the First Soviet Theatre, among other abstract works. In 1920 he worked as a decorator at the Summer Theatre of the Red Army and organised the Orenburg UNOVIS group.

In 1921, supervising a train evacuating starving children, he arrived in Smolensk where he met the Polish artists Katarzina Kobro and Vladislav Strzeminskii, followers of Kazimir Malevich. Later the same year he returned to Moscow and he subsequently sent works to the *First Russian Art Exhibitions* in Berlin (1922) and Amsterdam (1923). From 1925 to 1928 he showed his cosmic abstract compositions at the first, second and fourth exhibitions of the Society of Studio Artists.

At the end of the 1950s and during the 1960s he focused on cosmic abstract painting.

Ladovskii, Nikolai Aleksandrovich (1881–1941)

Born in Moscow, Ladovskii attended the Moscow Institute for Painting, Sculpture and Architecture between 1914 and 1917.

He worked at the Mossovet architecture studio in 1918–20 and for a decade from 1920 he was at VKhUTEMAS, where he established a research laboratory. He was a member of ZhivSkulptArkh and INKhUK, where he organised the Architects' Working Group (1921). In 1923 he became a founding member of ASNOVA and in 1928 of ARU.

Ladovskii worked on housing development and on planning the Moscow Metro system. He participated in the competitions for the Soviet Pavilion at the 1925 Paris *Exposition Internationale des Arts Décoratifs et Industriels Modernes* and the Palace of Soviets in Moscow (1931).

- S.O. Khan-Magomedov, *Nikolai Ladovskii*, Moscow, 2007.

El (Lazar) Markovich Lissitzky (1890–1941)

Born in Polchinok in Smolensk province, El Lissitzky attended the technical colleges in Darmstadt, Germany (1909–14) and Riga (1914–16).

From 1917 to 1924 he illustrated Yiddish picture books. He taught architecture and graphic design in Vitebsk in 1919, when he adopted Suprematism and joined UNOVIS. In 1919–20 he began working on his *Proun* project, while in 1920 he became a member of IZO in Moscow.

In 1922 he emigrated to Berlin, where he published the journal *Veshch/Gegenstand/Objet* with Ilia Ehrenburg, as well as his book *About 2 Squares*. He was one of the organisers of the *First Russian Art Exhibitions* in Berlin (1922) and Amsterdam (1923). He illustrated Vladimir Mayakovskii's *For the Voice* (1923), Aleksei Kruchenykh and Mikhail Matiushin's *Victory Over the Sun* (1923) and published his book *The Isms of Art 1914–24*, with Hans Arp.

El Lissitzky taught at the Moscow VKhUTEMAS from 1925 to 1930. He was appointed head of design for the Soviet pavilions in Cologne (1929) and Leipzig (1930) and designed horizontal skyscrapers. In 1930 he published his paper *Russia: An Architecture for World Revolution* and from 1932 he was a regular contributor to the magazine *USSR in Construction*.

- S. Lissitzky-Küppers, *El Lissitzky: Life, Letters, Texts*, London, 1980 and 1992.
- N. Perloff (ed.), *Situating El Lissitzky: Vitebsk, Berlin, Moscow*, Los Angeles, 2003.
- E.L. Nemirovskii (ed.), *El Lissitzkii: Konstruktor Knigi* (*El Lissitzky: Constructor of Books*), Moscow, 2006.
- J. Milner, *El Lissitzky: Design*, Woodbridge, 2009.

Malevich, Kazimir Severinovich (1878–1935)

Born in Kiev, Malevich studied at the city's School of Art in 1895–96 and in Fyodor Rerberg's private studio in Moscow from 1906 to 1910.

From 1907 he contributed works to Union of Youth exhibitions and from 1910 he participated in avant-garde shows including *Jack of Diamonds* (1910), *Donkey's Tail* (1912) and *Target* (1913). In 1913 he worked with Mikhail Matiushin and Aleksei Kruchenykh on staging the Futurist opera *Victory Over the Sun*, for which he designed costumes and sets.

After a period when he experimented with Cubofuturism and Transrational Realism, as well as creating a short series of works under the label of *Alogism*, he showed Suprematist pieces for the first time at *The Last Exhibition of Futurist Painting: 0.10* in St Petersburg (1915), proposing a new movement in painting which he supported with his essay 'From Cubism and Futurism to Suprematism: The New Realism in Painting'. Together with artists such as Liubov Popova, Ivan Kliun, Nadezhda Udaltsova, Olga Rozanova and others, he founded the Supremus group (1916–17) and prepared a journal, which was never published.

In 1918 he was appointed as a professor at SVOMAS and in 1919 he began teaching at the School of Art in Vitebsk, where he replaced Marc Chagall as head after they argued over theoretical issues. In Vitebsk he organised UNOVIS (Affirmers of the New Art), which aimed at promoting the theory and practice of Suprematism, and soon established branches in other cities. In 1919–20 he held a one-man show, *K.S. Malevich: The Path from Impressionism to Suprematism*, in Moscow.

In 1922 he settled with his group in St Petersburg and became the director of a department at INKhUK. At the same time he created Suprematist architectural models (*Architectons*) and published theoretical studies on Suprematism. From the late 1920s he returned to painting but in a post-Suprematist, realistic style.

- C. Douglas, *Swans of Other Worlds: Kazimir Malevich and the Origin of Abstraction in Russia*, Ann Arbor, 1980.
- A. Shatskikh (ed.), *Kazimir Malevich: Sobranie Sochinenii v piati tomakh* (*Kazimir Malevich: Collected Works in Five Volumes*), Moscow, 1995–2004.
- J. Milner, *Kazimir Malevich and the Art of Geometry*, New Haven, 1996.
- E. Petrova, I. Karasik (eds), *V Kruge Malevicha* (*In Malevich's Circle*), St Petersburg, 2000.
- A. Nakov, *Kazimir Malewicz 1878–1935: Catalogue raisonné*, Paris, 2002.
- *Kazimir Malevich: Suprematism*, M. Drutt, N. Gurianova, J.-C. Marcade, V. Rakitin, exh. cat., Guggenheim Museum, Berlin, 2003.
- I. Vakar, T. Mikhienko (eds), *Malevich o sebe. Sovremenniki o Maleviche. Pisma, Dokumenty, Vospominaniia, Kritika* (*Malevich on Himself. Contemporaries on Malevich. Letters, Documents, Memoirs, Criticism*), 2 vols, Moscow, 2004.
- *Kazimir Malevich in the State Russian Museum*, E. Petrova, exh. cat., State Russian Museum, St Petersburg, 2006.
- C. Douglas, C. Lodder (eds), *Rethinking Malevich: Proceedings of a Conference in Celebration of the 125th Anniversary of Kazimir Malevich's Birth*, New York, 2007.

Medunetskii, Konstantin Konstantinovich (1899–1934)

Born in Moscow, Medunetskii attended the Stroganov Institute of Industrial Art (1914–17) and SVOMAS (1918–19) in Moscow.

A founding member of OBMOKhU, he participated in the group's exhibitions in 1919, 1920, 1921 and 1923. In 1919 he joined INKhUK and in 1920 he became a member of the First Working Group of Constructivists. He collaborated with the Stenberg brothers in the production of Revolutionary festivals and the organisation of an exhibition at the Poetov café in 1922; this was accompanied by their declaration 'Constructivism', submitted to INKhUK later that year.

In 1922 he also took part in the *First Russian Art Exhibition* in Berlin and he worked at the Teatr Kameny until 1924. In 1925 he participated in the Paris *Exposition Internationale des Arts Décoratifs et Industriels Modernes*. From the late 1920s until his death he worked mainly as a stage designer.

Nikritin, Solomon Borisovich (Salmon Solomon Levi) (1898–1965)

Born in Chernigov in Ukraine, Nikritin attended Kiev School of Art (1909–14) and continued his training in the private studios of Leonid Pasternak in Moscow, Aleksandr Iakovlef in St Petersburg (1914–17) and Aleksandra Exter in Kiev (1918–20). From 1920 to 1922 he was at VKhUTEMAS in Moscow.

In 1921, with Aleksandr Labas, Sergei Luchishkin, Kliment Redko, Mikhail Plaksin and Aleksandr Tyshler, he founded the Projectionist (later Electroorganism) group, which held an exhibition at the Museum of Painterly Culture in Moscow in 1922. He participated in the *First Russian Art Exhibitions* in Berlin (1922) and Amsterdam (1923) and in the *First Discussion Exhibition of the Associations of Active Revolutionary Art* in Moscow (1924), signing the Projectionists' declaration in the catalogue.

From 1922 he worked as head of the department of analysis at the Museum of Painterly Culture and from 1922 to 1930 he taught at the School of Art Education in

Riazan. In the 1930s and 1940s he designed exhibitions and museum interiors and continued to produce paintings based on his theory of Dialectical Realism.

- *Spheres of Light – Stations of Darkness: The Art of Solomon Nikritin (1898–1965)*, N. Adaskina, J.E. Bowlt, N. Misler, M. Tsantsanoglou (eds), exh. cat., SMCA-Costakis Collection, Thessaloniki, 2004.

Popova, Liubov Sergeevna (1889–1924)

Born in Ivanovskoe near Moscow, Popova studied in the private studios of Stanislav Zhukovskii, Ivan Dudin and Konstantin Iuon in Moscow in 1907–08 and in 1912–13 at the Académie de la Palette in Paris.

In 1912 she worked in Vladimir Tatlin's workshop and from 1914 she participated in avant-garde exhibitions, making significant contributions to Cubofuturism, Suprematism – as a member of Kazimir Malevich's Supremus group in 1916–17 – and Constructivism. She worked in theatre, creating stage sets for Fernand Crommelynck's *The Magnanimous Cuckold*, produced by Vsevolod Meyerhold in 1922, and Sergei Tretyakov's *Earth in Turmoil* (1923).

As well as designing textiles for the First State Textile Print Factory in Moscow, she was a graphic designer and provided illustrations for posters, magazine covers, books and porcelain. A member of INKhUK, she taught at VKhUTEMAS, where she started a new programme of practical artistic education.

- D. Sarabianov, N. Adaskina, *Popova*, New York, 1990.
- *Liubov Popova*, M. Dabrowski, exh. cat., Museum of Modern Art, New York, 1991.
- *Rodchenko and Popova: Defining Constructivism*, M. Tupitsyn, V. Todoli (eds), exh. cat., Tate Modern, London, 2009.

Puni, Ivan Albertovich (1892–1956)

Born in Kuokkala near St Petersburg, Puni attended the Académie Julian in Paris (1910–12).

He became a member of the Union of Youth in 1912, illustrated

Futurist books and took part in *Tramway V: The First Exhibition of Futurist Painting* and *The Last Exhibition of Futurist Painting: 0.10* (both 1915), to which he contributed Suprematist works. He took part in the exhibitions of the Jack of Diamonds group (1916–17) and in shows of the Art Bureau in St Petersburg (1915–18).

In 1919 he taught at the Vitebsk School of Art and in 1920 he emigrated to Berlin, where he worked as a graphic artist and art critic. In 1921 his work was presented in a one-man show at Der Sturm gallery and in 1922 he contributed paintings to the exhibitions of the Novembergruppe in Berlin and Dusseldorf. He also took part in the *First Russian Art Exhibition* in Berlin (1922). From 1924 he lived and worked in Paris.

Rodchenko, Aleksandr Mikhailovich (1891–1956)

Born in St Petersburg, Rodchenko attended the Kazan School of Art (1910–14) and the Stroganov Institute of Industrial Art in Moscow.

In the mid-1910s his painterly compositions and constructions were shown in avant-garde exhibitions and in 1918 he held his first one-man show, at the Leftist Federation Club in Moscow. From 1918 he worked for IZO, and from 1919 to 1920 he was a member of ZhivSkulptArkh. In 1919 he took part in the *Tenth State Exhibition: Non-objective Creation and Suprematism* in Moscow and the following year he was a founding member of INKhUK and started teaching at VKhUTEMAS/VKhUTEIN, a role he maintained until 1930. A member of the Productivist group, he showed work at the OBMOKhU exhibitions (1920, 1921) and in 1925 he designed a workers' club which was exhibited at the Paris *Exposition Internationale des Arts Décoratifs et Industriels Modernes*.

Rodchenko was also involved in typography, photography, photomontage and stage design. He worked on the journals *LEF* and *Novyi LEF*, and collaborated with Vladimir Mayakovskii on advertising campaigns and illustrations for poetry publications. In the 1930s he

worked as a graphic designer for the magazine *USSR in Construction* and he subsequently returned to painting.

- D. Elliot, *Rodchenko and the Arts of Revolutionary Russia*, New York, 1979.
- G. Karginov, *Rodchenko*, London, 1979.
- S.O. Khan-Magomedov, *Rodchenko: The Complete Work*, London and Cambridge, Mass., 1986.
- A. Lavrentiev, *Rakursi Rodchenko* (*Rodchenko's Foreshortening*), Moscow, 1992.
- A. Lavrentiev, *Rodchenko Photography 1924–1954*, Edison NJ, 1995.
- M. Tupitsin, *Aleksandr Rodchenko: The New Moscow*, New York, 1998.
- C. Brockhaus, S.O. Khan-Magomedov, A. Lavrentiev, *Alexander Rodchenko: Spatial Constructions*, Stuttgart, 2002.
- *Aleksandr Rodchenko: Painting, Drawing, Collage, Design, Photography*, A. Lavrentiev, M. Dabrowski, P. Galassi *et al*, exh. cat., Museum of Modern Art, New York, 2005.
- A. Lavrentiev, J.E. Bowlt (eds), *Aleksandr Rodchenko: Experiments for the Future – Diaries, Essays, Letters and Other Writings*, New York, 2005.
- *Rodchenko: Constructing the Future,* E. Petrova, J.-C. Marcadé, exh. cat., Caixa Catalunya Obra Social, Barcelona, 2009.
- J. Milner, *Rodchenko: Design*, Woodbridge, 2009.

Stenberg, Vladimir Avgustovich (1899–1982)
Stenberg, Georgii Avgustovich (1900–1933)

Born in Moscow, the Stenberg brothers studied at the Stroganov Institute of Industrial Art from 1912 to 1917 and at SVOMAS in Moscow from 1917 to 1920. They worked as a team until Georgii's death.

Originally stage designers, they were involved with the production of Revolutionary festivals such as the 1918 May Day celebration in Moscow. They were founding members of OBMOKhU and participated in its exhibitions in 1919, 1920, 1921 and 1923.

Members of the Moscow INKhUK (1920) and of the

First Working Group of Constructivists (1921), they organised an exhibition at the Poetov café and submitted their paper 'Constructivism' to INKhUK in 1922. They worked at the Teatr Kameny (1923–24) and designed posters using photomontage and offset-printing techniques. In 1928 they supervised the decoration of Moscow's Krasnaya ploshchad (Red Square) for the celebration of the anniversary of the October Revolution and from 1929 to 1932 they both taught at the Moscow Architectural Institute.

After Georgii's death Vladimir continued to work in poster design.

- *2 Stenberg 2: La période laboratoire (1919–1921) du constructivisme russe/The Laboratory Period (1919–1921) of Russian Constructivism*, A. Nakov, exh. cat., Annely Juda Fine Art, London, 1975.
- *Stenberg Brothers: Constructing a Revolution in Soviet Design*, C. Mount, P. Kenez, exh. cat., Museum of Modern Art, New York, 1997.
- S.O. Khan-Magomedov, *Vladimir i Georgii Stenbergi (Vladimir and Georgii Stenberg)*, Moscow, 2008.

Stepanova, Varvara Fedorovna (1894–1958)

Born in Kaunas (Kovno), Lithuania, Stepanova trained at the School of Art in Kazan (1910–11) and in the studios of Ilia Mashkov and Konstantin Iuon (1912–13), and at the Stroganov Institute of Industrial Art (1913) in Moscow.

She participated in the *Fifth State Exhibition: From Impressionism to Non-objective Art* and the *Tenth State Exhibition: Non-objective Creation and Suprematism* (both in Moscow in 1919) and in 1920 she exhibited with Wassily Kandinsky, Aleksandr Rodchenko and Nikolai Sinezubov. She was represented in the Moscow exhibition *5x5=25* (1921) and in the *First Russian Art Exhibition* in Berlin (1922). During the years 1917–19 she wrote *zaum* poetry. In addition she created non-representational collage and calligraphic books.

In 1918 she joined IZO, and between 1920 and 1923 she was an active member of INKhUK. In 1922 she designed the costumes and sets for Aleksandr Sukhovo-Kobylin's *Death of Tarelkin*, in which, under the direction of Vsevolod Meyerhold, she produced variations on robot-like constructions of the human figure. She also designed sets for Vitalii Zhemchuzhnyi's *An Evening of the Book* (1924).

In 1923–24 she began working with Liubov Popova as a designer at the First State Textile Print Factory in Moscow. From 1923 to 1928 she was closely associated with the journals *LEF* and *Novyi LEF*, edited by Osip Brik and Vladimir Mayakovskii. She was a member of the Productivist group with Rodchenko, Popova and Vladimir Tatlin. She also taught in the textile department at VKhUTEMAS from 1924 to 1925. In 1925 she took part in the *Exposition Internationale des Arts Décoratifs et Industriels Modernes* in Paris.

From the mid-1920s Stepanova focused on typographic and poster design as well as on cinematography. In the 1930s she worked for several magazines including *USSR in Construction*. She started painting again in the late 1930s.

- A. Lavrentiev (ed.), *Varvara Stepanova: A Constructivist Life*, London, 1988.
- P. Noever (ed.), *Aleksandr M. Rodchenko, Varvara F. Stepanova: The Future Is Our Only Goal*, Munich, 1991.
- A. Lavrentiev, *Varvara Stepanova*, Moscow, 2008.

Tarabukin, Nikolai Mikhailovich (1889–1956)

Born in Moscow, Tarabukin attended the Faculty of History and Philosophy at Moscow University.

A prominent art historian and theoretician, he lived in Omsk in 1918–19 and in 1920 worked at SVOMAS in Tver with Antonina Sofronova and Mikhail Sokolov. In 1921 he participated in the debates on Constructivism and Productivism in INKhUK. His theoretical works included *From the Easel to the Machine* (1922), *For a Theory of Painting* (1923) and *The Art of Today* (1925).

Tatlin, Vladimir Evgrafovich (1885–1953)

Born in Kharkov, Tatlin trained at the Moscow Institute for Painting, Sculpture and Architecture (1902–03) and the Penza School of Art (1905–10).

He established his workshop in Moscow in 1911 and took part in avant-garde exhibitions, showing his first painterly reliefs at *The Last Exhibition of Futurist Painting: 0.10* in St Petersburg in 1915. From 1918 he was head of IZO, and in 1919 he taught at the Moscow SVOMAS, transferring to the St Petersburg branch later that year, where he started work on his *Monument to the Third International*.

In 1923 he became a member of INKhUK. He worked as a stage and costume designer for Velimir Khlebnikov's play *Zangezi* (1923) and taught in the department of theatre, cinema and photography at Kiev School of Art (1925–27). On his return to Moscow he took up teaching in the wood and metalwork faculty at VKhUTEIN. In 1929 he began to work on his manually operated flying machine, the *Letatlin*.

He subsequently continued to work for theatre and returned to figurative painting.

- J. Milner, *Vladimir Tatlin and the Russian Avant-Garde*, New Haven and London, 1983.
- L.A. Shadowa, *Tatlin 1885–1953*, Weingarten, 1987.
- *Vladimir Tatlin, Retrospektive*, J. Harten, A.A. Strigalev, exh. cat., Stadtische Kunsthalle, Düsseldorf, 1992.
- J. Harten (ed.), *Vladimir Tatlin: Leben, Werk, Wirkung, ein internationals Symposium*, Düsseldorf, 1993.
- *Tatlin and After*, L. Becker (ed.), exh. cat., SMCA-Costakis Collection, Thessaloniki, 2001.
- N. Lynton, *Tatlin's Tower: Monument to Revolution*, New Haven and London, 2009.

Vialov, Konstantin Aleksandrovich (1900–1976)

Born in Moscow, Vialov trained in Moscow at the Stroganov Institute of Industrial Art (1914–17), SVOMAS (1918–20) and VKhUTEMAS (1920–24).

A member of the Concretivist group, he took part in the *First Discussion Exhibition of the Associations of Active Revolutionary Art* in Moscow in 1924. The following year he joined the Society of Studio Artists and contributed to its exhibitions until 1928. His work as a stage designer included plays such as Vasilii Kamenskii's *Stenka Razin* (1924). He also designed books and posters. In the late 1920s he turned to landscape painting and during the three decades from 1930 he became a distinguished marine painter.

BIOGRAPHIES: ARCHITECTS

Aleshin, Pavel
(1881–1961)

Born in Kiev, Aleshin graduated from the Petersburg Institute of Civil Engineering in 1904 and from the Imperial Academy of Art in 1917. From 1900 to 1917 he travelled extensively in Western Europe, visiting, among other countries, Germany, Austria, Switzerland, France and Italy.

Kiev provided the main focus of Aleshin's career. His most important work was the Pedagogical Museum (now the Teachers' House) of c. 1910, a building rich in Classical and Renaissance motifs. After the Revolution he was initially in charge of reconstruction in Kiev and was appointed chief architect for the Kiev area. He was involved in numerous projects in the 1920s including the plan for the development of Settlement KhT3 for 113,000 people in Kharkov, which had replaced Kiev as Ukraine's capital. Few of these projects were built.

Aleshin built his first Soviet Doctors' Housing Cooperative in Kiev in 1927–30 (Cat. 76). In the 1930s he designed a second Doctors' Housing Cooperative (1932–35) and the Institute of Physics and was responsible for the reconstruction of the Grand Hotel in Kiev. NDBdeM

Barkhin, Grigorii Borisovich
(1880–1969)
Barkhin, Mikhail Grigorevich
(1906–1988)

Born in Perm, Grigorii Barkhin graduated in architecture from the Imperial Academy of Art in St Petersburg in 1907. His son Mikhail was born in Bobruisk and graduated from MVTU as an engineer-architect in 1929. From the mid-1920s father and son collaborated closely.

Grigorii Barkhin's pre-1914 work embraced both the Neoclassicism of St Petersburg and, for a church project, the Georgian vernacular. After the Revolution he was involved in the architecture and urban planning of workers' housing. His 1924 design for a People's House at Ivanovo-Voznesensk adheres to an avant-garde idiom in which the different functions are clearly articulated in the plan and the variety of cubic and cylindrical forms, while the exterior is animated by a play of different square and rectangular windows set in unornamented surfaces. The Barkhins' joint design for the Izvestia Building in Moscow (1925–27; Cat. 65) shows a further working out of these principles, but within the limits of a constricted urban site.

The Barkhins submitted designs for theatres and other large auditoriums at Rostov-na-Donu, Ekaterinburg and Minsk in the early 1930s. These sought both to reflect aspirations about the social cohesion of the audience without the hierarchical seating arrangements of traditional theatres and to improve the interaction between audience and performers. Mikhail Barkhin worked with the avant-garde theatre director Vsevolod Meyerhold to devise new principles of theatre design, illustrated in his plan for a proposed Meyerhold Theatre in Moscow. Virtually all these projects were abandoned, however, as official views turned against progressive theatre.

Grigorii Barkhin worked on the General Plan for the Reconstruction of Moscow (1933–37) and on the renewal of Sevastopol (1944–47). A writer on architecture, he published *The Workers' House and the Garden Settlement* and *The*

Modern Workers' Dwelling in the 1920s and *The Architecture of the Theatre* in 1947. An active participant in MAO, he sat on numerous competition juries. NDBdeM

Barutchev, Armen
Konstantinovich
(1904–1976)

Born in St Petersburg, Barutchev graduated from the city's VKhUTEIN in 1927. He also studied film directing.

After an early involvement in a group under Igor Fomin researching the development of the communal economy for the Leningrad Soviet, Barutchev worked on plans for factory kitchens. From 1928 to 1933, together with Izidor Gilter, Iosif Meerzon and Iakov Rubanchik, he designed the Narvskii Factory Kitchen and Department Store (Cat. 72) in the Narvskaia Zastava area of the Kirovskii district of St Petersburg and similar schemes in the Vyborgskii, Vasileostrovskii and Moskovskii districts.

The factory kitchen, created to provide meals for large numbers of local workers and inhabitants, was a key element in the attempt to restructure daily life, to strengthen the role of the community at the expense of that of the family, and to free women from their daily household tasks. Appropriately for their novel function, the buildings are among the most overtly avant-garde in St Petersburg: highly asymmetrical, with a horizontal emphasis and large areas of glass. The Modernist Narvskii Factory Kitchen stands across Stachek ploshchad from Aleksandr Gegello and David Krichevskii's contemporary but Classically influenced A.M. Gorky Palace of Culture.

Barutchev and his three partners also established the

St Petersburg cell of ARU, an organisation founded in 1928 by Nikolai Ladovskii with the intention of moving beyond the design of individual buildings for a new society to that of whole towns and communities. In later years Barutchev worked on a range of major public buildings and was an active participant in Giprogor, an important town-planning institute. After 1945 he worked again on St Petersburg's suburban developments. NDBdeM

Felger, Mark Davidovich
(1881–1962)

Born in Odessa, Felger graduated from the Imperial Academy of Art in St Petersburg in 1912 and by 1914 he had already built an apartment block in the city. He worked with Sergei Serafimov and Samuil Kravets on the Gosprom Building in Kharkov (1929; Cat. 63) and he subsequently designed buildings in St Petersburg including a residence for the Red Textile Workers' Cooperative and student housing for the Polytechnic Institute. NDBdeM

Fomin, Igor Ivanovich
(1904–1989)

Born in Orel, Igor Fomin was the son of the architect Ivan Aleksandrovich Fomin (1872–1936). He graduated in architecture from the VKhUTEIN in St Petersburg in 1926.

From around 1928 he worked with teams of architects designing buildings in the city's suburbs based on new ideas about restructuring the lives of the urban proletariat. He first worked under the leadership of L.B. Rudnev on two large *profilaktorii* (clinics and dispensaries) in the Kirovskii and Nevskii districts.

In 1930–32 he built a school on Stachek prospekt. From 1931 to 1935 he worked with V.G. Daugul and B.M. Serebrovskii on the House of Soviets in St Petersburg's Moskovskii suburb. These designs were characteristic of the city's avant-garde architecture in the late 1920s.

St Petersburg had been the main centre for a Classical revival in the post-Revolutionary era, and Igor Fomin's father had been the leader of the movement. While the influence of the avant-garde architecture of Moscow became more marked as the decade advanced, important groups of St Petersburg architects did not entirely embrace the ideas of the more radical movements. So while Igor Fomin's buildings express strong horizontality, this is often interrupted by contrasting vertical elements such as staircases, and he uses continuous banded fenestration sparingly. While surfaces are plain and undecorated, pitched roofs often appear, and occasionally a cornice. His Lensovet Communal House of 1934 (with Evgenii Levinson; Cat. 81) maintained the austere, undecorated surfaces of his more radical earlier buildings but introduced an axial symmetry with a grand entry and rich materials that marked a significant new phase in the city's post-Revolutionary architecture.

Fomin continued to work with Levinson through the later 1930s on large housing projects on Moskovskii prospekt and Ivanovskaia ulista. These retained the symmetry, imposing appearance and rich materials of the Lensovet Communal House but included increasingly explicit references to the traditional Classicism of St Petersburg, with façades decorated with colonnades and mouldings and capped with elaborate cornices.

After 1945 Fomin designed important Classically influenced buildings in St Petersburg and directed the planning of Leningrad State University. NDBdeM

Gegello, Aleksandr Ivanovich (1891–1965)

Born in Ekaterinoslavl in Ukraine, Gegello graduated from the St Petersburg Institute of Civil Engineering in 1921 and from the city's VKhUTEIN in 1924. He had worked as an assistant to Ivan Fomin from 1915 and his 1923 entry in the competition for the Arcos Building in Moscow reflected a simplified Classicism derived from his teacher.

From 1925 to 1935 Gegello worked on buildings for an important development around the Narvskaia Zastava area in the Kirovskii district of St Petersburg. This constituted an early practical attempt by the authorities to design a new way of life for the urban proletariat. Gegello collaborated initially with Aleksandr Nikolskii and Grigorii Simonov on workers' housing on Stachek prospekt (1925–28) and Traktornaia ulitsa (1927; Cat. 79), which placed apartments in three- or four-storey blocks around large planted courtyards.

At the same time Gegello, working with David Krichevskii, designed the A.M. Gorky Palace of Culture in St Petersburg. By flanking the large central auditorium with the library and rooms for sports and cultural activities, the architects retained the basic format of a traditional theatre. However, the extremely plain appearance – again with highly simplified Classical references – proclaims the seriousness of the building's purpose.

Gegello worked with Krichevskii in the 1930s on such projects as the Technical Studies Building (1930–32) and the I.I. Gaza Palace of Culture (1931–35). In these, Classical references disappeared in favour of a broader espousal of the avant-garde. In the Gigant Cinema (1933–35), however, the architects reverted to their earlier approach.

In the later 1930s Gegello designed schools in St Petersburg and after 1945 he became involved in the restoration of the city's historic buildings. NDBdeM

Ginzburg, Moisei Iakovlevich (1882–1946)

Born in Minsk, Ginzburg was the son of an architect. As a Jew in Russia, he had only limited access to higher education. He trained as an architect initially in France and then at the Accademia di Belle Arti in Milan, graduating in 1914, and as an engineer–architect at Riga Polytechnic, graduating in 1917. Settling first in the Crimea, he produced designs which conformed with his Classical training though his manipulation of undecorated masses showed an engagement with international developments and in particular with the work of Frank Lloyd Wright.

In Moscow from 1921 Ginzburg began, through writing, teaching and design, to formulate a vision of an architecture of the future appropriate to the post-Revolutionary era. *Style and Epoch* (1924) articulated an avant-garde position influenced by Heinrich Wölfflin's view that architects should shape an architecture for contemporary circumstances. The primary task of the post-Revolutionary architect was to develop appropriate forms of housing and places of work for the proletariat. The engineer, whose decisions about design and materials aim at optimal functionality, provided one key to solving these problems. Yet Ginzburg, drawing on the ideas of the psychologist Wilhelm Wundt, also maintained the importance of the aesthetic, writing that 'various elements of form… engender emotions of satisfaction or dissatisfaction within us'. Sending Le Corbusier a copy of his book inscribed '*Hommage cordial de l'auteur*' he expressed his broad adherence to Le Corbusier's vision, though there were many differences of emphasis.

Ginzburg and the Vesnin brothers founded OSA in 1925 to bring together architects sympathetic to these views. They also acted as joint editors of the journal *SA* (1926–30), which juxtaposed articles on new projects in the Soviet Union and Western Europe, promoting Soviet architecture as part of an international avant-garde project.

In his work on housing Ginzburg developed types of dwelling unit based on an analysis of the occupants' needs, applying a functional approach to daily life that owed much to Frederick Winslow Taylor's writings on industrial processes. Ginzburg distinguished between needs that could be fulfilled communally and those that should be addressed within the living 'cell' and put his ideas into practice in such schemes as the Narkomfin Communal House in Moscow (1930; Cat. 75) and 21 Malyshev ulitsa, Ekaterinburg (1929–31; Cat. 80).

A wide range of other projects and competition entries flowed from Ginzburg during the late 1920s, often produced in cooperation with other architects of the OSA group. He developed movable living units for 'non-urban' settlements and also turned his attention to planning issues, ultimately becoming convinced by the programme of the Disurbanist school.

In the early 1930s, as the state intervened increasingly to encourage historicist styles and traditional building methods, Ginzburg defended the avant-garde. At the First Congress of Soviet Architects in June 1937, which was called to seal state control of architecture, Ginzburg spoke for an hour in defence of architects' independence and compared construction methods in the USA favourably with those imposed by the Soviet Five Year Plan. But in the work of his later years he too was eventually obliged to conform to the new aesthetic regime. NDBdeM

- S.O. Khan-Magomedov, *M.I. Ginzburg,* Moscow, 1972.

Golosov, Ilia Aleksandrovich (1883–1945)

Born in Moscow, Golosov graduated as an architect in 1912 from the Moscow Institute for Painting, Sculpture and Architecture. While still a student he worked as an assistant to several architects and artists and was also engaged in book design and production. Two projects for houses were constructed in 1912–13 and he acted as a military engineer for several buildings behind Russian lines during World War I.

After the Revolution Golosov worked in the studios of the Moscow Soviet and as a teacher at VKhUTEMAS, where he co-directed an architecture studio with Konstantin Melnikov. In the early 1920s he developed a new theory and pedagogical approach, arguing that form must be determined by architectural design and construction. This contrasted with the position of his Constructivist colleagues, who argued that building form was determined by function.

He entered experimental designs for several competitions in the early 1920s, notably the Palace of Labour in Moscow (1923), the Leningradskaia Pravda Building in Moscow (1924) and the Soviet Pavilion for the 1925 Paris *Exposition Internationale des Arts Décoratifs et Industriels Modernes*, which Melnikov won. From the mid-1920s into the 1930s, working primarily on his own, he continued to enter competitions and win many prizes. His most notable built projects include the House of Textiles (1925) and the Elektrobank (1926) and the Rusgertorg Buildings (1926). After completing the Zuev Workers' Club in Moscow (1926; Cat. 87) he went on to design several communal housing complexes in Moscow, Volgagrad, Briansk and Rostov-na-Donu between 1927 and 1932.

From 1933 Golosov was head of the Moscow Soviet's architecture studios, where he was an active participant in debates about the organisation of Soviet architecture. At this time he began to include traditional architectural forms in his designs, as in an apartment block on Oktiabrskaia ulitsa in Nizhnii Novgorod (1938). During World War II he designed memorial structures and in his last years he worked on his book, *Foundations of Modern Architectural Composition,* which remained unfinished on his death. MC

Iofan, Boris Mikhailovich (1891–1976)

Born in Odessa, Iofan studied at the Odessa School of Art before going to Rome where he graduated from art school and then in 1917 from the Scuola di Applicazione per gli Ingegneri. He remained in Rome, designing a number of small villas and sketching Renaissance buildings, before returning to the Soviet Union in 1924.

He came closest to the architectural language of the avant-garde in a sanatorium

designed for Barvikha near Moscow (1929–34), a building largely defined by its curving balconies and extensive areas of glass. His VTsIK Residential Complex, built for high-ranking officials of the Communist party on the Bersenevskaia naberezhnaia in Moscow (1928–31; Cat. 82), makes a claim to modernity with its plain surfaces and technical innovation but clearly seeks to impose itself by its size, balanced disposition of large masses of masonry, symmetry and simplified Classical references.

Iofan's skill in developing monumental buildings to dominate the urban landscape was most fully deployed in a series of designs for the Palace of Soviets developed between 1931 and 1934. Working with Vladimir Gelfreikh and Vladimir Shchuko, Iofan entered this international competition for a building housing several auditoriums, the largest with a capacity of 15,000. It was intended to replace the recently demolished Cathedral of Christ the Saviour (begun in 1832 but not consecrated until 1883) on a prominent Moscow riverside site (now again occupied by the cathedral, which was rebuilt in 1992–2000). The proposal by Iofan's team was selected from 272 submissions; the final scheme showed a square plinth surmounted by a series of drums of decreasing diameter and increasing height drawing the eye up to the culminating 70-metre statue of Lenin. Although it remained unbuilt, the selection of Iofan's project signalled the Soviet regime's abandonment of the avant-garde and its conversion to the monumental rhetorical architecture characteristic of Stalinist Neoclassicism.

Iofan's design for the Soviet Pavilion at the 1937 Paris *Exposition Internationale des Arts et Techniques dans la Vie Moderne*, an imposing upwardly thrusting structure in a Neoclassical idiom surmounted by Vera Mukhina's dynamic sculpture *Worker and Collective Farm Girl*, reformulated the same themes. A model of Iofan's final design for the Palace of Soviets was displayed inside.

In the 1960s Iofan returned

to a more Modernist idiom for a housing complex on Sherbakov ulitsa in Moscow. NDBdeM

- I. Eigel, *Boris Iofan*, Moscow, 1978.

Kolli, Nikolai Dzhemsovich (1894–1966)

Kolli was born in Moscow. In 1918 he designed the Red Wedge, one of many pieces of temporary street scenery used in popular celebrations of the Revolution. He graduated from VKhUTEMAS in 1922 where he had trained under Ivan Zholtovskii, whom he assisted in the design of a wooden Neoclassical pavilion for a 1923 trade exhibition. In 1924–25 he worked on workers' housing and the industrialisation of construction using prefabricated components.

From 1927 to 1932 Kolli worked on the DneproGES Dam and Hydroelectric Power Station (Cat. 68). Between 1929 and 1936 he was the senior Russian architect assisting in the design and construction of the Tsentrosoyuz Building (Cat. 64), working first with Le Corbusier and Pierre Jeanneret in Paris and then in Moscow to adapt Le Corbusier's innovative ideas – on, for instance, heating and cooling the building – to the realities of Soviet technology. Kolli subsequently supervised its construction.

From 1933 to 1941 Kolli was head of the No. 6 Architectural Workshop of the City of Moscow, which produced designs for the stadium in the city's Izmailovo district, the Bolshoi Kamenii and Novoarbatskii Bridges over the Moskva River and a sanatorium at Sochi. Kolli designed stations for the new Moscow Metro; his Kirovskaia Station (1935–36) retains a clean geometry that would shortly give way to a more ostentatious aesthetic. He was active in the post-1945 reconstruction of Moscow and continued to work on housing and on the industrialisation of construction.

Kolli's engagement with Western Europe was reflected in his role as Russian representative (with Moisei Ginzburg) at CIAM in 1930 and his presence in Rome at the International Architectural

Conference in 1935. In 1962, following Khrushchev's reinstatement of architectural Modernism, an article by Kolli initiated the rehabilitation of Le Corbusier in the Soviet Union. NDBdeM

Kravets, Samuil Mironovich (1891–1966)

Born in Vilnius, Kravets graduated from the St Petersburg Polytechnic Institute in 1917. He collaborated with Sergei Serafimov and Mark Felger on the Gosprom Building in Kharkov (1929; Cat. 63). His most notable other work was for the Moscow Metro: between 1935 and 1945 he was involved in building several stations including Kropotskinskaia Station (originally Dvorets Sovetov; 1935), with Aleksei Dushkin and I. Likhtenberg. NDBdeM

Ladovskii, Nikolai Aleksandrovich (see page 254)

Le Corbusier, born Charles-Edouard Jeanneret (1887–1965)

Born in La Chaux-de-Fonds, Switzerland, Le Corbusier was an architect, planner, theorist, polemicist and a leading figure in the Modern Movement in architecture. He was greatly interested in the Soviet Union and was an architect of major importance to the Soviet avant-garde.

Between 1920 and 1924, while he was joint editor (with Amédée Ozenfant) of the review *L'Esprit nouveau*, Le Corbusier was already making use of the sparse information reaching France to report on Soviet cultural developments. After Franco-Soviet diplomatic relations were resumed in 1924, the Soviet Union participated in the 1925 Paris *Exposition Internationale des Arts Décoratifs et Industriels Modernes*; the extensive show of avant-garde Soviet architecture and the striking Soviet Pavilion by Konstantin Melnikov confirmed Le Corbusier's interest. Between 1926 and 1930 Jean Badovici's journal *L'Architecture vivante*, with which Le Corbusier was closely associated, regularly discussed and illustrated the major achievements of contemporary

Soviet architecture. At the same time avant-garde architects in the Soviet Union were taking an increasing interest in Le Corbusier. His ideas on town planning were discussed in the first issue of SA in 1926 and he featured regularly in the journal until it ceased publication in 1930.

Tsentrosoyuz, the Central Union of Consumer Cooperatives, was planning the construction of a new headquarters. In addition to holding an open competition, the Union invited Le Corbusier to submit a proposal (Cat. 64). The office building would be his biggest project to date. He felt that the Soviet Union, with its centralised planning, state ownership of land and sympathy for advanced ideas in architecture, might offer him opportunities to realise large-scale projects that were not available to him at that time in the West.

Between 1928 and 1930 Le Corbusier made three trips to Moscow to supervise work on the final designs for the Tsentrosoyuz Building; in 1928 he developed cordial relations with the leaders of OSA, the Vesnin brothers and Moisei Ginzburg, and with other OSA architects. Ivan Nikolaev's Textile Institute Student Housing (1929–30; Cat. 78) clearly shows the stamp of his influence and Ginzburg and Ignatii Milinis' 1930 Narkomfin Communal House (Cat. 75) incorporated all of Le Corbusier's recently formulated 'five points'. The term 'Corbuzianizm' would come to be applied derogatorily by Soviet commentators to these works.

By the early 1930s, however, the tide was turning against the avant-garde and Le Corbusier's Tsentrosoyuz Building was beginning to be heavily criticised. His 1930–31 proposal for the Palace of Soviets was passed over, along with other avant-garde designs. Le Corbusier launched a vigorous attack on the three joint winning projects, seeing them as regressive references to the Renaissance rather than examples of progressive and egalitarian architecture. This episode marked the end of his active engagement with the Soviet Union. NDBdeM

Leonidov, Ivan Ilich (1902–1961)

Born in the Tver district, Leonidov was the son of a farmer. He was apprenticed to an icon painter before beginning art studies, first at SVOMAS in Tver and then at the Moscow VKhUTEMAS, where he gravitated towards architecture under the influence of Aleksandr Vesnin.

Leonidov realised very few projects. His 1927 graduation project was a proposal for the Lenin Institute, a large library and study centre. The austere towering rectangle of the book depository, horizontal rectangular forms of the institute buildings and sphere of the large auditorium proclaim his preoccupation with geometry. Leonidov announced the building as 'answering the needs of contemporary life through maximising the possibilities of technology' and envisaged conveyor systems to transfer books from the store, mobile partitions to create a range of spaces within the auditorium and internal communication equipment to enable staff to work together on projects. The spherical auditorium suspended in a steel structure springing from a single pier and supported by hawsers is an external expression of the building's futuristic technology. Writing in SA, Moisei Ginzburg criticised the scheme's economic impracticability and deployment of unnecessarily technical solutions. However, he praised Leonidov for moving beyond building design to address the broader problem of shaping public space.

Leonidov's subsequent major designs (all unbuilt) would share these characteristics and his 1934 project for the Commissariat for Heavy Industry in Moscow proposed a highly ambitious reshaping of the area around the Kremlin.

His desire to deploy architecture for utopian ends became evident in his design for a Palace of Culture for the Proletarskii district of Moscow (1930). He suggested that the centre would be the headquarters of a cultural revolution, a means of spreading political knowledge and cultural development within its district.

His proposal for Magnitogorsk, a new industrial city, envisaged a linear plan with living zones penetrating the surrounding countryside interspersed with areas for recreation. This aligned him with the Disurbanist tendency of urban planning. His later City of the Sun, developed after 1945, reveals a more mystical dimension to his utopianism.

His design for the Artek Young Pioneers Camp, from the second half of the 1930s, integrated five complete camps of the same layout into the natural features along four kilometres of the Black Sea's undulating coastline. At Ginzburg's Ordzhonikidze Sanatorium at Kislovodsk (1934–37; Cat. 91) he designed the garden amphitheatre and the staircase, which binds the sanatorium and grounds into a single composition. This was one of a very small number of realised projects.

Leonidov's interplay of geometric forms seems to owe much to Kazimir Malevich's Suprematist work. His distinctive drawings, using a range of different washes and hatchings and sometimes working in white against a black background, enrich the geometrical forms of his designs.

Closely associated with OSA, an editor of SA from 1928 to 1930 and a collaborator with Ginzburg in the 1930s, Leonidov produced work that was distinct from that of other OSA members in its preoccupation with geometry and its extreme utopianism. This would leave him exposed to particularly vicious attacks during the reaction against avant-garde architecture from the late 1920s. NDBdeM

- A. Gozak and A. Leonidov, Ivan Leonidov: The Complete Works, ed. C. Cooke, London and New York, 1988.

Levinson, Evgenii Adolfovich (1894–1968)

Born in Odessa, Levinson studied under Ivan Fomin and Vladimir Shchuko at the St Petersburg VKhUTEIN, graduating in architecture in 1927.

Early in his career he produced both theatre designs and book illustrations. In spite of his training with St Petersburg's leading exponents of Classical architecture, his first important projects placed him firmly within the city's avant-garde. His cooperative housing project (with A.M. Sokolov) of 1930–32 and Palace of Culture (with B.O. Muntz) of 1931–38, both constructed on Kirovskii (now Kamennoostrovskii) prospekt, have severe and strongly asymmetrical exteriors, impressive areas of glass or continuous banded fenestration and a strong horizontal emphasis.

Levinson worked with Igor Fomin on the Lensovet Communal House (1934; Cat. 81) and other projects throughout the 1930s. After 1945 he continued to work in the Classical manner, as in his Pushkinskaia Station on the Moscow Metro. After the mid-1950s, however, in response to Khrushchev's programme to replace Stalin's bombastic Classicism, he returned to modern materials and the flatter, plainer Modernism of his earlier work. NDBdeM

Meerzon, Iosif Aizikovich

Born in St Petersburg, Meerzon graduated from the city's VKhUTEIN in 1927. While practising as an artist he worked for Vladimir Tatlin on the construction of his Monument to the Third International (1919–20).

From 1928 to 1933 Meerzon worked with Armen Barutchev, Izidor Gilter and Iakov Rubanchik on four factory kitchens in St Petersburg, including the Narvskii Factory Kitchen and Department Store (Cat. 72). He also worked with Barutchev in the later 1930s on public buildings in Saransk and Kronstadt. He was associated with Barutchev on projects for Giprogor, the important town-planning institute. NDBdeM

Melnikov, Konstantin Stepanovich (1890–1974)

Born on the outskirts of Moscow into a poor family of peasant origin, Melnikov served a short apprenticeship as an icon painter and was then apprenticed to an engineering firm, one of whose owners noticed his talent for drawing and sent him to the Moscow Institute for Painting, Sculpture and Architecture. He graduated initially in painting and then in 1917 in architecture.

From 1918 he worked in a Mossovet architectural studio under Aleksei Shchusev and Ivan Zholtovskii but his early projects for housing schemes show him abandoning the Classicism of his teachers. His most fully worked-out plan has terraces of small houses set diagonally to the main axis, giving the scheme its name, 'The Saw'. The terraces are not parallel to each other but diverge. The houses feature plain surfaces.

In his pavilion for the Makhorka tobacco firm at the 1923 *All-Union Agricultural Exhibition* Melnikov developed this exuberant angularity by giving different parts of the pavilion different heights and setting the sloping roofs at right angles to each other. Irregular fenestration and an external staircase – crowded with visitors in some photographs – add to the sense of animation. The construction is entirely of timber, the first evidence of Melnikov's abiding interest in combining traditional materials with avant-garde design. His Soviet Pavilion for the 1925 *Exposition Internationale des Arts Décoratifs et Industriels Modernes* in Paris would also feature timber construction, an animated roofscape and an external staircase. However, it achieved a more logical design by simplifying the plan into a rectangle bisected by stairs rising and descending across its centre. The pavilion was widely praised by progressive French critics, one noting its 'simplicity, cheapness, rationality and welcoming appearance'.

During the second half of the 1920s Melnikov completed five workers' clubs in the Moscow region for the Rusakov (1927; Cat. 85), Frunze, Kauchuk, Pravda and Burevestnik trades unions. He favoured interiors with large flexible spaces, sometimes using movable panels, and opposed the Functionalist tendency to create a large number of highly specialised areas. This gave him the freedom to mould bold internal volumes and create dramatic exteriors.

His own house, consisting of two interlocking cylinders, was designed on the same principles (1927–31; Cat. 83). His garages – Bahkmetevskaia, Novo Ryanskaia and Gosplan (1936; Cat. 73) – on the other hand, though still characterised by dramatic exteriors, are based on a careful analysis of vehicular movement.

Despite being briefly associated with ASNOVA, Melnikov appears a rather solitary figure, his beliefs about the design process differing from the main groupings of 1920s architects. Heavily criticised in the 1930s for his 'Formalism', he was largely excluded from employment and teaching and no significant buildings were constructed to his design during the last 40 years of his life. His reputation was somewhat rehabilitated when his work was shown in a brief exhibition and featired in an article in the professional press in the mid-1960s. NDBdeM

- S.F. Starr, *Melnikov: Solo Architect in Mass Society*, Princeton, 1978.
- S.O. Khan-Magomedov, *Konstantin Melnikov*, Moscow, 2007.

Mendelsohn, Erich (1887–1953)

Born in Allenstein, East Prussia (now Olsztyn in Poland), Mendelsohn trained as an architect in Berlin before graduating from the Munich Technische Hochschule. In Munich he came into contact with Wassily Kandinsky and other artists of the Blaue Reiter circle. He initially considered a career in stage design but after service as an engineer in World War I he started an architectural practice in Berlin.

His Einstein Tower observatory in Potsdam (1920–24) owes much to Art Nouveau, its fluidity of form made possible – despite appearances – by rendered brick rather than concrete. Like other German architects of the time, Mendelsohn believed in the healing power of form and in the role of architecture in cultivating a more spiritual world than that which had led to a catastrophic war. At this time he was also involved with a number of leftist

groupings of architects such as Arbeitsrat für Kunst and the Novembergruppe.

His Weichmann Department Store in Gleiwitz and the Haus Sternefeld in Berlin (both 1923) are marked by a major shift to square geometric forms, with similarities to the work of De Stijl in the Netherlands. However, he tended always to unify the faces of his buildings with sweeping horizontals which add a sense of movement, as in the Schocken Department Store in Chemnitz (1928), where he used a curved front with uninterrupted horizontal bands of glass or concrete.

In 1925 Mendelsohn was invited to design the Red Banner Textile Factory in St Petersburg (Cat. 71). His 1931 proposal for the Palace of Soviets took the simplification of the Schocken building even further with two vast hemispherical auditoriums on either side of a long rectangular central section.

In 1929 Mendelsohn published *Russland–Europa–Amerika*, photographs from his three visits to the Soviet Union and the USA. While the images of the USA focus on its modernity, the photographs of the Soviet Union contrast earlier Russian architecture with that of the 1920s, while the text notes the attempt to create a new world moving from absolutism to state socialism. Privately, Mendelsohn criticised modern Soviet architects for discarding the spiritual qualities of earlier Russian architecture in favour of the rational Modernism that had developed in Europe and the USA. Nor was he receptive to the social experiments of the Soviet Union, unlike many of his German contemporaries. His reserve towards the Soviet Union was increased by the failure to respect his design for the Red Banner Textile Factory and he would eventually disavow any connection with the finished building.

When Hitler took power in 1933 Mendelsohn, who was Jewish, left Germany, abandoning a successful practice with 40 employees. He moved to Britain and with Serge Chermayeff designed the De La Warr Pavilion in Bexhill-on-Sea (1935). He was

subsequently invited to Palestine where he designed major medical and university facilities before leaving for the USA in 1941. In his last years he designed a number of buildings for the Jewish community. NDBdeM

- E. Mendelsohn, *Russland–Europa–Amerika. Ein architektonischer Querschnitt*, Berlin, 1929.
- K. James, *Erich Mendelsohn and the Architecture of German Modernism*, Cambridge, 1997.

Merzhanov, Miron Ivanovich (1895–1975)

Born in Rostov-na-Donu, Merzhanov interrupted his education at the St Petersburg Institute of Civil Engineering to serve in World War I and eventually graduated from VKhUTEIN in 1930.

He is best known for his role as Joseph Stalin's personal architect, a position he held from 1931 to 1941. Works he completed for Stalin include a dacha in Kuntsevo, where the Soviet leader died in 1953, and a summer residence in Matsesta on the Black Sea. His public commissions included the Voroshilov Sanatorium in Sochi (1930–34; Cat. 90), where he adopted planning and formal principles developed for communal housing to create a new type of building, the Socialist leisure resort.

Merzhanov was arrested in 1942 on political charges. During his ten-year prison sentence he continued to work as an architect in the gulags, designing numerous buildings around the Black Sea, Krasnoiarsk and Komsomolsk-na-Amure. MC

- A.A. Akulov, *Arkitektor Stalina: dokumentalnaia povest (Stalin's Architect: A Documentary)*, Riazan, 2006.

Nikolaev, Ivan (1901–1979)

Born in Voronezh, Nikolaev studied the principles of Rationalist architecture under Viktor Vesnin and Aleksandr Kuznetsov at MVTU. He graduated in 1925. His theories and ideas on form moved further towards

Rationalism and Functionalism when, as a student at VKhUTEMAS, he became a member of a creative group that met weekly from 1923 to 1928 to discuss new developments in Soviet art, theatre, poetry and architecture. Nikolaev was later to collaborate with many members of the group, which included the architects G. and V. Movchan, V. Kalish, Anatoli Fisenko, Evgenii Popov and S. Turgenev.

Working under the direction of Aleksandr Kuznetsov, Nikolaev assisted with the design of the Central Institute of Aerodynamics and Hydrodynamics in Moscow (1924–28; Cat. 74). This led to further work on industrial buildings including the All-Union Electro-Technical Institute in Moscow (1927–29; with Fisenko, L. Meilman, G. and V. Movchan) and the Red Talka Textile Mill in Ivanovo (1927; with Boris Gladkov). He also designed the experimental Textile Institute Student Housing in Moscow (1929–30; Cat. 78).

Towards the end of his career Nikolaev became increasingly interested in education, focusing primarily on architecture. He was a prolific writer and produced a number of books on architectural history, notably *Architecture of Roman Aqueducts*. In 1956 he was elected a member of the Academy of Architecture. He acted as director of the Moscow Architectural Institute from 1958 to 1970. MC

Nikolskii, Aleksandr Sergeevich (1884–1953)

Born in Saratov, Nikolskii trained in the architecture studios at the St Petersburg Institute of Civil Engineering, graduating in 1912. As a winner of the gold medal in architecture for his final project he travelled in Italy for a year, studying architectural monuments. On his return he worked as an assistant to the architects Vasilii Kosiakov and Alexii Bubyr and helped design and construct several churches in Tallinn. In 1920 he returned to St Petersburg to teach at the Institute of Civil Engineering, where he promoted an experimental curriculum.

After the Revolution Nikolskii became a member of INKhUK,

where he encountered the formal experiments of Kazimir Malevich's Suprematism. These had a great influence on his work throughout the 1920s when he was involved with the reconstruction and design of structures for Soviet railways. Nikolskii was also heavily influenced by the pre-Revolutionary movement Cubofuturism and was a member of ZhivSkulptArkh, an organisation formed with the goal of synthesising painting, sculpture and architecture.

Considered overtly avant-garde by more traditionalist architects, Nikolskii was by 1925 head of an architectural studio working for the Leningrad Soviet's planning department. There he applied formal innovation to the development of workers' housing districts. His housing projects on Stachek prospekt (1925–28) and Traktornaia ulitsa (1927; Cat. 79), designed with Aleksandr Gegello and Grigorii Simonov, feature three- or four-storey courtyard buildings that combined traditional construction methods and materials with innovative plans and exterior forms.

Nikolskii continued to teach throughout the 1920s and in 1926 he took charge of the St Petersburg branch of OSA. During this time he entered several experimental designs in competitions, including those for the Central Telegraph Office (1925), an OSA-led competition for a communal house for workers (1927), and the Lenin Library (1928), all in Moscow. These designs remained on paper but he did complete a project, begun in 1927, for a hundred-thousand-seat stadium for the Park of Culture and Leisure in St Petersburg.

His status within the architectural community was underscored when he was the only St Petersburg architect invited to submit designs for the first round of the 1931 competition for the Palace of Soviets in Moscow. By the early 1930s political centralisation reached the architectural profession, dissolving independent unions and individual practices in the creation of a single Union of Soviet Architects. Nikolskii became an active member of

the Union in the mid-1930s and continued to produce designs for schools and other public buildings.

During World War II he designed camouflage for military targets and several monuments and memorial arches. MC

Orlov, Georgii Mikhailovich (1901–1985)

Born in Kursk, Orlov graduated from MVTU in 1926. His teachers there, Viktor Vesnin and Aleksandr Kuznetsov, introduced him to the principles of rational and functional construction of space. When OSA formed in 1925 Orlov became secretary and contributed to its publication, *SA*.

His training in functional and structural efficiency equipped him to design industrial buildings. He worked on several projects, notably the DneproGES Dam and Hydroelectric Power Station (1927–32), which he designed with Aleksandr Vesnin, Nikolai Kolli and Sergei Andrievskii (Cat. 68). As the first major industrial project of the initial Five Year Plan it symbolised the success of Stalin's will to give concrete form to Socialist progress. It was also the only project of its nature to be completed using the OSA group's simple geometric, formal vocabulary and functional approach to design. This project included designs for the workers' town of Zaporozhye, which was to be a Socialist City (*Sotsgorod*), a practical realisation of the principles of Functionalism in urban planning. Here Orlov contributed to the plans for workers' housing, a mass kitchen and dining hall, and an open-air theatre.

In 1944 he was called to lead reconstruction of the DneproGES Dam and Hydroelectric Power Station after it was damaged in World War II. Orlov's work translated into commissions to build several more hydroelectric power stations including those in Kahoka (1951–54), Kremenchug (1955), Cheboksary (1958), Kaunas (1961) and Bratsk (1967).

In the 1960s and 1970s he both headed and was secretary of the Union of Soviet Architects. He also taught at the Moscow Architectural Institute from 1933 until his death. MC

Osmak, Vasilii (1870–1942)

Born in Gogolev, Osmak received a diploma from the University of Kiev and graduated from the St Petersburg Institute of Civil Engineering in 1895.

He worked almost exclusively in Kiev, where his built works include School No. 71, Polevoi pereulok (1930s), a workers' club on Lipskaia ulitsa (1930), an apartment house on Taraskovskaia prospekt (1930) and the diving board and pool at the Kiev Dinamo Sports Club (1935; Cat. 89.2). MC

Pasternak, Aleksandr Leonidovich (1893–1982)

Born in Moscow, Pasternak was the son of the painter Leonid Pasternak and brother of the author Boris Pasternak. He graduated from the Moscow Institute for Painting, Sculpture and Architecture in 1917 and from the Moscow Institute of Civil Engineering in 1921. He was a member of OSA from 1926 to 1931.

In the mid-1920s, as a member of the Socialist Settlement Section of the State Planning Committee Gosplan, Pasternak was engaged in research on town planning. This work included an examination of the sociologist Mikhail Okhitovich's principles of Disurbanisation, which equipped Pasternak for his 1930 competition entry for Green Town near Moscow, which he submitted as a member of the OSA team.

Pasternak also worked on the rational design of communal housing. In 1928 he worked under Moisei Ginzburg for the Typological Section of the Committee for Construction, developing transitional types of dwelling as part of the move towards communal living. This research provided the basis for his designs for experimental living units on Gogolevskii bulvar in Moscow (1930), completed with M. Barsch. It also led him to design a communal-housing complex surrounding a garden courtyard in Ekaterinburg with Ginzburg (1929–31; Cat. 80). MC

Pen, Semen Samoilovich
(1898–1970)

Pen graduated from the St Petersburg Institute of Civil Engineering in 1925. He is known for his work in Azerbaijan, which includes the Palace of the Press in Baku (1932; Cat. 66) and the Dzerzhinskii Building Workers' Club (1930; later the Rotfront Printing Workers' Club). He is an example of an architect producing avant-garde work in the Soviet provinces at a time when architecture in the major urban centres was moving back towards traditionalism and eclecticism. MC

Popov, Evgenii Mikhailovich
(1901–1965)

Born in Medun, Popov trained at MVTU, graduating in 1927. In common with other graduates of this school, he became particularly involved with the design of industrial buildings. He worked with Boris Gladkov, another graduate of the institute, on textile factories in Leninaken and Bogorodsk in 1927–28 and with Sergei Muravaev and Vladimir Zlatolinskii on the AMO Automobile Factory in Moscow (1928–33). As in other work by this group, the large flat surfaces of the AMO Automobile Factory are animated by varied fenestration.

Popov later gravitated to the circle of Moisei Ginzburg and OSA, working with Solomon Lisagor to design one of a series of six communal dwellings in Saratov whose internal plan was based on that developed by Ginzburg and Ignatii Milinis for the Narkomfin Communal House (Cat. 75). Adopting a similar Corbusian visual language, the complex consisted of a communal block and a dwelling block with a combination of units designed for those choosing to live communally and those living in a traditional family structure. Popov later worked with Ginzburg on aspects of the Ordzhonikidze Sanatorium at Kislovodsk (Cat. 91). NDBdeM

Reisher, Moisei
(1902–1980)

Born in Troitsk, Reisher graduated from Tomsk Technical Institute in 1926. His known work

is in Ekaterinburg in the Urals, where he designed a water tower for the Socialist City of Uralmash (1929; Cat. 70) as well as two student-housing projects for the Ural Polytechnic Institute and the Road-Transport College (both completed by 1938). He was the only locally trained architect who remained in the Urals rather than moving to Moscow or St Petersburg. MC

Rubanchik, Iakov Osipovich
(1899–1948)

Born in St Petersburg, Rubanchik graduated from the city's VKhUTEIN in 1928. He became a member of ASNOVA and was one of the few members of the group who lived and worked in St Petersburg.

From the 1920s Rubanchik assisted in planning a new type of building, the communal kitchen. This included the Narvskii Factory Kitchen and Department Store (Cat. 72) and similar schemes designed with Armen Barutchev, Izidor Gilter and Iosif Meerzon in the Vyborgskii, Vasileostrovskii and Moskovskii districts of St Petersburg between 1928 and 1933. The innovation of these buildings lay in combining the mass kitchen with a communal eating area and shopping centre.

He also worked with Barutchev on a project for a communal house on Matveev pereulok in St Petersburg. MC

Serafimov, Sergei Savvich
(1878–1939)

Born in Trabezund, Serafimov graduated from the Imperial Academy of Art in St Petersburg in 1910. He was later a member of OSA.

His most notable design was the Gosprom Building in Kharkov (1929; Cat. 63), where he worked with Mark Felger as a member of a team led by Samuil Kravets. This was built as the focal point of the new Socialist capital of the Ukraine. It is considered to be a landmark in the formal development of Soviet administrative buildings because it combined several bodies under one roof: around 25 institutions occupied a complex composed of four large units linked by covered skywalks.

Working with Maria Zandberg-

Serofimova, Serafimov also completed designs for the House of Design and Construction Organisations in Kharkov (1930–33), which maintained the avant-garde aesthetic at a time when the mood was increasingly shifting back towards traditionalism. MC

Shchusev, Aleksei Viktorovich
(1873–1949)

Born in Kishinev, Shchusev studied under Leon Benois and Ilia Repin, graduating from the Imperial Academy of Art in St Petersburg in 1897. For his gold-medal-winning diploma project he was awarded a sixteen-month study trip to Europe, which he undertook in 1898–99. He also travelled to North Africa and Central Asia.

His pre-Revolution designs display his Classical training and interest in medieval Russian architecture. Later, however, he incorporated elements from the Style Moderne, the Russian Art Nouveau movement, into designs for churches that were built between 1908 and 1912, and for the Kazanskaia Station in Moscow, completed in 1913.

After the Revolution Shchusev was actively involved in official organisations, teaching and administration throughout Moscow's architectural community. In 1918 he became a member of the architectural section of the Commissariat for Education and he was later to teach at VKhUTEMAS. He and Ivan Zholtovskii established and ran the architectural and urban planning office of Moscow City Council. He also chaired MAO, a group that was responsible for running several important architectural competitions in the 1920s and 1930s. From 1926 to 1929 he was director of the Tretyakov Gallery in Moscow.

His most important designs of this period are the three mausoleums for Lenin, which he conceived in quick succession (Cat. 92). Two were temporary wooden structures, the first very simply constructed and the second fully realised in 1924; the final, permanent stone version of 1929–30 still sits in Moscow's Red Square. All three designs display simplicity of form combined with references to Classical architecture. However,

in the final version, Shchusev paired down the Classical elements to emphasise the geometric composition rather than historical references, signalling his embrace of the more innovative trends of the time. His other designs from this period, notably his competition entry for the Moscow Central Telegraph Office (1925) and the Narkomzem Building (built 1928–33), reflect the influence of such avant-garde architects as Aleksandr Vesnin.

Shchusev both ran and participated in the competition for the Palace of Soviets in Moscow in 1931. His entry showed a movement back towards a more eclectic and traditional language of architecture in line with the official promotion of Socialist Realism in literature and the visual arts.

In 1946 he became the first director of the State Research and Scientific Museum of Russian Architecture in Moscow, the central archive of Russian and Soviet architectural drawings after it established its autonomy from the Soviet Academy of Architecture. It was given his name following his death in 1949. MC

Shekhonin, Nikolai
(1882–1933)

Shekhonin is known only as the architect of the Pishchevik Club, built for food-industry workers in Kiev (1931–33; Cat. 88). MC

Shukhov, Vladimir Grigoriavich
(1853–1939)

Born in Graivoron in the Kursk region (now the province of Belogorod), Shukhov graduated from MVTU in 1876. He then travelled to the USA to research recent developments in American technology, visiting the 1876 Philadelphia World's Fair and mechanised factories in Pittsburgh.

Best known as an engineer, Shukhov is credited with inventing a structural system based on a steel-lattice shell, which he applied to covered bridges, water towers, radio towers and vaulted roofs. His earliest work, however, was as chief engineer of Russia's first oil pipeline (1878) and his achievements in this area were significant in the development of the country's oil industry. He was also responsible for engineering and constructing railway bridges and covered bridges, for which he devised a light arch system (1892).

Shukhov's innovative steel-lattice shell system made it possible to build lightweight yet rigid structures that lent themselves easily to many applications. His first use of the system, in 1895, was for a water tower in the shape of a series of stacked hyperboloids. After the Revolution a similar structure was employed for the Shabolovka Radio Tower in Moscow (1922; Cat. 62). With its striking shape and impressive height, it remains a landmark on the city skyline.

In 1929 Shukhov was elected an honorary member of the USSR Academy of Science. MC

Simonov, Grigorii Aleksandrovich (1893–1974)

Born in Troitsk, Simonov studied at the Imperial Academy of Art and the St Petersburg Institute of Civil Engineering, graduating in 1920.

He helped to design several important new Socialist building types in the city. His first completed project was for a hospital in Vyshnii Volochëk (1926). He was later an assistant to Aleksandr Nikolskii and Aleksandr Gegello on the workers' housing in Traktornaia ulitsa (1927; Cat. 79) and designed the school on Tkachei ulitsa (1927–29; Cat. 84).

In the 1930s he developed his ideas about communal housing and entered competitions. Among his successes were a design for a residential block for the Association of Pre-Revolutionary Political Deportees in St Petersburg (1932). The brief, set by the city council as an All-Union open competition, was for a collective dwelling for two thousand workers. Simonov produced a complex design that comprised interconnecting housing blocks, each with a clearly defined domestic and social purpose where individuals, families and couples without children were allocated different-sized units. The scheme included a communal building with a theatre,

sports facilities and dining hall. Simonov later applied similar conventions to the city's Batenin housing scheme (1936). MC

Sokolov, Veniamin Dmitrievich (1889–1955)

After graduating from the Imperial Academy of Art in St Petersburg in 1918, Sokolov worked primarily on developing new types of buildings that responded to the needs of Socialist society. His executed designs included a clubhouse for building workers in St Petersburg (1930) and the Dinamo Sports Club in Moscow (1929–34). He is best known for the experimental Chekist Housing Scheme in Ekaterinburg, on which he worked with Ivan Antonov and Arsenii Tumbasov (1929–32; Cat. 77). MC

Tumbasov, Arsenii Mikhailovich (1901–1974)

Tumbasov graduated from Ekaterinburg Arts and Industrial Graphics College in 1918 and from Tashkhent Art Technical College in 1922. He designed the Chekist Housing Scheme in Ekaterinburg with Ivan Antonov and Veniamin Sokolov (1929–32; Cat. 77), in which the living units were arranged around a semi-circular court, with the communal areas at each end. MC

Vesnin, Aleksandr Aleksandrovich (1883–1959)

Born in Lurevets, Aleksandr Vesnin studied at the Moscow Practical Institute and graduated from the St Petersburg Institute of Civil Engineering in 1912. He was the youngest of three brothers and worked in collaboration with both Viktor and Leonid on many successful projects during the 1920s and 1930s.

Before the Revolution he was involved in painting, which he studied under the 'impressionist' artists Konstantin Iuon and Ivan Tsionglinksii between 1907 and 1911 and with the Constructivist artist and designer Vladimir Tatlin from 1912 to 1913. After 1917 he continued to develop his interest in non-objective painting, participating in

the *Tenth State Exhibition: Non-Objective Creation and Suprematism* in 1919 and the Constructivist painting show *5x5=25* in 1921, both in Moscow.

His interest in art took him into theatre design. He produced sets and costumes for several productions by Aleksandr Tairov at the Teatr Kameny in Moscow, most notably *The Man Who Was Thursday* in 1923. The sets featured an asymmetric, industrially inspired skeletal construction. They were designed with moveable parts and a series of platforms, stairs and lifts that could be rearranged in various combinations, reflecting Vesnin's Functionalist ideas.

Vesnin became a professor at VKhUTEMAS in 1921, teaching painting and drawing. He later became head of the architecture studio. In 1922 he joined INKhUK, and between 1923 and 1925 he was a contributor to the avant-garde group and journal *LEF*. Through these organisations and his work in theatre he developed an aesthetic that emphasised such basic plastic elements as material, line, plane and colour to produce designs with a focus on economy and the use of modern technology.

In 1924 he designed the cover for Moisei Ginzburg's book *Style and Epoch*, which established the theoretical basis of Constructivist architecture; Vesnin's new formal aesthetic was combined with a theoretical programme that contributed to the formation of OSA in 1925. Vesnin was not only a founding member OSA but was also the chief editor and a regular contributor to its periodical *SA*.

He and his brothers submitted entries to several architectural competitions. Though unbuilt, these represented many of his most notable projects, including the Palace of Labour (1923), the Leningradskaia Pravda Building (1924) and the Lenin Library (1928), all in Moscow. Built projects included the Mostorg Department Store on Krasnaia Presnia ulitsa in Moscow (1927), communal housing in Volgograd and Kuznetsk (1929–30) and the Palace of Culture in Moscow (1932). The DneproGES Dam and Hydroelectric Power Station (designed with Nikolai Kolli,

Georgii Orlov and Sergei Andrievskii, 1927–32; Cat. 68) represents not only Vesnin's first important industrial project but also a major achievement of Stalin's First Five Year Plan.

After their competition entry for the Palace of Soviets in 1931, Vesnin, his brother Viktor and Moisei Ginzburg publicly expressed their dislike of the return to traditionalism in Soviet architecture. After his final project, the Commissariat for Heavy Industry (1935), Vesnin returned to Expressionist figurative painting. MC

- S.O. Khan-Magomedov, *Alexander Vesnin and Russian Constructivism*, London, 1986.

Vesnin, Leonid Aleksandrovich (1880–1933)

Born in Nizhnii Novgorod, Leonid Vesnin graduated from the Imperial Academy of Art in St Petersburg in 1909. He was a member of OSA and was involved in developing the Functionalist approach to architectural design and in exploring its practical application.

While much is known about his younger brothers Viktor and Aleksandr (see above), there is little biographical information about Leonid. However, he did work on several important projects with his brothers, and his solo buildings include the Surakhani district Palace of Culture in Baku, Azerbaijan (1929; Cat. 86).

He also taught architectural design at MVTU. MC

Zholtovskii, Ivan Vladislavovich (1867–1959)

Born in Moscow, Zholtovskii graduated from the Imperial Academy of Art in St Petersburg in 1898 and then taught architecture at the Stroganov Institute of Industrial Art in Moscow. The strong influence of Italian Renaissance architecture, especially the work of Andrea Palladio, can be seen in several of his pre-Revolutionary designs, and he translated Palladio's *I quattro libri dell'architettura* into Russian.

In 1918 he was given a leading position in the planning of New Moscow. A year later he was made head of the architectural section at the Commissariat for Public Education, where, with Aleksei Shchusev, he trained several young avant-garde architects including Ilia Golosov, Panteleimon Golosov, Konstantin Melnikov, Nikolai Ladovskii and Nikolai Kolli. Since the department was responsible for most architectural activity in Moscow, including the administration of competitions, Zholtovskii was able to assert his preference for the Classical style. He did so for the 1923 Palace of Labour competition, where he favoured a historicising project by Noi Trotskii over a structurally and formally innovative design by the Vesnin brothers.

During the early 1920s, when little construction was taking place, Zholtovskii concentrated on education and research into urban planning. His design work from this time includes the entrance gates to the *All-Union Agricultural Exhibition* (1923) and a competition entry for the House of Soviets (1927), both in Moscow.

He maintained his traditionalist stance throughout the mid-1920s, despite the dominant trend towards Rationalist and Functionalist Modernism, though he was open to using Functionalist vocabulary for certain projects. Thus his MoGES Electric Power Station in Moscow (1926; Cat. 69) uses materials such as concrete and plate glass and a geometric massing of forms in the interior courtyard. This is counter-balanced, however, by the long river façade, which proclaims his debt to Classical sources. MC

FURTHER READING

Architectural Drawings of the Russian Avant-Garde, C. Cooke, exh. cat., The Museum of Modern Art, New York, 1990.

The Great Utopia: The Russian Avant-Garde 1915–1932, exh. cat., Schirn Kunsthalle, Frankfurt, Stedelijk Museum, Amsterdam, The Solomon R. Guggenheim Museum, New York, State Tretyakov Gallery, Moscow, 1992–93.

Russian Avant-garde 1910–1930: The G. Costakis Collection, A. Kafetsi (ed.), exh. cat., 2 vols, National Gallery of Greece, Athens, 1995–96.

Light and Colour of the Avant-Garde: The George Costakis Collection, M. Papanikolaou (ed.), J. Bowlt, C. Douglas, N. Misler, M. Tsantsanoglou, exh. cat., Martin Gropius Bau, Berlin, 2004.

Five Seasons of the Russian Avant-Garde: The George Costakis Collection, M. Tsantsanoglou (ed.), exh. cat., Museum of Cycladic Art, Athens, 2008.

Lost Vanguard Found: A Synthesis of Art and Architecture in Russia 1915–1935, M. Tsantsanoglou (ed.), exh. cat., SMCA-Costakis Collection, Thessaloniki, 2008.

S. Bann (ed.), *The Tradition of Constructivism (The Documents of 20th Century Art),* London and New York, 1974; second edition Cambridge, Mass, 1990.

M. Barkhin and Y. Yaratov, *Mastera sovetskoi arkhitektury ob arkhitektura (Masters of Soviet Architecture on Architecture),* 2 vols, Moscow, 1975.

J.-L.Cohen, *Le Corbusier and the Mystique of the USSR,* Princeton, 1991.

C. Cooke, *Russian Avant-Garde: Theories of Art, Architecture and the City,* London, 1995.

M. Gough, *The Artist as Producer: Russian Constructivism in Revolution,* San Francisco, 2005.

L.I. Ivanova-Veen (ed.), *From VKhUTEMAS to MARKHI: 1920–1936,* Moscow, 2005.

S.O. Khan-Magomedov, *VKhUTEMAS: Moscou 1920–1930,* Paris, 1990.

S.O. Khan-Magomedov, *Arkhitektura Sovietsokogo Avangarda (Architecture of the Soviet Avant-Garde),* Moscow, 1996.

S.O. Khan-Magomedov, *Pioniere der sowjetischen Architektur,* Dresden, 1983; English translation by A. Lieven, *Pioneers of Soviet Architecture: The Search for New Solutions in the 1920s and 1930s,* ed. C. Cooke, London, 1987.

S.O. Khan-Magomedov, *Ratsionalizm (Ratio-Architektura) –'Formalizm' (Rationalism [Rational Architecture] – Formalism),* Moscow, 2007.

S.O. Khan-Magomedov, *Suprematizm i Arkhitektura: problemy formoobrazovania (Suprematism and Architecture: Problems in the Development of Form),* Moscow, 2007.

C. Kiaer, *Imagine No Possessions: The Socialist Objects of Russian Constructivism,* Cambridge, Mass, 2005.

A. Kopp, *Constructivist Architecture in the USSR,* London, 1985.

C. Lodder, *Russian Constructivism,* New Haven and London, 1985.

V. Margolin, *The Struggle for Utopia: Rodchenko, Lissitzky, Moholy-Nagy, 1917–1946,* Chicago, 1998.

I. Matsa, *Sovietskoe iskusstvo za 15 let (Fifteen Years of Soviet Art),* Moscow and St Petersburg, 1933.

R. Pare, J.-L. Cohen, *The Lost Vanguard: Russian Modernist Architecture 1922–1932,* New York, 2007.

A. Rudenstine (ed.), *Russian Avant-Garde Art: The George Costakis Collection,* New York, 1981.

O.A. Shvidkovsky (ed.), *Building in the USSR 1917–1932,* London, 1971.

INDEX

All references are to page numbers; those in **bold** type indicate catalogue plates, and those in *italic* type indicate essay illustrations

268